Julian B

God's Democracy

God's Democracy
American Religion after September 11

Emilio Gentile

Jennifer Pudney and Suzanne D. Jaus, Translators

Religion, Politics, and Public Life

Under the auspices of the Leonard E. Greenberg Center for the Study of
Religion in Public Life, Trinity College, Hartford, CT

Mark Silk, Series Editor

Westport, Connecticut
London

Library of Congress Cataloging-in-Publication Data

Gentile, Emilio, 1946–
  [Democrazia di Dio. English]
  God's democracy : American religion after September 11 / Emilio Gentile ; Jennifer Pudney
  and Suzanne D. Jaus, translators.
    p. cm. — (Religion, politics, and public life, ISSN 1934–290X)
  Includes bibliographical references (p.   ) and index.
  ISBN 978–0–313–35336–9 (alk. paper)
1. United States—Religion—21st century. 2. Religion and politics—United States—History—
21st century. 3. September 11 Terrorist Attacks, 2001—Religious aspects. 4. United States—
Politics and government—2001– I. Title.
BL2525.G47 2008
200.973'090511—dc22   2008020077

British Library Cataloguing in Publication Data is available.

Library of Congress Catalog Card Number: 2008020077
ISBN: 978–0–313–35336–9
ISSN: 1934–290X

First published in 2008

Original Italian edition, *La democrazia di Dio*
© 2006, Gius. Latertza & Figli
Prima edizione 2006
© 2006, Emilio Gentile
per la lingua inglese

Praeger Publishers, 88 Post Road West, Westport, CT 06881
An imprint of Greenwood Publishing Group, Inc.
www.praeger.com

Printed in the United States of America

The paper used in this book complies with the
Permanent Paper Standard issued by the National
Information Standards Organization (Z39.48–1984).

10 9 8 7 6 5 4 3 2 1

Contents

Series Foreword

Alexis de Tocqueville, that acute foreign observer of democracy in Andrew Jackson's America, claimed that while religion took no direct part in Americans' government, it was nevertheless "the first of their political institutions." In Tocqueville's view, religion exerted its powerful political influence by schooling the citizens of the United States in the proper exercise of their freedom. This, he believed, was far preferable to the direct part played by the Roman Catholic Church in the politics of his native France.

In this exploration of the role of religion in George W. Bush's America, Emilio Gentile, another acute foreign observer, updates and adds a cautionary note to Tocqueville's assessment. A longtime student of Italian fascism and of religious politics in Western Europe generally, Gentile understands as few scholars do the ways that religion serves to bind national communities together in the modern world. Looking at religion in American public life from a transatlantic perspective, he provides a unique portrait of a country struggling to get a spiritual grip on itself in the wake of the traumatic attacks of September 11, 2001.

Those attacks made for a revival of what has come to be known as American civil religion. Rooted in the Protestantism that originally dominated the American religious landscape, American civil religion over the years grew into an inclusive faith that encompassed Americans of a great variety of religious traditions and enabled them to view their country as endowed with a sacred character that in no way excluded them. It was a religion that not only sacralized the nation in the abstract but even extended to such concrete manifestations of it as the national flag—Old Glory. It was hardly a surprise that the events of September 11 should revivify the cult of Old Glory, but the extent of that revivification was nevertheless remarkable.

Wars do have such effects on the souls of nations, and the "war on terror," as it came to be called, has been no exception. Previous American wars have, to varying degrees, connected the religious sensibilities of the populace to the nation's own purposes. America, conceived as a specially God-favored place that is also a beacon of hope and freedom to the rest of the world, has long seen itself as "God's democracy." What made the post-September 11 era different, however, was that well before the attacks of that day, the country experienced an unprecedented degree of faith-based partisanship in its politics. Simply put, religion had become directly engaged in government to a degree that, one may surmise, would have concerned Tocqueville.

Beginning in the 1980s, a resurgent evangelical Protestantism, consumed with concerns about liberalizing mores in the culture at large, began to associate itself with the Republican Party. On issues ranging from abortion and gay rights to prayer in the public schools and Darwinian evolution, conservative white evangelicals proved susceptible to a type of politics based on religious values, and with the active efforts of Republican political operatives, they quickly came to see the GOP as the instrument of those values. If the party did not often deliver on their policy desires, the mood music and the access to the ears of the powerful were never lacking. From the presidency of Ronald Reagan on, white evangelicals became the largest bloc of GOP voters, as well as the source of a major portion of party activists.

Partisan religiosity was not, however, restricted to them. Beginning in the 1990s, a substantial division opened up in the American electorate as a whole between the more and the less religious, regardless of denominational affiliation. By 2000, voters who said they attended worship at least weekly were voting Republican in presidential and congressional races by a margin of 60 percent to 40 percent; less frequent attenders were voting Democratic by about the same amount. In a word, religious "values" were increasingly seen by Americans as the special province of the GOP, while the Democratic Party seemed to have become, if not a bastion of irreligion, then at least unfriendly to the issues that most of the country's most religious citizens defined as most important. In the culture wars of the late twentieth century, the Democrats were arrayed on the secular side.

The attacks of September 11 thus came at a moment when religion was not spread evenly across America's public landscape. President Bush himself was more than familiar with the partisan uses of religion. In 1988, not long after his own adult conversion, he chose to participate in his father's successful campaign for president by working on outreach to religious voters. Although he was not the most favored candidate of the Religious Right in the 2000 GOP primary campaign, he understood religious conservatives and knew how to appeal to them as one of their own. Two decades of garnering votes on the basis of religious faith had created a machine by which the distress of September 11 could be exploited.

And exploit it the Bush administration did. What Gentile shows is how a revival of American civil religion began to be transformed from a common American cause into something more like a political religion—no longer an inclusive faith designed to bring all Americans under a single spiritual umbrella but a partisan creed that could be used as a weapon against those Americans who were not prepared to enlist in the Cause of Bush.

In the event, the effort proved of limited success. The ability of American society to resist totalistic religious ideologies proved stronger than seemed possible in the immediate aftermath of the attacks. No less important, the manifest failure of the Bush administration to bring the war in Iraq to a swift and success-ful conclusion undermined what Gentile terms President Bush's "messianic nationalism." By the 2006 midterm elections, the Bush enchantment was, to all intents and purposes, over. Two years after that, Americans seemed hardly aware that they had recently been flirting with an "exclusive and intolerant political religion."

God's Democracy provides an authoritative account of how that nascent political religion came to be. Written originally to explain America in the September 11 era to Italians, the book captures a period in America's religious history that will be pondered—and wondered at—for years to come.

Mark Silk

Director
The Leonard E. Greenberg Center for
the Study of Religion in Public Life
Trinity College
Hartford

Preface

This book examines the consequences of the terrorist attack of September 11, 2001 on American religion, a civil religion based on the belief that the United States is a nation blessed by God, originating from a design of Divine Providence, with a mission to defend and spread "God's democracy" throughout the world. I intend to use this expression to define the Americans' concept of democracy, which has a religious matrix and is constantly inspired by religion, maintaining that freedom is a gift of God. Since the times of the first president, George Washington, all the United States presidents have ended their inaugural addresses by calling on God to bless America, and no president has failed to mention, at least once, his faith in Almighty God, in the divine origin of American democracy, and in the United States' providential mission. The American president is not only the nation's political leader, he is also the pontiff of its civil religion. Studying American religion helps to understand American politics, especially after September 11, even though this is not an easy task for European observers, who have to cope with various seemingly paradoxical situations, mainly due to the symbiosis between religion and politics.

The United States is a country of paradoxes. The most paradoxical American paradox may be the high level of religious fervor that distinguishes the people of the star-spangled republic from other peoples of the most industrialized and modernized countries in the contemporary world, while the Americans can boast their primacy for having confirmed and respected the lay principle of the separation between state and church. Since the year 2000, however, many Americans, both lay and religious, have feared that the "separating wall," using Thomas Jefferson's metaphor, between the state and church, may be seriously damaged by the attacks of a religious right. The latter found a political leader in President George W. Bush, elected in 2000 and reelected in 2004, who was determined to instill the values of a traditionalist, religious, conservative, and fundamentalist view in American society, culture, institutions, and home and foreign policies. In fact, as this book will show, the "separating wall" between state and church has never separated religion and politics, which have always lived in symbiosis in the United States, with the full approval of most of the population. Almost all Americans declare they are Christian, but the United States, which in the twentieth century became the greatest imperial power in human history, with the richest economy and the strongest armed forces, has not carried out the Beatitudes preached by Jesus in his Sermon from the Mount. Furthermore, up to 1960, no Catholic person could be elected president. Up to 2000, no Jew had been proposed as candidate for the vice presidency. All the American presidents elected up to now have declared their faith in God, and in our times it seems impossible that an atheist may be elected as president of the United States, and predictably this situation will continue for a long time to come. The majority of Americans would now be ready to elect a Catholic, a Jew, a woman, and perhaps even a black or a gay to the highest office of the state, but would absolutely refuse to vote for someone who says he is an atheist, even if most Americans are convinced that it is not necessary to believe in God to be a good American or a morally decent person. This, too, is an American paradox.

Then the September 11 tragedy was added to these paradoxes. Just when America had become the only undisputed superpower of the planet, the nation which had won two world wars and the Cold War, it was attacked, terrorized, and humiliated in the heart of its territory, by 19 young fanatical Muslims. Armed with box cutters, they seized four American airplanes and, invoking the name of God, flew them in a suicide attack straight into the most important symbol of United States military power, the Pentagon, and into the Twin Towers of the World Trade Center, universal emblems of American civilization. Nowadays some suspect that what happened on September 11 in America was the fruit of a plot hatched at the summit of the Bush administration. This book does not deal with the events of September 11, nor with plots, but with how the Americans who believe in God reacted to the terrorist attack.

At the dawn of the twenty-first century the American nation suddenly found itself living in the age of empire and terror at the same time, discovering that it was vulnerable although protected by two oceans and the most powerful armed forces in the history of mankind, unrivalled in the world. However, the September 11 terrorist attack did not cause only a profound psychological trauma and political upheaval, it also affected the Americans' religious feeling, that is, their attitude towards God, the meaning and aim of existence, and their idea of good and evil. Millions of appalled Americans crowded the churches, synagogues, mosques, and temples, trying to relieve their sorrow and fear through prayer. Many wondered if God had abandoned America. Some fundamentalist preachers upheld that the terrorist attack was a sign that God no longer protected the Americans, punishing them for their sins. On the contrary, the president of the United States stated that America was a good nation, attacked by evil men who wanted to destroy God's democracy and set up an empire of evil. Bush declared "war on terror" to free the world of evil, appealing to God to bless Americans, once again called to fight to save mankind, as they did in the last century. The terrorists wanted to destroy America in the name of God, the American president began the war against the "axis of evil" maintaining that God was on America's side, and the American nation was fighting terrorism to follow the plans of Divine Providence. This, too, is a paradoxical situation.

The fusion between religion and nationalism is one of the distinctive features of God's democracy. The September 11 tragedy gave rise to an unexpected ferment in religious and patriotic feeling, just when many right- and left-wing American intellectuals were complaining about the nation's moral crisis, fearing for its unity. For over a decade civil religion in the United States seemed reduced to a halfhearted ritual. After September 11 it was suddenly rekindled, mainly due to President Bush, one of the most religious American presidents—as such, he is the protagonist of this book.

The main subject of the book is the attempt of the Republican presidency and the Religious Right to turn American civil religion into an American-style political religion, using the September 11 tragedy to arrogate the monopoly of defining good and evil to themselves, as well as the exclusive prerogative of defining the values and principles of "real Americans." They fostered the revival of the myths of civil religion, from the myth of the "chosen people" to the myth of the "manifest destiny" of the nation to carry out a mission, following a traditionalist and fundamentalist view of religion and politics. It was a new experience of sacralizing politics, one strongly criticized and opposed by lay and religious circles, starting off a passionate debate on the nature, meaning, and function of civil religion in a democracy. Also those who criticized and opposed American religion in the age of empire and terror play a leading role in this book.

This work is therefore a natural follow-on of the book *Le religioni della politica: fra democrazie e totalitarismi,* published by Laterza in September 2001 (Emilio Gentile, *Politics as Religion,* translated by George Staunton [Princeton: Princeton University Press, 2006]). The fact that *Politics as Religion* was published at the same time as the September 11 tragedy was pure coincidence, but it contributed to the birth of this book, the fruit of an intellectual need and personal emotion. I had been studying American religion for some time, that is, since I became aware of it not through books but through direct experience, during my first stays in the United States in 1974 and 1976. In the following years, when I stayed there either on holiday or to study or teach, it was important for me to examine American religion closely, as it was one of the first and most lasting experiences of sacralizing politics in a Western democracy. One of these stays ended on the morning of September 10, 2001, after I had taken part in a meeting on the historical work of George L. Mosse, organized by the Mosse Program at the University of Wisconsin, in Madison. I had intended to make a stop in New York on the eve of my return to Italy, but it was impossible. When I returned to Italy the following day, I saw the terrorist attack and its consequences on television. If I had stopped over in New York, my fate may have been as a witness, a victim, or a survivor of the terrorist attack. Indeed, for over a quarter of a century I have always gone up the Empire State Building on the evening I arrive, and on the following morning up one of the Twin Towers of the World Trade Center, to say hallo to the city. I love it because my maternal grandfather lived there for over 50 years in the 1900s. He was an immigrant who became an American citizen, son of an Italian-American immigrant who was the forefather of American families of Italian origin now down to the third or fourth generation. During my childhood, New York and America were constantly present in my imagination, through memories, parcels, letters, postcards, photographs, and magazines, and they were more familiar to me, without my ever having been there, than Italy or Rome. Consequently, I have always felt an instinctive liking for the United States and Americans, which, over the years, turned into a need to know and understand them better.

I mention these personal details so the reader will know that this book is not only the fruit of intellectual curiosity, but is marked by my emotional involvement in the September 11 tragedy. Emotion certainly influenced the way I carried out this research, but I made a great effort to prevent my liking for America from influencing this attempt at a historical, critical, and rational analysis of the myths of American religion, as they were and are now, to better understand the America of today and of the near future. The reader will decide if this effort has been successful.

E. G.

Acknowledgments

Writing a book may be the only occasion when it is a pleasure to incur debts and then pay them back, even though inadequately. The memory of Phil Cannistraro is alive in these pages. Over the years and almost up to the eve of his premature death, he helped me to study American religion with his culture, experience, and advice, waiting for, and curious to see, the final results, which were reached without the comfort of his opinion. On the contrary, a work containing the imaginary, parallel biographies of Benito Mussolini and Adolf Hitler as emigrants to New York will never see the light. We had begun to write it by chance, treating ourselves to the pleasure of an invented story, to break away from depressing real history every now and then.

I owe a great deal to Maria Fraddosio and John Tortorice, who were never impatient with me but supported my efforts affectionately, giving valuable help in my search for books and articles, enhancing my finds with their own curiosity. After reading the manuscript, Stanley Payne who approved, and Walter Adamson who disapproved, gave me useful suggestions to reflect on opinions and interpretations that they did not agree with. I thank them for this, naturally exonerating them from any responsibility for the content of the book. Mark Silk and I discussed American civil religion a great deal, and my debt towards him grew after he read and commented on the manuscript. Furthermore, it is owing to his friendly insistence that I managed to finish the book. Also Marina Cattaruzza contributed to its completion, with her friendship, trust, and sensitivity in the study of political religions.

The most substantial financial support was offered by the University of Berne which awarded me the Hans Sigrist Prize 2003. Special thanks go to the directors and officials of the libraries where I carried out most of my research: the Memorial Library of the University of Wisconsin, the Wisconsin Historical Society, the New York Public Library, the Chamber of Deputies Library, the Senate of the Republic Library, the Alessandrina Library, and the Department of Political Studies library in the Faculty of Political Science of the University of Rome "La Sapienza." The periods of study in the United States as First Visiting Scholar of the Mosse Program at the University of Wisconsin–Madison, and as

Distinguished Visiting Fellow of the Leonard E. Greenberg Center for the Study of Religion in Public Life at Trinity College in Hartford, were the most fruitful for studying and observing American religion, before and after September 11. My gratitude goes to both institutions for giving me the opportunity to work in an environment favorable for research.

——— 1 ———

America Violated

A Peaceful Dawn

On Tuesday, September 11, 2001, the day was fine and began with New York's usual frenzied activity. The Twin Towers of the World Trade Center on the southern coast of Manhattan Island stood out, shining white against a limpid blue sky, while the host of 50,000 people who worked there daily began to flock into their respective 110 floors. The towers contained 15 business floors, the offices of 285 companies, 9 chapels, and 2 restaurants. Every day about 70,000 people visited the two buildings which had dominated the city's panorama since 1973, proud symbols of America's business and economic power.

Also in the United States capital the day began with its usual tempo. The 23,000 employees of the Pentagon were already at work in the enormous, imperious building, built during the Second World War as the seat of the defense department of the greatest military power in history, as inaccessible as a fortress. It was the same scene at the White House, the United States president's residence. However, the head of the CIA (Central Intelligence Agency), the American counterespionage organization, was not to give his usual daily report to the president that morning, informing him of the latest news gathered all over the world by the CIA's information network. George W. Bush, ensconced in the White House just eight months before, was in Florida campaigning for his education policy.

The weather was fine everywhere on the eastern coast of the United States. Airliners took off regularly. American Airlines Flight 11 to Los Angeles left Boston at 7:59 A.M.; United Airlines Flight 175 took off at 8:14 A.M. for the same destination; also, American Airlines Flight 77 headed for Los Angeles after taking off from Washington at 8:20 A.M., while United Airlines Flight 93 left Newark for San Francisco at 8:42 A.M., half an hour late. There were 19 young non-American Arabs among the passengers on board the four planes, all of them in the United States with temporary visas. Mohammed Atta, a 39-year-old Egyptian engineer who had graduated in Cairo and done a postgraduate course in Hamburg, was traveling on Flight AA11, in business class. Atta had been in the United States over a year; he had attended a flight school in Florida. On each of the other flights there was a young Arab who had learned to fly a commercial jet airplane at an American flight school. An uneventful trip was expected for everyone on the morning of September 11, in the first year of the third millennium.

The twenty-first century began as an "American century": the United States had become the undisputed world superpower after the collapse of the Soviet empire and the end of the USSR, decreed by the Soviet leaders in December 1991. On October 23, 1999 the *Economist* wrote that the United States towered over the world like a colossus—it dominated business, trade, and communications, it had the strongest economy in the world, and its military strength was unrivalled.[1] At the end of 1999, the French secretary of state, Hubert Védrine, stated that the supremacy of the United States then embraced economics, finance, the armed forces, lifestyle, language, and mass-produced products, which flooded the world, consequently conditioning minds and fascinating even its enemies.[2]

At the beginning of the third millennium, the United States was an empire, the mightiest known in history—a "hyperpower" both attractive and frightening, present everywhere in the world with its flag, soldiers, economy, and culture. The dynamic and seductive, sophisticated and popular "American way of life" was emulated and hated, wielding its power to charm over all peoples and in every continent, capable of working its way into every culture and society, changing them and leaving the mark of its lifestyle. And those who hated America were fascinated, resorting to imitation to fight it.[3]

The Empire of Democracy

The idea of empire is usually associated with a single power conquering territory and peoples, then subduing and exploiting them. America considers itself a democratic nation, founded on the principles of liberty, equality, and happiness as the inalienable rights of human beings, bestowed on all of them by the Creator at birth. That is why the Americans refuse to call their country an empire and indignantly reject the accusation that they are imperialist, that is, a people that conquers, subdues, and exploits other peoples. At the end of the nineteenth century, in the age of European imperialism, the United States imitated the colonial powers of the Old Continent and conquered new territories outside its own continent, after the war against Spain in 1898–1899. The United States thus acquired the Philippines, Hawaii, some of the Samoan Islands, Cuba, and Puerto Rico, but its colonialism was limited: Cuba became an independent republic as an American protectorate in 1899, the Philippines were set on their way to independence in 1935, achieving it definitively in 1946, and in 1959 Hawaii became the fiftieth state of the United States.

However, there is another idea of empire, associated with the expansionist policy of a power which exercises its hegemony without conquering territories, setting itself up as a superior model of civilization and political, social, and economic systems, which are then to be transplanted in other countries as a civilizing mission to benefit humanity. Nowadays there are some Americans who are more willing to call their power an empire in the second meaning of the term, a "benevolent empire,"[4] because the term fits in with the view they have of America's role and destiny in the twenty-first century. This view dates back to the origins of the United States; its founders were convinced from its birth that it was a nation chosen by God to be a model for the world and to redeem mankind.[5] The founding fathers used the word "empire" to define the new republic's authority and propensity to carry out a mission. Under the banner of this myth, the United States expanded across the continent during the nineteenth century, from the Atlantic to the Pacific Ocean, from the borders of British Canada to the Caribbean Sea.[6] Various interlinked reasons were given to justify the conquering of the continent—which was carried out through treaties, purchases, and wars, and by wiping out the American Indians—the need to guarantee security for the "sacred experiment" of democracy and make it invulnerable to the greed of despotic and corrupt Europe; the need to satisfy the hunger for land of a nation with a rapidly growing population; and the carrying out of a "manifest destiny," that is, a civilizing mission entrusted by God to Americans.[7]

Religion accompanied and blessed the United States when it expanded across the continent, and continued to bless it when it crossed the oceans.[8] American missionaries preceded or followed traders and soldiers; the evangelizing spirit united with capitalist interests and geopolitical strategy. Urging for a crusade in the name of God, to make the world safe for democracy, inspired American intervention in the two world wars and during the Cold War.[9] For a long time men of religion in the United States rarely spoke out against these war operations, and then only halfheartedly. Only during the war in Vietnam did they protest more frequently.[10]

After the Second World War, the United States became a superpower in a state of "cold war" with the Soviet Union, the other superpower, competing for the military, political, economic, and cultural hegemony of the planet. The United States was then called an "empire without imperialists,"[11] because it refused to recognize its imperial role and continued to consider itself a beneficial power, uncontaminated by imperialist ambitions or the totalitarian aberrations of the godless communists. Nevertheless, the United States resembled an empire more and more during the half century of cold war, even though it was a democratic empire. In 1986 the historian Arthur M. Schlesinger Jr., who had been President John Kennedy's adviser, wrote that nobody could doubt that an American empire existed. It was an "informal" empire, the historian explained, not colonial politically, but all the same abundantly equipped with imperial paraphernalia: armies, ships, bases, proconsuls, and local collaborators scattered everywhere over this unfortunate planet.[12]

At the end of the 1900s, it seemed that the "end of history" had arrived, that is, the universalization of Western liberal democracy as humanity's final form of government, as the American expert in politics Francis Fukuyama stated in 1989.[13] However, four years later another American expert, Samuel P. Huntington, observed that the possibility of setting up a new world order, one founded on Western liberal democracy, was threatened by the danger of a clash of civilizations between different cultures and religions, which could spark off a global war.[14]

In the last decade of the twentieth century, America's future seemed to depend solely on the choices it made. The last two United States presidents before the new millennium, Republican George H. W. Bush (1989–1993) and Democrat William J. Clinton (1993–2001), had nothing in common except the view of a world made in the image of God's democracy. After the end of the Soviet Union, Bush aspired to a "new world order" founded on peace and harmony among nations. Clinton dreamed of a world of cooperating democracies. However, in a world where unfortunately there were still numerous regimes that denied freedom and human rights, both presidents had to decide on military interventions.[15] In February 1991 with the consent of the United Nations, Bush led a coalition of Western, Japanese, and Arab military forces in a war in the Persian Gulf to free Kuwait, occupied the year before by Saddam Hussein, the ambitious Iraqi dictator who aspired to supremacy in the Middle East. In four days the coalition forces drove the invader out of Kuwait and invaded Iraq, but they ended the war leaving the Iraqi tyrant in power. In the following 10 years he continued to challenge the United States and the United Nations with bellicose arrogance. Eight years later in 1999, backed by the Atlantic Alliance, Clinton ordered the U.S. Air Force to intervene with and bomb Serbia, forcing the dictator, Slobodan Milošević, to stop the ethnic bloodbath in Kosovo.

At the end of the twentieth century, the road to spreading and making it safe for God's democracy throughout the world was still fraught with obstacles, but the undisputed power of the United States seemed capable of overcoming them.

The Millennium Nightmare

At the beginning of the first century of the third millennium, the Americans were convinced that their military power excluded the possibility of being threatened again by a dangerous enemy, as the Soviet Union had been to them for half a century. The Americans celebrated the end of the Cold War, relieved and satisfied, hoping to be able to enjoy the profits of peace now that the expenditure for national security had been reduced with the end of the Soviet military threat.[16] In spite of the moaning and groaning of the millenarist prophets, both religious and lay, who continued to complain and deprecate the spiritual and moral decadence of American society and who predicted looming catastrophes, the Americans entered the new millennium fairly satisfied with being the richest and strongest nation in the world. They felt unconquerable and invulnerable, while new experts in international political strategy called "neoconservatives"—who supported a Messianic realism that did not exclude using military force—planned the coming of a "new American century," where spreading democracy would ensure the planet's stability with a *pax americana*. The neoconservatives believed that the United States should no longer hold back from carrying out an imperial role, that is, averting the growth of any other power capable of threatening America's world supremacy, even taking up arms if necessary. One of the main aims of their strategy was to prevent Saddam Hussein's Iraq from becoming such a threat. The last two presidents of the United States in the twentieth century were urged to adopt this strategy for a "new American century," but neither of the two paid any attention to the neoconservatives' plan.[17]

However, the end of the millennium raised anxiety and fears. The passing from the second to the third millennium was awaited by some sectors of religious and popular culture prophesying imminent catastrophes, fruit of a tradition of apocalyptic visions whose roots lay in the Puritan origins of the American nation. The American revolution had been interpreted as an apocalyptic event, and during all the 1800s, millenarian movements believed in the imminent return of Christ. Apocalyptic millenarianism continued into the 1900s, fostered by the catastrophic events of the First World War, the Great Depression, the Second World War, and the nightmare of a nuclear threat during the Cold War. In 1992 Paul Boyer, a historian of American culture, observed that not only had millenarian prophecies and beliefs survived the secular twentieth century, but they actually showed strong signs of revival as it closed.[18] In 1995 a Gallup poll revealed that 61 percent of adults and 71 percent of young people believed that the world was about to end or be destroyed. Humanity would be wiped out by a spate of catastrophes caused by global warming, AIDS, hunger, overpopulation, viruses, and other unimaginable biblical scourges. The Hollywood film industry prospered by producing apocalyptic stories.[19] Books about the end of the world were bestsellers in the United States, and one of the most successful was the *The Late Great Planet Earth* by Hal Lindsay, published in 1970. He maintained that the Bible's prophecies for the end of the world were about to take place, and that the battle of Armageddon was approaching and inevitable. Seven and a half million copies of the book were sold in the 1970s, and up to the 1990s 28 million copies were sold in 52 languages.

Some religious movements following the Judaic-Christian version of the premillenarian belief foresaw depraved and corrupt American society as being destined to end catastrophically—to make way for rebirth, the return of Christ, the coming of the millennium, the final war between the forces of good and evil, the Last Judgment, the end of history, and the eternal triumph of God's reign. President Reagan loved apocalyptic prophecies. During the Gulf War in 1991, 15 percent of Americans declared they believed the war was the beginning of the Apocalypse and that it would bring Armageddon closer. A book by John F. Walvoord, published in 1974, called *Armageddon, Oil and the Middle East Crisis,* was updated and republished in December 1990: 600,000 copies were sold up to February 1991.[20]

Belief in the end of the world was widespread, especially among the fundamentalist evangelicals:

> Nurtured by the dense network of colleges, seminaries, Bible schools, publishing houses, Christian bookstores, radio and television programs, and churches by the tens of thousands that sustain the vast subculture of late-twentieth-century U.S. evangelicalism, the conviction that God's plan for human history lies encrypted in ancient biblical texts remains very much alive as the century draws to its close. From pulpits, cassette tapes, orbiting communication satellites, and the pages of millions of paperbacks, the ancient cry rings out as it has for hundreds of years: "He Is Coming Soon."[21]

The fundamentalist evangelicals supported the traditional values of Christian America rigidly and considered the secularized America which had emerged from the crisis and the transformations of the 1960s to be a materialistic, hedonist, and pagan country. They accused it of having driven religion out of politics and public life, forbidden Christian symbols in state institutions, barred prayer from schools, spread evolutionistic theories, legalized abortion, and fostered feminism, pornography, and homosexuality. That was why America now risked an inevitable, imminent punishment from the wrath of God, asserted television preachers like Jerry Falwell and Pat Robertson, foreseeing that a nuclear war would carry out the Bible's prophecies. According to a survey made by the magazine *U.S. News & World Report,* published on December 19, 1994, 61 percent of those interviewed had no doubts about Christ's second coming, and 53 percent of these believed that the world would end in the twentieth century in accordance with the Bible's prophecy. "No part of our history has gone for long without a fresh application of the patterns of apocalypse. And the ending of a century in the year 2000 (or, as some more accurately put it, in 2001) is bound to create that feeling of history taking a corner that always stimulates apocalyptic thinking," wrote Garry Wills, the historian of American culture, in 1990.[22] However, a few years later Daniel Wojcik, a scholar of American apocalypticism, pointed out that "if the years 2000 and 2001 pass uneventfully, perhaps the emphasis in American millennialist beliefs will shift from visions of the world as irredeemably evil and inevitably doomed to more optimistic views in which human beings are compelled to bring about millennial transformations through their actions, confronting crisis and working to overcome suffering in the tradition of postmillennial social reformists of the nineteenth century."[23]

In actual fact, at the end of 1999 the disaster the Americans mainly feared was technological, abbreviated to "Y2K," which simply stood for "Year 2000," with the "K" indicating "thousand." This did not refer to a new weapon of mass destruction, nor to the virus of a mortal pandemic, but was used to define the risk that computers all over the world would be blocked at midnight on December 31, 1999 with disastrous consequences in the financial, economic, and social sectors, because their memories had not been prepared in advance to distinguish between the numerals "1900" and "2000" when dating any operation.

The possibility of a computer catastrophe caused by the so-called "millennium bug" was taken very seriously. The American government set up a special President's Council on Year 2000, to prevent the disastrous effects of the millennium bug. It was even feared that the Y2K effect would enable Russian computers to launch nuclear missiles against America. However, there was no catastrophe. "Remember Y2K? A Nostalgic Look at the Disaster That Never Was," was the joking title of the popular *Time Almanac 2001,* recalling the millennium bug.

Election Ennui

At the beginning of the third millennium, the Americans' lives seemed destined to go ahead uneventfully: "2001 will be a year in which the world becomes a richer and sharply more decent place," was what the English magazine the *Economist* predicted in its 2000 yearbook.[24] Forecasts for the United States were comforting. The American economy was enjoying its longest period of growth in history. Poverty and unemployment were at their lowest level for the last 30 years, and the federal budget could count on hundreds of millions of dollars on the credit side. "America is the dominant power in the world, militarily, economically and culturally. Its companies and icons are everywhere, yet its soldiers—although targets of terrorism all over the world—are nowhere engaged in combat." However, the magazine added, "into this paradise has come a note of sourness. When America's 43rd president is sworn in on Saturday January 20th, many Americans will feel unable to share his moment of triumph."[25]

The year 2000 had been a presidential election year in the United States, but most Americans were unenthusiastic about the clash between the two candidates, the Democrat Albert A. Gore and the Republican George W. Bush. The eight years of Clinton's presidency had ended with many religious and conservative Americans disgusted and offended by the scandalous conduct of an immoral president who lied and had even dared to defile the sacrality of the Oval Office, the United States president's office, with his sexual behavior. The Religious Right had fought vainly to have the president, a lecherous sinner, removed from office through impeachment. However, the new presidency of the Republican Bush also began under a cloud. There were rumors of a scandal regarding the elections, not sex, for the very controversial way Bush had won over the Democratic candidate, who had received the majority of votes with over half a million more than Bush. In fact, when voting ended on November 7, a month of political and legal battles followed, while the votes were recounted rather chaotically in the state of Florida, where the governor was Bush's brother. In the end, on December 9, the federal Supreme Court brought the dispute to an end, assigning the victory to Bush with a majority of just one vote, decided by the judges who had been nominated by Republican presidents. Thus George W. Bush, son of the 41st president of the United States and with the same name, became the 43rd president. The Democrats contested the decision of the Supreme Court and raised doubts about the new president's legitimacy, but on December 13 Gore accepted defeat, publicly acknowledging his rival's victory in a sober speech to the nation on television. This was how the struggle for the presidency, which the *Time Almanac 2001* called "Election Ennui," came to an end.

Terrorism Was Not Frightening

The same almanac mentioned the name of Osama bin Laden twice, as a rich militant Islamic extremist protected by the Taliban in Afghanistan, and furthermore that the American government had requested his extradition as he was believed to be involved in the terrorist attacks of August 7, 1998, against the American embassies in Kenya and Tanzania. However, the almanac forgot that 10 years earlier the United States had supported bin Laden with arms and money when he fought in the Islamic resistance against Russia's occupation of Afghanistan. Offspring of a very wealthy Saudi family, bin Laden had abandoned his affluent way of life to dedicate himself to Islamic radicalism and aggressive asceticism. He was converted to anti-American terrorism after the Gulf War because he thought that the presence of American troops in Saudi Arabia, the sacred cradle of Islam, was sacrilege.

That was when bin Laden began to hate the United States profoundly and ruthlessly, as the Islamic radicals believed it was the great Satan, an evil power both corrupt and corrupting that spread its poison throughout the world. It did so by means of its depraved customs and morals and by spreading pornography and sexual freedom; and furthermore, by protecting the state of Israel, it was trying to destroy Islamic civilization on its own territory. In 1992 bin Laden began his terrorist campaign against the West by founding the terrorist organization al Qaeda, which had its training camps in Afghanistan, then ruled by the extremist regime of the Taliban. The aim was to free Arab lands of the infidels, unite all the believers in Islam, and set up a Muslim community based rigorously on religious radicalism.

In 1998, bin Laden declared a holy war on the United States, inciting Muslims all over the world to gain paradise by killing as many Americans and Jews as possible, everywhere, without making any distinction between civilians and servicemen. He also announced terrorist attacks in the United States.[26]

However, on the morning of September 11 it is likely that most Americans, including those who were flying, did not know who bin Laden was. Islamic terrorism did not frighten them more than the millennium bug at the turn of the millennium. During the 1990s, Gallup polls showed that fewer than 10 percent, and often even fewer than 5 percent of Americans, gave the greatest importance to defense and national security. Also the two candidates for the presidency spoke little about terrorism during the electoral campaign. In his first electoral speech, Bush said that his presidency would give top priority to tracking down terrorists on American territory and fighting them back, but in the three debates between the two candidates, the subject of terrorism was not discussed.[27] Neither the U.S. Congress nor the mass media paid much attention to the danger of terrorism.[28] The word "terrorism" was not even in the list of "key words" given by the *Time Almanac 2001*.

Current Issues

On the morning of September 11, terrorism was not America's main worry. Summer was nearly over, and according to the press, the news that had upset the summer holidays the most was that shark attacks on bathers had been unusually frequent on the southern coasts. However, at the end of the summer, America's greatest worry was probably the economic situation. Since the end of 2000, a period of economic recession had begun; there was a debit balance, unemployment was increasing, and the price of oil was rising—while to keep to the electoral program, the new administration continued undeterred to cut taxes, a move which had already poured 80 percent of its benefits into the pockets of 2 percent of the richest tax payers. "There's a hint of panic in the air, and this can lead to bad politics," commented the *New York Times* on September 11.[29] Consequently the president was losing consent. His "honeymoon" with the Americans, as the first period of a new presidency is called, was shorter than in the past. Spring and summer polls had shown a constant drop in public approval ratings, and they were still dropping on the eve of September 11.[30]

However, on that morning, the authoritative American newspaper gave importance to other issues. A group of scientists of the National Academy of Sciences, an eminent scientific organization, had made public a long report in favor of the federal government's financing research on new series of stem cells extracted from human embryos, in order to develop their potential efficacy in treating serious illnesses like Parkinson's disease, Alzheimer's disease, diabetes in the young, and cancer.[31] The scientists maintained that over a hundred million Americans could benefit from this research. The newspaper declared that this request would probably stir up a political debate, because the new president, a very religious evangelical conservative, supported the "culture of life" and was therefore against both abortion and research on human embryonic cells, because he believed that this meant killing potential individuals. On August 9, in a speech to the nation on television, Bush said that every human embryo is unique, with the unique genetic potential of a human individual, and that he felt morally obliged, as president, to protect and encourage respect for life, in America and the world.[32] The president had decided not to allocate federal funds, although he permitted research to be continued on cells already extracted.

The influence of the new presidency's traditionalist and religious conservatism also made itself felt in other fields. On the morning of September 11, the airplane passengers who read the *New York Times* found the news of unrest among the students in the state of New York, because the government had decided to oblige all public schools to adopt a "code of conduct" which regarded also what clothes the schoolchildren wore: scanty clothes were forbidden. Furthermore a scholastic district in Massachusetts had forbidden girls to wear very low-cut tee shirts.[33] A similar code of conduct had been adopted by the North Carolina government, with a law that allowed schools to display the Ten Commandments.

On the morning of September 11, certainly more important news was the end of the electoral campaign in New York with six candidates taking part to succeed the mayor, Rudolph Giuliani, a popular but controversial personage, famous for having reduced crime by adopting harsh measures in one of the most violent cities in the world. The electoral campaign had ended the day before and the polls were to open on the morning of September 11.

In the meantime, President Bush was under fire from the Democrats who attacked his missile defense plan. According to the Democratic Senator Joseph R. Biden Jr., president of the Senate Committee on Foreign Relations, not only would the space defense plan cost astronomical figures, but it would also sacrifice national security to a theological belief, nullifying 40 years of efforts in a policy of weapon control. Furthermore, it would trigger clashes between the United States and its allies and create tension with Russia, while it would definitely not offer the protection promised by its supporters. The senator ended by saying that the administration would do better to modernize the air force.[34]

Imperial Worries

These were the main news items on home affairs that Americans read in their most authoritative newspaper on September 11. There was no alarming news from abroad, even though the new president's style and the new administration's foreign policy had created some trouble in the United States' international relations.

Bush had no experience in international politics; he knew little about other countries and geography in general. "Nobody needs to tell me what to believe. However, I *do* need someone to tell me where Kosovo is," he said during the electoral campaign, and he was not joking.[35] Apart from frequent visits to Mexico when he was governor of Texas from 1994 to 1999, Bush had made only short trips overseas.

As presidential candidate, Bush had said that his foreign policy would give priority to national interest, in harmony with, and inspired by, Woodrow Wilson's internationalism, further declaring that the United States had a great goal to guide it—to turn this age of American influence into generations of democratic peace.[36] Bush refused to consider the United States an imperial power. In 1999 he said that America had never been an empire, and even when it had the chance to become one, it refused, preferring greatness to power and justice to glory.[37] When Bush mentioned foreign policy, which was not the main subject of his electoral campaign, he promised he would collaborate with America's strong democratic allies in Europe and Asia to spread peace; that he would foster the full development of democracy in the western hemisphere, united by a free market; that he would defend American interests in the Persian Gulf and encourage peace in the Middle East, guaranteeing Israel's security; and that he would keep the contagious spread of weapons of mass destruction under control.

Once the presidency was won, it was clear the new administration would follow a unilateral tendency in foreign policy, inspired by a realism aimed at asserting the supremacy of American interests over international bodies and agreements.

On the morning of September 11, the barometer of the international situation did not forecast stormy weather for the United States, even though there had been a few brief, isolated storms in the last few months in its relations with Russia and China, and there had been some clouds in those with its Western allies. The latter did not like the new administration's beginning with a unilateral tendency, its refusal to ratify the Kyoto Protocol on curbing greenhouse gases, or its decision to take up the plans for a new space defense system again. At the beginning of 2001, following the arrest of an FBI (Federal Bureau of Investigation) agent who had sold information to the Russian leaders for 15 years, a dispute arose between the Russian and American governments which called to mind the times of the Cold War. Washington expelled 50 Russian diplomats accused of counterespionage, and Moscow retaliated likewise. Then the situation calmed down. At the beginning of April there was another international clash, between the American and communist Chinese governments, after a collision between an American spy plane and a Chinese military jet plane. The Chinese plane crashed and the pilot was killed, while the crew members of the American plane, forced to land on the island of Hainan, were held prisoner somewhere unknown. At that time relations between the two nuclear powers were already troubled, because China had threatened military retaliation if Washington agreed to Taiwan's requests for anti-missile weapons. The spy plane incident heightened the tension. Beijing accused the United States of violating China's national sovereignty, demanding official apologies as well as compensation for damages and the pilot's death, while Washington protested that the incident had taken place in international space, so refused to make its apologies, demanding that the American crew be released immediately. The crisis between the two countries could easily have worsened, but after about 10 days of difficult negotiations, a compromise was reached which saved the faces of both powers. The United States president expressed his sincere regret for the Chinese pilot's death, and the American crew was consequently freed.

On the morning of September 11, the main international news in the *New York Times* concerned the Middle East. In Istanbul a woman had blown herself up in the commercial and tourist center of the city—two police officers were killed and bloody pieces of the woman's body were flung everywhere. "There was blood all over the place, it was terrible," was how a woman office worker described the scene after the explosion. There was other news from the Middle East: the Iranian government rejected the United States' accusation that it was frantically looking for foreign technology to produce weapons of mass destruction, pointing out that Iran had been the victim of chemical weapons during the war against Saddam Hussein's Iraq which had been backed by the United States. The newspaper reported that for the Iraqi government's part, it accused the American and British air forces of killing eight civilians during a missile attack in the so-called "no-fly zone," set up by the United Nations after the Gulf War in 1991 to keep the aggressive Iraqi dictator under control. In the meantime, Israel went ahead with building the dividing wall between the Palestinian and Israeli territories, decided on by the Sharon government to prevent terrorist attacks, while the series of Palestinian suicide bomb attacks continued, with Israel retaliating.

The American administration was more worried about the news from Afghanistan. The *New York Times* reported that the White House had no sure information about the death of Ahmed Shah Massoud, the leader of the United Front, the last force that opposed the Taliban regime. Massoud was the victim of a suicide attack made by two Arabs who had introduced themselves as journalists. "This is a gift sent by God," a Taliban commander commented, "I'm really pleased." The Afghan government denied it was involved in the attack. Nevertheless, the daily commented, anything confirming that the murderers were Arab would prove that those who maintained that foreign Arabs, like Osama bin Laden, played a constantly greater part in decision making among the Taliban, were right.[38]

A Predicted but Unconsidered Risk

Since 1992, bin Laden had been closely observed by the United States, as the American government thought that he, above all, inspired the new anti-American terrorism. In the last eight years there had been numerous Islamic attacks against American targets, in Africa and the Middle East, but only one had been made on American territory. In New York on February 26, 1993, a truck bomb exploded in a garage of the World Trade Center. There could have been thousands of victims, and the police thought it was a miracle that there were only six dead and just over a thousand injured. Those guilty of the attack were discovered and convicted. Ramzi Yousef, the terrorist who had placed the bomb, said he had hoped to kill 250,000 people, to avenge the Palestinians and punish the Americans for supporting Israel. Two hundred twenty-four people, including 12 Americans, were killed in the attacks on the United States embassies in Africa. The latest attack made by Islamic terrorists against American targets was on October 12, 2000, with a suicide attack against the ship *USS Cole* in a Yemen port, where 17 sailors were killed. President Clinton had given orders to hunt down bin Laden and kill him; consequently the al Qaeda bases in Afghanistan were bombed.[39]

The millennium bug had had repercussions on the problem of terrorism as well: it was feared that the bug could cancel computer data files and block communications between anti-terrorist agencies, thus encouraging terrorists to act.[40] The American government was warned and all the counterterrorism agencies were mobilized. Some Islamic terrorists who were planning to carry out attacks in the United States were arrested. An Arab loaded with explosives destined to blow up the Los Angeles airport was discovered at the Canadian border. Then the anti-terrorist alarm was called off, and terrorism was no longer on the agenda. No Gallup poll results, either during 2000 or the first eight months of 2001, considered the issue of terrorism important enough to be worth investigating on a national scale.

However, during the first half of 2001, federal agencies reported the danger of new Islamic terrorist attacks against United States interests. On June 30, a CIA report maintained that bin Laden was planning a large-scale attack against the United States with catastrophic consequences, and another report on August 6 repeated that bin Laden was determined to strike the United States on its own territory. Nevertheless, in the following days the imminent danger of a terrorist attack was not discussed by the president or his advisers, and from May to September not even the press or television paid it any attention. The main news about anti-terrorist initiatives in the days preceding September 11 regarded security measures in military bases abroad and warnings to Americans not to go to Arab countries.

Terror in the Heart of America

The 19 Arabs who were flying over the United States on the morning of September 11 were certainly thinking about bin Laden.

It was just after 8:00 A.M. President Bush was going by car to a primary school in Sarasota, Florida, to be present at a reading exercise of the schoolchildren there. At 8:50 A.M., as he was about to enter the school, he was privately informed that an airplane had crashed into the North Tower of the World Trade Center at 8:46 A.M. It was thought to be an accident. At 9:05 A.M. the president was sitting in class among the pupils when his private secretary entered the classroom and whispered in his ear that a second plane had hit the other tower: America was under attack. While he was heading for the airport, Bush learned that a plane had crashed into one side of the Pentagon at 9:37 A.M., reducing it to rubble. Later, when his plane had taken off, he was told that a plane had crashed in a field near Shanksville, Pennsylvania, at 10:03 A.M. Perhaps the terrorists wanted to fly the plane into the White House or the Capitol, but had been prevented by some passengers who rebelled after finding out about the attack on the World Trade Center from their cell phones—the plane ended up crashing to the ground.

The 19 Arabs on board the 4 planes carried out the terrorist attacks. They overcame the crews and killed the pilots with small knives and cutters, then flew the planes like missiles into the most important symbols of American power and wealth. The sequence of the second attack on the World Trade Center was seen live on television by America and the rest of the world, while the tower which had been struck first burned like a torch.

It took six years and eight months, from 1966 to 1973, to build the towers, whose structures were capable of resisting even if hit by the largest airplanes of that period. In its September 24, 2001 issue *Newsweek* commented that when the towers were raised 30 years before, they were greeted as the first buildings of the twenty-first century—instead, they were its first victims.[41] The two towers disappeared from New York's skyline in 1 hour and 40 minutes, the length of time between the first attack and the collapse of the second tower. The South Tower was the first to collapse, at 9:59 A.M. producing a gigantic cloud of dust, smoke, and debris, which spread, whirling violently like a volcanic eruption, blotting out the sky and enveloping thousands of terrified people fleeing in a suffocating darkness that spread for nearly a mile around, raining down innumerable fragments and scattered papers which floated haphazardly and lazily in the tumult of the dense cloud. This horrendous scene was repeated at 10:28 A.M. when the North Tower imploded. In a few hours the World Trade Center became Ground Zero, the name given to places where an atomic explosion has taken place. At 10 30 A.M. on September 11, a monstrous and shapeless "third tower" took the place of the white and slender twin towers. This mass of smoke and fire was produced by 1,800,000 tons of debris, shapeless blocks of concrete, mixed with an intricate forest of broken girders and twisted steel gratings, which once made up the elegant external structure of the two towers, now looking like the mutilated rib cages of shattered skeletons. Thousands of people, men and women of 80 nationalities, hundreds of firemen who had raced to the two buildings, together with dozens of policemen, rescuers, and passersby, died—were wiped out—in this heap of debris.[42]

Rescue operations began immediately, arduous and risky because of gas leaks, explosions, collapsing walls, and fires, and continued feverishly and uninterruptedly round the clock for days, in the hope of finding survivors. Then hope gave way to desperation and horror. Digging in this mountain of rubble as high as seven stories, few bodies were found while scraps of human remains were continually being pulled out. The work to remove the tons of debris went on for a year and was carried out with compassionate care, in an effort to find even the tiniest fragment of human remains and the slightest sign that could make it possible to identify the victims. Straight after the two towers collapsed, the mayor, Mr. Giuliani, ordered 30,000 coffins, preparing for the most dreadful possibility that few had managed to escape before the collapse. Fortunately a later body count turned out to be much lower. After six months 287 bodies and 18,937 fragments of human remains had been recovered, which allowed 972 victims to be identified. In the summer of 2002, when the works to clear out the site ended, less than half of the victims' remains had been identified, while thousands of human fragments were still waiting to undergo DNA tests for identification: almost 20,000 of them made it possible to identify 1,092 victims. The bodies of 1,731 human beings were dispersed. About 3,000 people perished at the World Trade Center, as well as 343 firemen and 60 police officers. One hundred twenty-five died at the Pentagon, and 256 passengers of the four airliners were killed. Only 18 people were pulled out alive from the ruins of the World Trade Center: 12 firemen, 3 police officers, and 3 civilians, all of them saved by September 12.[43]

A Grief-Stricken Community

On the morning of September 11, the United States was a seriously bewildered nation tottering on the brink of chaos.[44] For the first time in the history of civil aviation all airplanes were ordered to land, flights were cancelled and airports closed, as were government and public buildings, financial centers, the Wall Street exchange, offices, and schools. The United States seemed to be paralyzed.

When the Americans first heard the news that a plane had crashed into one of the World Trade Center towers, they were amazed and incredulous. A witness who was going to work when he heard that a plane had struck the World Trade Center said:

> There was no panic, just puzzlement: how *does* a plane, on a sparkling day, crash into a skyscraper so tall you can see it for miles? Something felt wrong. I hurried upstairs, logged on to America Online and turned on CNN.
> Minutes later, I watched a jetliner zoom across the television screen and explode as it crashed into the Trade Center's second tower.[45]

Over two hundred million Americans followed, on television and at the same time, every moment of the tragedy at the World Trade Center after the first plane attacked. Over 60 percent of them confessed that, even though they were anguished and horrified by what they saw, they could not take their eyes off the screen, which continued to show the sequence of the terrorist attacks and repeats of the towers collapsing, the scenes of terror, panic, and horror among the fleeing people.

Like on-the-spot witnesses of the tragedy, this is how Americans saw flames and smoke billow out of the top of the North Tower and the second plane fly into the South Tower, exploding inside the skyscraper and producing an enormous ball of fire. They saw groups of people clinging to the windows of the two skyscrapers, surrounded by smoke and flames, and men and women jumping off into space to escape from an atrocious death, falling towards a death just as atrocious. A witness who worked in an adjacent building said he had seen at least 14 people jump off.[46] Bodies and objects falling from the towers struck and killed some people on the ground as well. Soon after, millions of Americans saw the two towers suddenly and unexpectedly collapse with thousands of people still imprisoned inside, while crowds of men and women swarmed along nearby streets, fleeing in the desperate search for refuge under a dense rain of debris and sheets of paper and with an enormous cloud of suffocating dust looming over them, following and then enveloping them like a monster killer. And when the cloud began to clear up, revealing the terrifying sight of the mass of ruins towering above the place where the World Trade Center had stood, millions of Americans saw firemen, police officers, and civilian volunteers moving like whitened specters on the mountain of rubble, looking for survivors among hidden chasms and tottering heaps of concrete and steel girders. They saw the bloody faces and tortured bodies of the injured, and a stream of people leaving Manhattan crossing Brooklyn Bridge, like an exodus of survivors fleeing the horrors of a war.

Then during the day and night of September 11, the day after, and the following days, the Americans saw hundreds of men and women of every race and age with grief-stricken faces, sometimes silently showing photographs of their loved ones who worked in the World Trade Center, imploring people for information in the desperate hope that somebody could reassure them that these loved ones had survived. The streets and squares around Ground Zero were turned into sacred places by the crowd gathered in prayer day and night, keeping vigil with burning candles. At the same time numerous small altars appeared everywhere, along the sidewalks and the gratings enclosing gardens, on the walls of buildings and in subway stations. Each altar held the picture of a person missing in the World Trade Center, with flowers around it, the American flag, and messages of sorrow, memories, and faith. While the site was being cleared, the Americans saw human remains recovered from the rubble, and they followed the silent ceremonies with firemen and police officers rendering honor to the bodies of their companions, wrapped in the Stars and Stripes and saluted as fallen in battle. When the body of a fireman was recovered, the machines were stopped, a "deathly silence" fell, and everyone took off their helmets and saluted the body wrapped in the American flag, which was carried away religiously by companions. The ritual was repeated many times during the day, the night, and the following day.

Seeing both the catastrophe and the mourning at the same time turned the Americans into a single grief-stricken community, which plunged suddenly from its pride and sense of security in an unbeatable nation to the terror of a nation attacked and horribly wounded in the very heart of its power, discovering that it was vulnerable. "We are all in the Third Tower now, which rose instantly from the collapse of the other two," wrote Nancy Gibbs, the *Time* journalist.[47]

No Longer Invulnerable

Humiliation for being taken by surprise and for the success of the terrorist aggression was added to the terror and horror of the catastrophe, to the sorrow for the victims. The terrorists were treacherously knowledgeable when they chose their emblematic targets, to inflict not only sorrow for a ruthless carnage on the great Satan, in the name of God, but also a symbolic mortal blow to its power, pride, and prestige, at the same time humiliating the infidel and blasphemous Western civilization which the United States represented. Probably when choosing the targets to attack, the terrorists saw the two towers as symbols of the infidels' religion, so their attack was meant to be a kind of divine punishment against Western idolatry. After all, the American press itself called up the Promethean fascination of the World Trade Center towers after September 11:

> The towers inspired awe and fascination. The building was also emblematic of our country's deepest aspirations. Skyscrapers are an American invention, and the World Trade Center was among the last to reflect something of the visionary ideals of progress and technology that so defined the last century. How high can we build? How high can we fly? Can we reach the moon?[48]

The two towers were so majestically imposing that they gave off an aura of sacredness; one felt awed and fascinated, they were the cathedrals of America, the minister of a church in New York stated on September 16; and now the cathedrals had disappeared.[49]

Together with thousands of unaware and innocent people, the feeling that America was inviolable was also a victim of the terrorist attack on the Pentagon and the two towers. The theologian Peter Ochs said that the greatest shock for his students, six months after the terrorist attack, was to discover that America was vulnerable: "I didn't know that *we* could be attacked."[50] In a few hours the way Americans perceived the world was radically changed:

> Our national world, as we understood it—standing alone, virtually invincible—no longer exists. Foreign powers, however they are ultimately defined, have breached our borders, and there can be no absolute promise that they will never do so again. We must reconstruct our understanding of our nation and its meaning in our lives. We must defend it in its newly recognized vulnerability.[51]

This is what Joanne B. Freeman, teacher of history at Yale University, wrote on September 28, reminding her readers that only in the early years of the republic had Americans felt vulnerable in the same way, fearing the power of the enemy they had fought against to gain independence. In 1814 the British army occupied and torched Washington; however, since then, the Americans had not undergone an attack on their territory. Protected by two oceans and the most powerful military apparatus the world has ever known, the American nation felt inviolable. Only Hollywood films about catastrophes had thought up war attacks on the United States, carried out by Soviet infiltrators, madmen aspiring to dominate the world, or aliens—but the United States always won. On the contrary, at the beginning of the twenty-first century, just when the United States was at the height of its power, undisputably superior to all the nations in the world, 19 Islamic terrorists dedicated to suicide and armed with small box cutters, managed to seize 4 American jetliners and turn the apocalyptic nightmare of the imaginary catastrophes into terrifying reality.

Americans had gotten used to small doses of fear in their lives: fear caused by crimes, natural disasters, and even their home-produced terrorism, like what happened in Oklahoma City. But they were not prepared *for this, U.S. News & World Report* commented on September 24. The magazine added that not even the Japanese attack on Pearl Harbor, brought up by many commentators, was comparable to the shock of September 11, because Americans knew their enemy at Pearl Harbor; they knew his address—but they did not know who this enemy was; they did not have his address. This is the terror of terrorism: the enemy can work beside you, with you. In the following days, the death of five people caused by the bacillus of anthrax, sent by mail to newspapers and Senate offices, made Americans even more afraid of being exposed to an invisible, lethal terrorist threat.

Those who drew up the report of the National Commission on Terrorist Attacks wrote that September 11 was a day of shock and unprecedented suffering in the history of the United States, that the nation was unprepared, and that at 8:46 A.M. on the morning of September 11, 2001, the United States was a nation transformed.[52] Fareed Zakaria, editor of *Newsweek,* observed that September 11 was the end of the end of history for the United States.[53] The myth that the United States was invulnerable had collapsed, nothing would be the same any more. These words, continually repeated, revealed a tragic and hostile world, and the tragedy of September 11 violently awakened the Americans to this reality.

Fear and Anger

Edward T. Linenthal, a historian of American religion and culture, compared the perception of reality after September 11 to the sight of a "fractured landscape": he had the feeling Americans lived in an alien landscape, foreboding and terrifying, and were looking for the resources to face it, and find a new normality.[54] A poll carried out in the first weeks after the attack revealed that 7 out of 10 Americans were depressed and a third suffered from insomnia. Their sense of security had been profoundly shaken. Fear would reign among them for a long time, a Kansas City psychoanalyst declared at the end of September.[55] Even if the passing of time tended to alleviate the depression, *U.S. News & World Report* observed in November, the traumatic effects had left a feeling of anxiety when perceiving reality and imagining the future.[56] At the end of 2001, the psychologist Garland DeNelsky commented that what had happened on that terrible Tuesday had drastically changed the lives of Americans, an immense change which was probably irreversible, because the new combination of potentially devastating technology, ideological extremism, and fanatics ready to commit suicide for their cause made any scenario of mass deaths and suffering for the people conceivable. Another mortal terrorist attack against this nation, God forbid, the psychologist added, would wound its already diminished sense of security even more deeply.[57]

According to some approximate estimates, at least 40,000 people among the survivors, witnesses, and rescuers suffered severe psychological traumas caused by the terrorist attack. Based on collective traumatic experiences in the past, it was expected that at least a third of the people more directly involved in the September 11 tragedy would be disturbed after the trauma because of stress, with recurring nightmares, and would be incapable of recalling the experience of the tragedy without living it again physically.[58] Research carried out in the following months showed that many Americans had reacted to September 11 with emotional suffering, fear, depression, and anguish, naturally more acute among the inhabitants of New York and the direct witnesses, but also widespread among the millions of Americans who had seen the tragedy on television. Research carried out between October and December in the state of New York, in Connecticut, and in New Jersey, revealed that 75 percent of those interviewed complained of traumatic symptoms, while 48 percent declared they were above all angry, even furious. According to a poll of the *New York Times* and CBS News, in the days straight after September 11, 85 percent of Americans were in favor of military action against those who had organized the terrorist attack, and 75 percent thought military action was right even if it involved killing innocent people.[59] Some representatives of the Republican right brutally expressed their desire for revenge, like the writer Ann Coulter, who had lost a friend in the attack on the Pentagon: "We should invade their countries, kill their leaders and convert them to Christianity. We weren't punctilious about locating and punishing only Hitler and his top officers. We carpet-bombed German cities; we killed civilians. That's war. This is war."[60] The Republican Senator John McCain, a hero of the Vietnam War who had competed with Bush for the Republican candidacy in the 2000 elections, expressed the Americans' anger in less brutal words when he stated that, after shedding a tear for the future victims of the war, it was necessary to undertake to kill as many enemies as possible and as quickly and ruthlessly as possible, because they had started a war not wanted by America, and the blame for innocent victims would fall on them.[61]

Two months after September 11, a nationwide survey showed that almost 45 percent of adults and 35 percent of children still had stress symptoms. Six months later, people who had not been directly involved in the tragedy still suffered from its traumatic effects, which appeared as anxiety and fear of new terrorist attacks capable of striking them and their loved ones directly. All over the country, people feared that an invisible enemy was present, capable of using even nuclear devices and bacteriological weapons to spread death and destruction in the United States. However, as William Langewiesche, a correspondent of *The Atlantic Monthly* observed, in the weeks following September 11 the Americans' fear arose not so much from the terror of death as from the sensation that collective control was lost, from the impression they were being dragged headlong into an apocalyptic future which their society was not prepared for.[62]

And the President Spoke

On September 11, the president of the United States was picked up in Florida and for the whole day moved from one military base to another on the presidential airplane and escorted by fighter planes for fear of another attack, keeping contact with the vice president, who carried out his functions in the anti-atomic bunker of the White House. Only in the evening did the president return to the capital.

After learning that a second airplane had crashed into another tower of the World Trade Center, Bush had no doubt that America was under attack, and he decided that the United States was at war. At 9:30 A.M. on September 11, he made his first brief comment to the nation, broadcast from the primary school in Sarasota, saying, "Today we've had a national tragedy. Two airplanes have crashed into the World Trade Center in an apparent terrorist attack on our country.... Terrorism against our nation will not stand."[63]

A few hours later, speaking from an air base in Louisiana, the president assured the Americans that the government was doing everything necessary to protect America and the Americans. "The resolve of our great nation is being tested. But make no mistake: we will show the world that we will pass this test. God bless."[64] At 8:30 in the evening, in his message to the nation from the Oval Office, Bush said that the terrorist attack was aimed at America's way of life, its freedom, intending "to frighten our nation into chaos and retreat. But they failed, because our country is strong." America, he said, "was targeted for attack because it was the brightest beacon for freedom and opportunity in the world. And no one will keep that light from shining. Today, our nation saw evil, the very worst of human nature. And we responded with the best of America, with the daring of our rescue workers, with the caring for strangers and neighbors who came to give blood and help in any way they could." The government was ready to pursue and punish the culprits. No distinction would be made between the terrorists who committed these crimes and those who protected them. "America and our friends and allies join with all those who want peace and security in the world, and we stand together to win the war against terrorism."[65] On the morning of September 11, the "accidental" president, as he was called sarcastically for the way he had obtained the presidency, turned into the supreme commander and head of the nation at war.

The age of empire had become the age of terror for violated America.[66]

—— 2 ——

Where Was God?

He Was Not in Lisbon

On November 1, 1755, the city of Lisbon was almost completely destroyed by an earth- and seaquake. There were tens of thousands of victims among the population of 250,000 inhabitants. Many died while they were in church attending mass for All Saints' Day. A fire raged for almost three days, completing the destruction of the city and increasing the number of dead. This was not the first time that such natural catastrophes happened in the eighteenth century, affecting thousands of victims. There were 20,000 dead in the earthquake that destroyed Lima, the capital of Peru, in 1746, and 10 times as many in the two earthquakes in China at the beginning of 1700. The planetary distance away of these last two catastrophes may have attenuated the emotional impact on Europeans who, on the contrary, were profoundly shocked by the destruction of one of the most beautiful and prestigious cities in Europe, the rich and elegant capital of a colonial empire which extended from the Atlantic Ocean to the Indian Ocean, from Latin America to Africa and Asia. As Walter Benjamin commented on October 31, 1931, in a radio program on natural catastrophes, for Europe of the eighteenth century, calling Lisbon destroyed was rather like nowadays calling Chicago or London destroyed.[1]

The Lisbon earthquake triggered off a flood of religious, moral, and philosophical reflections that tried to answer a question which had arisen dramatically among Europeans: where was God when thousands of innocent lives were being wiped out violently by a natural catastrophe? Jansenists and Jesuits, Protestants and Catholics, clergymen and laymen tried to interpret the disaster in the light of their own theology, in an effort to reconcile mercy and divine omnipotence with the ruthless indifference of natural forces when slaughtering human beings. Some theologians explained that the Lisbon catastrophe was a manifestation of divine wrath which had struck an opulent and dissolute city, corrupted by the anticlerical Enlightenment. Others said it was a warning for all European society, which had strayed from God to follow the cult of human reason.

Also the followers of the Enlightenment movement, which was then at its climax, were shaken by the Lisbon earthquake. Voltaire, Rousseau, and Kant reflected on the problem of evil, on man's destiny, and on divine providence. What place had the divine design set out for the thousands of men, women, and children, unknowing and defenseless victims, who were randomly wiped out by nature's unpredictable damage, while other lives were saved just as randomly? How was it possible to reconcile natural evil with the concept of a universe created and regulated by a good, merciful, just, and almighty God? The Lisbon earthquake brutally raised doubts about the optimistic doctrine of divine providence, condensed into the axiom "all is well in the best of all possible worlds," which had been expounded in the *L'Essai de Theodicée, sur la bonté de Dieu, la liberté de l'homme et l'origine du mal* by the German philosopher Leibniz and in the poem "Essay on Man" by the English poet Alexander Pope. Theodicy tried to reconcile evil with divine good, maintaining that evil itself was a way that led to good in the designs of Providence. Voltaire railed at this doctrine, lashing out ironically. In a poem on the Lisbon disaster, he mocked Pope and Leibniz's axiom "all is well," belied by such a natural catastrophe: "these tremendous ruins,/This rubble, these scraps of flesh and wretched ashes,/These women, these children heaped up on each other,/These limbs scattered under the fragments of marble in the rubble."[2]

Before a tragedy of these proportions, Voltaire thought that claiming to justify evil in the name of a divine providence which always brought about good, was a detestable insult to human suffering and reason, just like the idea of an irascible God inflicting death and suffering on unknowing and innocent victims, to punish them for sins they had not committed. The French philosopher's conclusion was pessimistic, as he gave up looking for answers. God's mind is inscrutable, Voltaire stated: "The book of destiny is closed to our eyes. This is what the voice of nature has taught me."[3]

"Our Lisbon Earthquake"

Where was God on September 11, was what many Americans wondered. When the theologian Carol Zaleski commented on the first anniversary of the terrorist attack, she wrote: "September 11 is our Lisbon earthquake."[4] Zaleski referred to Voltaire's polemic against theodicy, noting that the Lisbon earthquake was the decisive experience for the Enlightenment's religion of reason, because it showed that no concept of a design sent by Providence or of a preordained harmony could come to terms with so much gratuitous horror.

The comparison between the Lisbon catastrophe and that of the World Trade Center was limited to the massacre of innocent people, because there was a substantial difference between the two catastrophes which was more alarming for religious consciences: the World Trade Center catastrophe was not caused by nature but was the consequence of voluntary actions, carried out by religious fanatics dedicated to death, who called upon God as their prerogative and compensation. Zaleski pointed out that despite this difference, the September 11 tragedy raised the same moral and theological problems that had been debated after the destruction of the Portuguese capital and which were now topical, because the Americans realized how uncomfortable they felt when justifying God's actions towards mankind, distinguishing between a saint and a fanatic or explaining why there was hope. She went on to say that from this point of view, September 11 had made Americans once again aware that religious optimism which tolerated everything was inadequate, as Voltaire discovered: there really was evil in the world.

Also the sociologist Elemér Hankiss made a comparison with the Lisbon earthquake, in a concise but acute analysis of the mythical and symbolic meaning that the events of September 11 could take on in American and Western thought, events which he called a negative miracle, an infernal prodigy of destruction:

> The impossible and unimaginable happened under our very eyes. The irrational broke into our world of Cartesian, Kantian rationality. The impact may prove to be as destructive as was that of the earthquake of Lisbon in 1755, which—according to the testimony of Voltaire—irreparably shook the faith of the Enlightenment in a harmonious and rational universe.[5]

According to Hankiss, the September 11 tragedy had profound symbolic repercussions because of what the United States represented in the Western world. In the preceding few decades, the United States had become the center of the world and held sway over the destiny of the West. The collapse of the World Trade Center, a symbol of glory for the Western world, undermined the triumph of the West by means of the very technology it had been so proud of as an emblem of its civilization.

Hankiss pointed out that such an event called up ancient catastrophic myths, deeply rooted in American and Western culture. Millions of people saw the frightening metamorphosis of an elegant silver airplane, a symbol of peace, freedom, and joy, into a terrible weapon of destruction, like the transubstantiation of a silvery angel into a ferocious demon. The desperate plunge towards death of the people who threw themselves off the towers in flames perhaps could be compared to the destiny of another Western symbol of human pride, Icarus, who fell to his death because he had risen too high, driven by his desire for power. The destruction of the two towers evoked the myth of the tower of Babel, God's intervention to punish human ambition which presumed to rival with his power. The fact that thousands of people from different walks of life, the powerful and rich together with the weak and poor, were wiped out at the same time, renewed the myth of the inflexible and capricious wheel of fortune. The events of September 11 confirmed the terrifying vision of human beings falling from the height of glory and success into the abyss of nothing, while the sudden absence of the two towers, which had stood out against the sky for 30 years, aroused a profound feeling of horror for the void, for life being wiped out. The mythical legacy of Western culture, concealed by its pretentious rationality, made the figure of Satan emerge again spontaneously from the horrible sight of destruction and death. Hankiss pointed out that many witnesses thought they saw the sneering image of the devil in the smoke and flames of the two towers.

The sociologist believed that all this spontaneously led the Judaic-Christian conscience to interpret the September 11 events through the apocalyptic myth of the struggle between God and the devil, between heaven and the kingdom of darkness. After the Cold War ended, we had hoped to be freed from this danger-ous and destructive dualism forever. On the contrary, it has come back forcefully as a consequence of September 11. The Manichaean pretension of those who identify themselves with God and their adversaries with evil, and who believe that their own truth is absolute and the only one, considering that doubting this truth or even trying to destroy it is a horrible sacrilege, emerged once more with the apocalyptic dualism. In short, Hankiss indicated a final mythical and symbolic effect of September 11 on Americans, that is, the end of the illusion of immortal-ity cultivated by the consumer society, the belief that even the fundamental prob-lem of human existence, death, would be resolved by man's power, by denying death.[6] On September 11, Western peoples were once again struck by the reality of death and were brutally made to face how fragile their lives were.

Living in a Fragile World

The Americans' reflections on the consequences of the terrorist attack were dominated by this new awareness of how fragile human beings were. The September 11 events were perceived by many observers as an apocalypse, not only in the meaning acquired by everyday language, as a synonym for catastro-phe, but in the original meaning of the word, that is, as the "revelation" of a looming turning point in history, destined to mark a profound, radical interrup-tion in man's destiny. Mary Marshall Clark, director of Columbia University's Oral History Research Center, held the opinion that those chosen for interviews among the survivors and witnesses of September 11 perceived its most important relevance as apocalyptic, an event that ended history as it was understood up to that moment.[7] However, for many theologians and scholars of religion, the apocalyptic significance of September 11 went beyond the perception of a break in history, to be understood as revealing that human lives are precarious in a fragile world. Karen Armstrong, a historian of religions, wrote that September 11 was a revelation in the original meaning of the word, because it "revealed" a reality that had always existed but which we had not seen clearly enough. The atrocities showed us how extremely precarious our position is in a world where most people feel underprivileged and defenseless.[8]

The philosopher Susan Neiman agreed that September 11 "underscored our infinite fragility,"[9] and brought up the comparison with the Lisbon earthquake again in the final reflections of a history of the problem of evil in modern consciousness. Modern thought had abandoned all references to Providentialism, acknowledging it was incapable of explaining the origin of evil after passing from the Lisbon catastrophe to the September 11 tragedy and on the way, the horrors of the two world wars and of genocides. Theodicy had been an attempt to give meaning to evil, to help face desperation. However, the Lisbon earthquake, like the World Trade Center catastrophe, had shown how vain every attempt was to link natural and moral evil to a providential design which made them rational, claiming to find a justification for human suffering in divine will.[10] Neiman pointed out that the terrorist attack on the World Trade Center was like natural catastrophes, because it could not have been foreseen, the attack did not make any moral distinction between victims or a difference between life and death, as in the slaughters caused by nature—it was left to fate to decide. This aroused a fear unknown up till then, because we had not understood the meaning of the word "terror." The shocking novelty of the September 11 catastrophe was the deliberate intention to plan an act of terror, meticulously and patiently preparing it for years, to inflict the greatest number of deaths and the most suffering possible on innocent people by means of suicide attacks.

It was not possible to apply the expression "the banality of evil" to the terrorists, as Hannah Arendt did to Adolf Eichmann, because what happened on September 11 "was hardly the product of mindless agents whose self-serving and self-pitying actions led to evils they never quite intended. On the contrary: the al-Qaeda terrorists knew exactly what they did.... Their goals were as perfectly calculated just as they were perfectly malicious."[11] Neiman concluded by saying that was why it became immediately clear that September 11 "was indeed a historical turning-point that would change our discussion of evil."[12]

The deliberate, conscious, and suicidal violence of the terrorists had revealed such vast proportions of evil that the categories worked out for it by modern thought offered no possibility of understanding it. And it was even more difficult for the Americans to understand this new reality of evil as it appeared in the terrorist attacks, because a long time ago they had dismissed the problem of evil from their daily lives. As Andrew Delbanco, the historian of culture, wrote in 1996, Americans suffered from a crisis of competence as regards evil, while never as in the world today have images of real horror been so widespread and terrifying. Americans do not have a language that links up their inner lives with the horrors they continually see in the world. The horrors of real war seem indistinguishable from war in video games, and when they are disgusted by horrible scenes, they change to another television channel.[13]

At the beginnings of their history, the Americans believed in evil as a consequence of original sin, and for a long time facing evil was a basic source of their identity. Delbanco stated that however, in recent times, the awareness that evil was real had begun to fade—evil had become a metaphorical abstraction, an epistemological problem,[14] that nobody even dared to call by its name, substituting it with neutral, technical expressions without metaphysical or ethical inspiration:

When American culture began, this devil was an incandescent presence in most people's lives, a symbol and explanation for both the cruelties one received and those perpetrated upon others. But by 1700 he was already losing his grip on the imagination—a process that has continued ever since.[15]

According to Delbanco, losing the awareness of evil had undermined the American identity, leaving Americans without precise and clearly-defined guidelines to direct their awareness of who and where they were. Evil had been removed from the present and sent back to the past, transfigured into mythical images of the age when the struggle against evil had galvanized the Americans, inspiring them with a shared moral purpose as happened during the Second World War, because at that time evil was easy to recognize and identify. Delbanco remembered President Clinton, who belonged to the generation of the Vietnam War and who had not done military service, walking on the Normandy beach on the day commemorating D-Day and commenting: "One watched the commemorative ceremonies with some measure of doubt about whether Americans were still equipped to recognize evil if it should be visited upon us again."[16] Modernity had made the devil invisible. Satan had become a "caricature of terror." A poll carried out in June 2001, showed that only 17 percent of Catholics, 18 percent of Methodists, 20 percent of Episcopalians, 21 percent of Lutherans, and 22 percent of Presbyterians believed that Satan existed.[17]

In an interview on the day after the terrorist attack on the World Trade Center, Delbanco again reflected on the problem of evil faced by Americans: would they still be able to avoid taking evil seriously after the tragedy of the World Trade Center? Delbanco explained that the new reality of evil which the Americans had become aware of, suddenly and violently, took the form of human beings capable of convincing themselves that there was good, an ideal, to which they had to dedicate their own lives, and before which the sorrow and suffering of others were unimportant, and, on the contrary, that they could be a price to pay in order to reach the goal. Evil is not being capable of seeing your victims as human beings, on the contrary considering them only as instruments, cogs in a wheel, numbers in statistics. "Yesterday we saw evil. We must face its challenge, stand against it."[18]

The reality of evil which the Americans' optimism had dismissed for so long, convinced as they were that they lived in the best possible country, had suddenly burst into their lives, embodied in a terrorist organization which caused a slaughter of innocent people, declaring it did so in the name of God. Such an event could not but create a dizzy feeling of bewilderment in a people that believed it was protected by God and suddenly found itself at the mercy of dark malevolent powers.

Had God Abandoned America?

The trauma Americans suffered from the September 11 tragedy was not only psychological, existential, and political but, for believers, also religious. "On September 11, 2001, even many who believed they had a firm hold on the Solid Rock were shaken and startled. Perhaps shaken not so much by the inadequacy of their faith, but by the sheer enormity of the destruction," the theologian Martha Simmons wrote in the preface of a collection of sermons by African-American ministers after the terrorist attack.[19]

The Americans are a religious people, the most religious of the highly industrialized nations. Over 90 percent of the United States population declare they believe in God or in a Higher Being. More than 80 percent of the Americans are professed Christians. Only 8 percent declare they are atheists. For such a religious people, the September 11 tragedy inevitably involved faith in God, especially considering how many Americans interpret God's role in the history and destiny of their nation.

Since the origins of this country's history, the myth that it enjoys special benevolence from Divine Providence, and that the United States was assigned a special mission to carry out on this earth to benefit all humanity, is rooted in American culture.[20] This myth reached the new world from England with the pilgrim fathers, and gained strength as the history of the United States evolved. Its rapid and amazing development in little more than a century to the standing of a world power, fortified the people's faith in providential protection, which even overcame serious crises like the war against Great Britain in 1812, the civil war of secession, the harsh struggles for civil rights against racism, the assassination of Kennedy, and the failure of the war undertaken in Vietnam. The end of the Cold War, the breakup of the Soviet Union, and achieving undisputed imperial supremacy confirmed that God continued to bless America also in the first century of the third millennium. Then suddenly and violently the terrorists attacked, destroying the greatest symbols of American civilization with the massacre of thousands of people. They too, in their ethnic and religious variety, represented the American nation, made up of different nations and faiths and founded on freedom of religion. The success of the September 11 terrorist attack suddenly made the myth that the United States was invulnerable collapse, and deeply upset the religious faith of the Americans who believed in an omnipotent, just, and merciful God. Many Americans were disconcerted and bewildered, wondering how it was possible to reconcile divine good with such a monstrous extermination of innocent lives, deliberately committed by fanatics convinced they were doing it in God's name.

Where was God while so many defenseless people were being wiped out so ruthlessly? Was God perhaps absent, impotent, or indifferent? Was God perhaps not good? These were the questions that many Americans asked themselves after September 11. Some relatives of victims felt they were losing their faith, others felt angry with God. A year after the tragedy, the wife of a fireman who died at the World Trade Center said, "I don't feel like speaking to him any more, because I feel so abandoned. I know God exists, I know I must forgive and go ahead, but I'm not yet ready to do so." A security guard who had known many of the victims was harsher: "I think I'm a good Christian, but now I consider God a barbarian." A young minister of the Episcopal Church who had been at Ground Zero right from the beginning to bless buckets containing fragments of bodies recovered from the heaps of rubble, stated that since that day he saw God's face as a blank surface.[21] Many Americans wondered why God left evil free to cause the death and suffering of innocent human beings. "There are times and experiences in our lives when we don't really see God or feel God's hand or presence or understand what God is doing...There are times when all of us, no matter how big and powerful and close our walk with the Lord, feel the absence of God in our situation....This experience is causing some people to feel disconnected from God," observed the African-American Methodist Reverend William Watley on September 16.[22] Others commented that perhaps God is good but impotent, or he is omnipotent but indifferent. "If he is all-powerful, why didn't he stop it [the terrorist attack]? Maybe he doesn't love us. Maybe he is punishing us. Maybe he is weak. Are we really so alone and endangered? Can't we trust him? Are we so terrifyingly alone?" is what the writer Frederica Mathewes-Green wondered.[23]

These were the doubts that inspired the theological reflections on the September 11 tragedy, "a dark day in the history of humanity," as John Paul II called it in the general audience on September 12. Also the pope wondered how anyone could carry out such savagely cruel acts, which showed that there are designs of unbelievable ferocity capable of destroying the normal life of a people in an instant, designs which sometimes emerge from the depths of the human mind.[24] Believers of every religion in America and all over the world were anguished by these doubts, which regarded the meaning of existence, man's destiny, and God's role in human events. It seemed that God had abandoned not only the Americans but all of humanity in the face of evil. America's tragedy was a human tragedy because, as the theologian Leroy Rouner remarked, in a very profound sense it does not make any difference where you live. Everyone, everywhere, now feels vulnerable anew. The problem for everyone is how to live with it, without being terrorized.[25]

Some of the American clergy and theologians reflected that feeling vulnerable and fragile after the September 11 attack took on existential and universal dimensions: the awareness of living in a world where evil is a reality and man's destiny an adventure, exposed to joy or sorrow, life or death by chance. In this fragile world, God himself is fragile, declared the Presbyterian theologian Frederick Buechner, meditating on the significance of the crucifix:

> It is not just the world we walk that is fragile, it seemed to say, but God also is fragile. It is not just the world that is vulnerable to the worst that mankind can do, but God also is vulnerable. The Twin Towers had been reduced to a smoldering mountain of rubble with who knows how many thousands of victims buried in it dead, dying, or alive, and what the cross under my shirt seemed to be saying was that one of the victims was God.[26]

God's Voices

As happened after the Lisbon disaster, faced with the American catastrophe there were no rational and theological answers to the question of how we can reconcile the reality of evil with the omnipotence and goodness of God. "Theodicy nettles us, but the bottom line is that it's irrelevant," Mathewes-Green declared: "The only useful question in such time is not 'Why?' but 'What next?' What should I do next? What should be my response to this ugly event? How can I bring the best out of it? How can God bring resurrection out of it?"[27] Despite this, many theologians and clergymen spoke to the Americans in the name of God when commenting on the September 11 events, explaining to them how they should interpret the tragedy of which they were victims according to divine will—even if "there are so many interpreters of the Word of God and they are often contradictory," as the Latin patriarch of Jerusalem observed on September 17:

> Some find in the Word of God love and mercy, and some find death and hatred.... This brings back the role of religion in our present world. It happened in history that religion has served to be a cause of wars. Today, too, religion is manipulated and God is prayed to overcome the enemy. In our country here, religion on both sides is having a big role in the conflict and in the cycle of violence. Religion cannot be a cause of wars. God is not the God of hatred and death.... It is a common responsibility of all religious leaders to free themselves, not to remain obedient parts of the political system, in order to be the voice of God, not of men, the God of mercy, righteousness, and love for all.[28]

On the same wavelength, an American minister criticized those who claimed to be God's voice, speaking in his name to express his will:

> In the weeks since the terrorist attacks of September 11, we have heard many voices claiming to speak for God. The terrorists claim that their holy war against the United States is in fact the will of God. Do they speak for God?
>   Television evangelists are claiming to speak for God as well....
>   So who does speak for God? Do our politicians who gathered on the steps of the Capitol to sing "God bless America"? Does our president, who gave the order to begin bombing Afghanistan?
>   Does your pastor speak for God?...
>   Who does speak for God? God speaks for God![29]

Indeed, judging from the voices of God heard during and after the September 11 events, we would have to conclude that God was everywhere and with everyone on that day: with the hijackers and the passengers, with the slaughterers and the victims, with the people imprisoned in the burning towers and those who managed to escape to safety. He was with those who jumped to their deaths and with the thousands of victims in the collapse of the two towers, with the Americans who wept and the Arabs who rejoiced for the enormous massacre at the World Trade Center, with bin Laden and President Bush, both of whom called on Him to guide their armies, lined up on opposite fronts, in the war against evil. Among so many voices speaking in the name of God, it was impossible to make out what was said by those who thought that silence was the only thing compatible with the tremendous cruelty of the September 11 tragedy:

This is time to be silent and filled with awe in the face of the power of evil and the enormity of mass death, and not to begin to extract redemption from it. To wriggle out of this horror in redemptive ways is false to the power of the event and dishonors the dead.[30]

Almost a year later, when reviewing a book entitled *Where Was God on September 11,* which quoted a dialogue between an Episcopal minister and an agnostic, the *New York Times* editorialist Peter Steinfels observed that when other peoples, in Asia and America, were faced with similar tragedies, nobody wondered where God was. Steinfels pointed out that God was not even present in the loving messages sent by some of the victims to their loved ones before dying, because their language was not religious but expressed simple, spontaneous, and human love. The title of an article by Steinfels was even more eloquent: "Where Was God? It Is a Question That Might Be Asked Every Day—Or Perhaps Not At All."[31] Evidently few listened to these solicitations to be humble, while many spoke on God's behalf. After all, people whose mission it was to answer the questions of the faithful tormented by doubt, to console the afflicted and encourage the desperate, could not be expected to remain silent. Nor could those whose vocation and profession involved studying good and evil, meditating on the mystery of God, and reflecting on the inscrutability of the divine designs, say nothing.

Many clergymen and theologians thought it necessary to reflect aloud on the September 11 tragedy, to comfort and help the Americans understand what it could mean for the fate of the nation in its relationship with God, even if not all of them said they spoke in God's name. For example, this was the case with the Episcopal bishop John Shelby Spong. Certainly few Americans were comforted by what he said, as after September 11 he announced the death of theistic God, that is, God conceived as a paternal entity, who watched over and protected humanity. Such a God is only a ghost of human hope. The image of the hijacked planes crashing into the buildings and killing thousands of people, jeopardizes theological claims. "The skies are empty of a protective deity ready to come to our aid. The God defined theistically has died. That is the lingering conclusion created by last week's events."[32] In other words, God as a supernatural being who lives above the heavens and is closely involved in the affairs of human history, who miraculously changes events to adapt them to some divine plan, is no longer credible. The terrorist tragedy could be the chance to free ourselves of the illusion that God is a magic potion made to save us, or a protective figure who controls our destiny or makes our fragile world safe. The bishop ended by saying that we must rid ourselves of the pious illusion of protective theism, which is a frightening conclusion but which reflects the reality we live in. However, the bishop's advice was not to resign ourselves in desperation to living without the comfort of God in a senseless world. As the Jewish philosopher Hans Jonas did when meditating on the concept of God after Auschwitz,[33] Spong urged people to form a new understanding of God and suggested considering him as a "wind" that flows through people's lives, an impersonal, vital force moved by the power of love.

The Scathing Critics

If millions of Americans in search of reassuring answers found little comfort when the Episcopal bishop declared the death of God as father and protector, a great many of them were outraged by some other voices of God, who said they saw the wrath of God against sinful America manifested in the terrorist attack.

What the Reverend Jerry Falwell, one of the most important representatives of the Christian evangelical Right, declared during a television interview on September 13, was met with a chorus of disapproval. The television program was conducted by the Reverend Pat Robertson, another leading representative of conservative evangelicalism and president of the television channel that broadcast the interview. The Reverend Falwell explained to the Americans that the September 11 tragedy had come about because God had taken away his protection of the United States, and that they were to blame—they had removed God from their lives, from society, from schools, and from politics. He went on to say that God had protected America wonderfully for 225 years: since 1812 this was the first time Americans had been attacked on their home ground, the first time, and with much worse results. Nor could the possibility of new attacks with more lethal weapons in the hands of these monsters, the various Husseins, Arafats, and bin Ladens, be excluded. What was seen on Tuesday, however terrible it was, could seem very little if God continued to raise the safety curtain and let America's enemies give it what it probably deserves. Falwell continued, saying that if God had stopped protecting America, it was the fault of the abortionists, pagans, feminists, gays, lesbians, and liberal associations like the American Civil Liberties Union, which had tried to secularize America.[34]

The Reverend Falwell's declaration caused such a flood of protests, even from President Bush, that he felt obliged to recant publicly, explaining that he thought only the hijackers and terrorists were responsible for the barbaric events of September 11.[35] Nevertheless, he did not recant his opinion of America's transgressions.[36]

If Falwell's theology lashed out at America's sins, the Reverend Robertson's was not very different in his introduction to the interview. The Reverend Robertson was much more detailed in denouncing the sins of the Americans, who were greedy for material possessions and interested in wealth, pleasure, and sex, while secularization gained momentum. Thirty-five or 40 million unborn babies were killed in America, the Supreme Court drove God out of schools, the Ten Commandments were expelled from courts of justice, and children were forbidden to pray at school. God was even insulted by the highest level of America's government, Robertson concluded, referring to Bill Clinton, and wondered: "Why did this happen? Well, it happened because Almighty God no longer protects us, and without protection we are all vulnerable, because we are a free society and therefore vulnerable." According to the reverend, thousands of Arab terrorists had already infiltrated America, ready to strike, and only the power of Almighty God could defend it.[37]

Robertson did not recant this opinion. On the contrary, about 10 days later he drove home that the September 11 tragedy had come about also because God no longer protected America:

> It also happened because God is lifting His protection from this nation and we must pray and ask Him for revival so that once again we will be His people, the planting of His righteousness, so that He will come to our defense and protect our nation.....
>
> We must have a spiritual revival. The churches need to be full....
>
> We have sinned against You, Lord. We ask You to forgive us. And that You might bring us to the place where we are truly sorry for our sins, and as a Nation we repent before You. And Almighty God, we ask for a spiritual revival, a cleansing of our Nation, a cleansing of the hearts of Your people.[38]

The Consolers

There were many clergymen and theologians who resolutely condemned the arrogance of those who presumptuously stood in judgment on the American nation in the name of God, claiming to know his will. The Episcopal Reverend Peter Eaton said that the September 11 tragedy was not divine justice but a barbaric act of human terrorism, and therefore it was senseless to maintain that God had "revoked" his protection because of America's sins, as if God usually protected the nation with a kind of heavenly Star Wars program.[39] The German theologian Jürgen Moltmann objected that after all, stating that God permitted the terrorist attack in order to punish secular, liberal, and homosexual America, was equivalent to saying that our God was the God of terrorism, and the terrorists were the servants who carried out God's orders. Moltmann added that instead of wondering where God was among those mass murderers, he should have been sought among the victims. Jesus wept when he saw that Jerusalem was about to be destroyed, in the same way a suffering God wept over the death of his beloved creatures at Ground Zero.[40]

Other clergymen and theologians explained that on September 11, God was neither absent nor indifferent nor impotent, but was somewhere (in his case meaning everywhere) grieving for what his children suffered. Like every good father, God weeps for his children. We do not know enough about God to understand what sadness he feels and how it is expressed. But God is sad, as the Scriptures tell us all the time, even if theologians find it difficult to explain, declared the Reverend Andrew M. Greeley, a sociologist and expert in politics.[41]

On the same wavelength, many clergymen and theologians explained that, on September 11, God was with the passengers on board the hijacked airplanes in their loving messages to their families, with the victims of the terrorist massacre, with the heroic firemen who lost their lives to save those of others, and with the families in mourning. He was with the rescuers and the millions of Americans who lined up to give their blood. He was with all the Americans who prayed to him seeking comfort in their sorrow and spiritual guidance, trusting that God would not abandon them in a world which had suddenly become alien and frightening.

However, not even the consolers offered the Americans only comfort and hope. Although their tone and reasons were certainly different from the stern rebukes of the scathing critics, they also admonished the Americans, urging them one and all to examine their consciences and search their hearts for their own responsibility for evil in the world, instead of accusing God or reproaching him for not preventing evil from harming America. Some clergymen answered those who wondered why God had not stopped the terrorist attack by saying that we could not expect God to be always present everywhere, ready to intervene and prevent evil from doing harm, almost as if he were a police officer permanently on duty. The problem of evil was not that God was impotent or indifferent before man's suffering; it concerned man's freedom, and therefore his responsibility. God had given man the privilege of free will, so he could choose between good and evil. God could not anticipate and prevent evil without depriving man of his freedom. All told, the reality of evil was the consequence of the freedom that God had given to human beings, because man's freedom was constantly exposed to the temptation of evil, was the explanation given by clergymen and theologians of every confession, and it was man who had to choose. The theologian Buechner observed that the return to chaos was a never-ending possibility.[42] This risk depended on human choices, not on divine responsibility, and especially the Americans had to be aware of this risk, just because they belonged to the richest and most powerful nation in the world, whose conduct directly or indirectly influenced the existence of all humanity.

Prophets of America

Although profoundly shocked by the September 11 tragedy, some clergymen and theologians, while trying to comfort the Americans, were little inclined to encourage them in an attitude of martyred innocence. The terrorists embodied evil but it was not only in them, nor did it act only through them.

As severe as the Bible's prophets, these clergymen and theologians stigmatized America's wealth and power, implicating American politics as responsible for fostering or even creating the conditions for evil to exist in the world, causing the spread of hostile feelings which developed into the bitter and ruthless hatred leading to the terrorist massacre. The terrorists were unconditionally condemnable, as they had deliberately caused the atrocious death of so many innocent people, and they could not in any way be justified. However the fact that the condemnation was unequivocally absolute should not have prevented the Americans from soul-searching on the origins and reasons for this hatred that had led to producing such ruthless enemies. Then they could have consciously decided how to face this new, terrible reality of evil revealed by the terrorist attack. Instead of wondering where God was when the terrorists attacked America, the Americans should have taken a humbler attitude towards God himself and wondered why there were some people who hated the United States so intensely, considering it the embodiment of evil, the great Satan.[43]

Moltmann thought that the answer was not difficult to find:

> The answer is a simple one: go out and ask the people who are evidently suffering under policies of your government. Learn to see yourselves in the mirror of other people's eyes, and especially the eyes of the victims. That is painful, and hurts the image of ourselves we cherish so much; but it helps us to wake up out of our dreams and to come face to face with reality.[44]

The president of the Catholic University of Notre Dame, Theodore Hesburgh, took the same attitude, and quoting Pope Paul VI, pointed out that 80 percent of world resources belonged to 20 percent of its population, and that the United States was not without blame for this terrible situation.[45] We are targets for the terrorists because we support dictators, slavery, and exploitation in the world, wrote Robert Bowman, president of the Institute for Space and Security Studies in an impelling letter to President Bush. We are not hated because we practice democracy, freedom, and human rights, but because we deny them to the peoples of developing countries.[46]

Of all the clergymen who demanded that the Americans do some soul-searching when turning to God for protection, theologians and African-American preachers were the most severe. In the time of terror, African-American preachers were those who spoke most frankly. This frankness was due to the long grievous history of attacks suffered, it derived from centuries of familiarity with the intransigence of evil.[47] In such distressing times, African-American preachers had to be this nation's conscience.[48] And this meant telling the Americans that evil was not only in bin Laden's terrorists but was within America itself, in its illusion of greatness, its lack of ethical values, and because it felt invincible.[49]

The theologian Robert Franklin warned that the Americans turned to religion for an answer to their anguished questions, but they only looked for it in rites and religious practices. However, there was another authentic dimension of religious faith which should not have been ignored at that time, that is, being capable of acknowledging one's own individual and national sins, in order to understand what part of responsibility could be attributed to the Americans themselves. Franklin said that the buildings attacked, the World Trade Center and the Pentagon, represented the opulence and military power which had caused poverty, death, and suffering in the world.[50] The September 11 tragedy was a prophetic warning to the American nation, an exhortation to carry out an act of humility and repentance for its arrogance and abuse of power towards other peoples.[51] Vashti Murphy McKenzie, the first woman bishop in the African Methodist Episcopal Church, said:

> It is amazing that at times...such as these we are forced to take a long hard look at who we are, what we value, what we deem important. We are compelled to examine what or in whom we really believe....Our way of life is now changed forever. The world looks different now. More than seeing through a glass darkly, we look through the lens of terror.[52]

The reasoning of a theodicy lacking in optimism emerged from the reflections of the African-American clergymen. God was certainly not responsible for the terrorist attack, nor had he "gone on holiday and left us to our own demonic destruction,"[53] said the Reverend Charles Booth, but he made use of every event to speak to our souls. It took a tragedy like this to make the Americans understand that their nation lived with the arrogance that came from a false sense of superiority; "God has strange ways of humbling us," but "we also recognize that God is calling the nation to repentance....America has sins that need to be forgiven. A lot of us don't want to admit it, but we have been a dirty nation...We can be a dirty nation," Booth said, referring to the Chile affair and the murder of Lumumba: "we created Osama bin Laden. Many of you have forgotten, but we trained the people in Afghanistan to be terrorists....Some of you all better watch whom you train. You better watch to whom you give your secrets. That stuff can come back to haunt you."[54] The Reverend Cain Felder added that materialistic America was guilty towards God, because it openly praised greed, raising temples to egoism and materialism, while few Americans realized there was a growing gap between rich and poor and among the different races. This revealed a decline in religious feeling and belief in the Bible's idea of a community founded on love. "White" America was guilty of these wrongs. After September 11 "white America has been 'niggerized,'" alluding to the fact that "the black masses in America live on a daily basis the fear and existential *angst* that comes from being socio-political victims of the oppressive racial preference networks in America."[55]

God Has Returned, Return to God!

Nevertheless, if there were Americans who were angry with God and felt they were abandoned by, or cut off from him, most believers did not lose their faith in God's goodness, despite the dimensions of the massacre caused by the terrorist attack and how diabolically the terrorists had planned and carried it out. "God had nothing to do with this," said a retired fireman, a Catholic, who had lost a son and many friends and coworkers at the World Trade Center on September 11, "there were a lot more people that could have been killed. He was fighting evil that day, like he does every day." The retired fireman explained that among firefighters fire is called "the devil"—"that day we fought the devil, and we saved a lot of people...But the devil's the devil."[56]

A great many Americans hoped to allay their grief and fear by seeking refuge in faith and prayer. On the day the terrorists attacked and in the following days, churches, synagogues, mosques, and temples were more crowded than they had ever been for over 50 years. On the morning of September 11, when evil appeared in the worst possible way, some ministers said that God had appeared in the best possible way, through an entire nation that turned to him in prayer everywhere—in the streets, schools, work places, and the seats of government.[57] On September 28, Peggy Noonan, who had collaborated with President Reagan in writing his speeches, announced that "God is back." "In 1964, *Time Magazine* famously headlined 'God Is Dead.' I hope now, at the very highest reaches of that great magazine, they do a cover that says 'God Is Back.'"[58] The Baptist theologian Peter Gomes noted that after September 11, people put aside abstract philosophical or theoretical issues and were once again drawn to places of worship in great numbers: "Every rabbi, minister, priest, imam or spiritual leader whom I know or have heard of reports, as can I, the incredible turn toward faith in this time of our current crisis. Probably not since the Second World War has there been such a conspicuous turn to the faith in our country."[59] According to a poll carried out on September 19, almost 70 percent of the Americans said they prayed more than in the past.[60] Bible sales increased by 45 percent, hundreds of thousands of books offering religious solace were sold, and visits to religious and spiritual web sites on the internet increased by 50 percent compared to the year before.[61] In November 2001, 78 percent of those interviewed, compared to 38 percent eight months earlier, thought that the influence of religion on American lives was growing, a percentage that was a leap forward compared to the last four decades, when it had never gone beyond 45 percent. It was even much higher than a similar poll in 1957, when 69 percent of Americans thought that the influence of religion was growing. Furthermore, at the end of 2001, 49 percent of Americans had an unfavorable opinion of atheists, against 32 percent who thought the opposite. In short, 73 percent of Americans continued to believe that God had not stopped protecting America.[62]

Many theologians and clergymen urged the Americans to derive new reasons for acting rightly from the wrong suffered in the ferocious terrorist attack. September 11 "is a call to conversion," declared the Reverend Jose Gomez.[63] The experience of this tragedy should be the beginning of a return to the religious values which had given rise to American democracy. This would be possible only if the Americans once again listened to God's words and put them into practice. Many clergymen and theologians repeated that it was only by returning to God's way and taking his words as guidance that America would be able to overcome the trauma of September 11 and continue its mission with renewed moral strength.

This was the same exhortation that, through the new American ambassador to the Vatican, John Paul II also addressed to President Bush in his message on September 13. The pope was convinced that "America's continued moral leadership in the world depends on her fidelity to her founding principles," to the values of freedom, self-determination, and equal opportunity, these being "universal truths, inherited from its religious roots," which gave birth to "respect for the sanctity of the life and dignity of each human person made in the image and likeness of the Creator."[64]

The pope warned that nevertheless, in order to continue its democratic mission in the light of the terrible challenge at the beginning of the new century, America had to realize that the crisis Western democracies were going through had spiritual origins. This crisis was caused by the spread of a materialistic, utilitarian, and basically inhuman outlook on life, tragically separated from the moral foundations of Western civilization. The pope took the cue from the September 11 tragedy to ask American democracy and Western democracies to do some soul-searching, to acknowledge their own responsibility in encouraging a view of life that led to moral decadence in their societies. He clearly intended to condemn abortion and euthanasia, which were the most serious aspects of this decadence. John Paul II cautioned that democracies should be guided by rigorous moral vision in order to survive and spread,

> a vision whose core is the God-given dignity and inalienable rights of every human being, from the moment of conception until natural death. When some lives, including those of the unborn, are subjected to the personal choices of others, no other value or right will long be guaranteed, and society will inevitably be governed by special interests and convenience.

The pope ended by saying that it was more urgent to strengthen the moral outlook and the determination essential to conserving a just and free society.[65]

The thread of the argument expounded by the head of the Catholic Church, calling for America's return to the religious roots of its democracy, was interwoven with the jeremiads of the American Protestant prophets, both the former and the latter of the opinion that the Western world was morally decadent. The subject of moral decadence was not new to either conservative or progressivist American culture, but after September 11 it became predominant in the reflections on the lessons that America could draw from the tragic experience which had made it brutally face the reality of evil. Profound soul-searching in the American nation and all the Western world should arise from the sorrow for the September 11 tragedy. Actually, apart from differences in tone and language, most of the religious and theological reflections on the September 11 tragedy, of both conservatives and progressivists, dealt with the Americans' "national sins," even though modulated according to different criteria, arguments, and aims. They also shared the same idea, even though differently interpreted and motivated, that this tragic experience should be the beginning of spiritual revival for America, through a return to the basic religious values which had originated American democracy.

Much had been said about the need for moral revival in America during the 2000 presidential campaign. The candidates of both parties presented themselves to the Americans as God-fearing men who wanted to bring God back into politics. Bush's arrival at the White House was interpreted by the Religious Right, which had strongly supported him, as God's return as America's leader. Furthermore, the September 11 tragedy gave President Bush the chance to take on the role of theologian of American religion, together with that of commander in chief of the nation at war. To understand how this happened and what the consequences were for American religion in the new age of terror, we must follow the path that Bush took to arrive at the White House. The president was convinced he had followed this way until reaching his goal victoriously because God had called him, and he had obeyed humbly, considering it his mission to bring about God's return to politics, by using his power and with the aid of his faith in Jesus Christ, for the revival of the nation.

3

At the White House

Son of the Father

Most of the Americans did not feel abandoned by God when the terrorists attacked their country, slaughtering innocent victims and destroying the myth that the United States was invulnerable. Nor did they think that God was absent during the attack or had allowed evil to act ferociously towards the American nation to punish it for its sins and induce it to repent, as the preachers of castigating theodicy maintained. The latter interpreted the thousands of innocent people who perished in the terrorist attack and the grief of the mourning families as just punishment for the Americans, who had abandoned the ways of the Lord. A poll carried out a few weeks after September 11 showed that 89 percent of the Americans refused to consider the terrorist attack as a sign that they had lost the protection that God had given the United States in the past.[1] Nor did their president think so. On the contrary, Bush told those who worked closely with him that he was convinced God continued to watch over the United States, especially at the most tragic time in its history, comforting and inspiring the Americans and their president through prayer.

Bush was a devout believer.[2] Fifteen years before he was elected president, he had found his faith in Christ again, dedicating his life to him. His faith accompanied him into politics, and his policies were inspired by his faith.

For almost 40 years Bush had lived in his father's shadow, his life marked by a series of mediocre events in every field.[3] Bush the father, son of Prescott Bush, a wealthy financier and influential Republican senator from the end of the 1940s to the middle of the 1960s, was a brilliant student, a hero of the Second World War when he was eighteen, and a successful entrepreneur in the oil industry, before entering politics in the Republican Party. He continued this career, despite a few defeats, right up to the White House, where he arrived as vice president to Ronald

Reagan in 1981, after being a deputy in the United States Congress, ambassador to the United Nations, head of the American legation in Beijing, and CIA director.

Bush the son was born in Connecticut in 1946, the firstborn of six children, and at the age of two was resettled in Texas where his father had moved, after graduating, to work in the oil industry. The popular, religious, and conservative culture of Texas contributed to forming his mentality and character much more than his studies in illustrious New England universities like Andover, Yale, and Harvard, the same ones attended by his grandfather and father. Young George made his mark by enlivening parties rather than as a brilliant student. He was not involved in the young people's rebellion in 1968, nor did it influence his Texan conservatism, which, on the contrary, was strengthened by it. In the Vietnam War years, Bush did his military service as a fighter pilot with the Texas Air National Guard and thus avoided going to fight against the Vietcong. After taking his master's degree in business and administration, he went back to Texas in 1975, and thanks to his father's circle of friends, entered the oil business, setting up a drilling company. In 1978 Bush the son wanted to take up politics also, standing for election for Congress as the Texas candidate, but was defeated. Nor was he fortunate in drilling for oil, but when his company went bankrupt, he managed fortuitously to emerge unscathed, even making quite a large sum out of it.

During this part of his life, Bush was not particularly religious. There were different branches of Christianity in his family's tradition. His paternal great-grandfather had been Catholic, and his father had belonged to the Episcopal Church but later became Presbyterian like his wife. When Bush the son was a boy he attended the Presbyterian Church, but when he married in 1975, he changed to the Methodist Church, which his wife belonged to—but religion was still not one of his passions, as alcohol then was. Bush drank and was often drunk because, as his friends said, when he began drinking, he was incapable of stopping. Neither his parents, nor his wife, nor the birth of the twins, nor the political renown of his father, who became vice president of the United States in 1981, managed to get him away from the bottle. Not even rediscovering his faith in Christ in 1985 was enough to give Bush the crucial incentive to give up alcohol, which he only did a year after returning to religious devoutness. What triggered his decision to give up alcohol forever were the terrible aftereffects of a hangover the day after his 40th birthday party, and the resoluteness of his wife, who was determined not to tolerate his drunken behavior any longer. Rediscovering his faith in Christ contributed to giving Bush the moral strength to definitively abandon the road to perdition in alcoholism.

Following the Son of God's Path

Bush revealed that he started following Christ's path in the summer of 1985, after a talk with Billy Graham, the famous evangelistic preacher and religious consultant of all the American presidents in the last 50 years, also a personal friend of the Bush family. Bush explained that the preacher put a mustard seed in his soul and started him off on a new road, on which he would dedicate his heart to Jesus Christ again.[4] A friend helped him enter an evangelical group belonging to the national organization called Community Bible Study (CBS), which met periodically to read and meditate on the Holy Scripture.

Bush frequently recalled his return to religion, and when doing so, the rediscovery of his faith in Christ and his giving up alcohol took on the meaning of a single extraordinary event—almost as if they revealed and announced a providential design which eventually pointed down the road to winning the presidency in 2000, lost by his father eight years earlier. "You know," he said, "I had a drinking problem. Right now I should be in a bar in Texas, not the Oval Office. There is only one reason that I am in the Oval Office and not in a bar. I found faith. I found God. I am here because of the power of prayer."[5]

Faith strengthened his will, put some order in his life, and gave it discipline and direction. The seed planted by Graham and his decision to give up alcohol began to bear fruit in 1988, when George W. Bush moved to Washington to help manage his father's presidential campaign. It was an important experience for the son's political formation because it taught him how complicated the Republican Party's organizational and electoral machinery was. It also brought out the good qualities of his character, like a strong will and tenacity, as well as organizing capability. Discovering religion again helped George W. Bush to gain the Religious Right's votes, as they were anything but unanimous in supporting Bush the father's candidacy, whom they considered an unreliable Republican because of his lukewarm religious conservatism. In fact, the most important champion of the evangelical Right, Pat Robertson, had entered the field against Bush the father, to compete for the Republican Party candidacy. Bush the son was very good at wooing and gaining the votes of the evangelicals and "born-again" Christians, because after returning to faith in Christ, he had learned to speak their language, showing he was one of them—a sinner redeemed by his personal experience of faith in Christ and determined to follow the way of the Son of God in every moment of his life and activities.

After the presidential campaign ended in victory, Bush the son returned to Texas, where he contributed to buying the Texas Rangers baseball team together with a group of wealthy financiers, friends of his father. He became the team's manager, although he had paid only a modest share. From then on baseball was his main activity, which served to increase his personal wealth and to make him popular in Texas. His father's defeat in the presidential election of 1992 led George W. Bush to take up politics again, so as to continue the family tradition. He stood for election as governor and won, contrary to the expectations of many. And he won again in 1998, the first time a governor was elected twice running in the history of Texas.

It was then that religious faith became Bush's political banner, as he believed that carrying out institutional functions was fulfilling a mission in God's service.[6] At the inaugural ceremony for the office of governor, with Billy Graham present, Bush called on God to help him because, he said, the duties he was taking on could be better accomplished "with the guidance of One greater than ourselves." After the inaugural speech there was a religious service, where a hymn chosen by Bush, called "A Charge to Keep," was sung. It was composed by Charles Wesley, brother of John Wesley the Protestant preacher, who founded the Methodist Church in the eighteenth century.[7] Soon after taking office, Bush sent a memorandum to all those who worked for him, informing them that he had put up in his office a painting by W. H. D. Koerner, *A Charge to Keep,* inspired by Wesley's hymn and with the same title, quoting the lines that said: "To serve the present age, My calling to fulfill: O may it all my powers engage To do my Master's will." "I thought I would share with you a recent bit of Texas history which epitomizes our mission. When you come into my office, please take a look at the beautiful painting of a horseman determinedly charging up what appears to be a steep and rough trail. This is us. What adds complete life to the painting for me is the message of Charles Wesley that we serve One greater than ourselves,"[8] Bush commented. His last official act as governor of Texas was to proclaim June 10, 2000 "Jesus Day," to honor the life and teachings of Christ, recognized by believers in all the religions in the world as an example of love, compassion, sacrifice, and service. "Jesus Day" would urge people to follow Christ's example in voluntarily carrying out good works for their own communities and fellowmen.[9]

His Favorite Philosopher

When Bush decided to stand for the 2000 presidential elections, he introduced his religion into the election campaign and it immediately became the most talked-about aspect of his candidacy. It all began almost by chance in Des Moines, the capital of Iowa, on December 13, 1999, during a television debate among the aspiring Republican candidates. The moderator had asked each of them to name his favorite political philosopher. The first candidate gave John Locke, the second the founding fathers. Perhaps Bush was not prepared for such a question, as when it was his turn, he answered: "Christ, because he changed my heart... When you turn your heart and your life over to Christ, when you accept Christ as your savior, it changes your heart. It changes your life. And that's what happened to me." When he was asked to explain to the viewers how Christ had changed his life, Bush answered that it was difficult to explain the experience, because only those who had gone through it could understand it. However, most of the audience present liked the fact that he cited Jesus and applauded, while the other candidates were taken by surprise, and five out of six of them also hastened to declare their faith in Christ and God.[10]

This episode sparked off widespread interest in Bush's religion and gave him enormous publicity, focusing attention on his religious convictions and how they could influence his political choices if he became president. Many thought that Bush's display of faith was an expedient for the elections to gain the votes of the Religious Right. After all, why not use the Son of God to help Bush's son appeal to voters, said Maureen Dowd, a *New York Times* editorialist.[11] However, whatever the real reason was for Bush's answer on Jesus as his "favorite political philosopher," it gave him the chance to make religion one of the main themes of the election campaign, even though, before the debate in Iowa, he had said: "I'm mindful of people in public office who say, 'Vote for me. I'm more religious than my neighbor.' I want to be judged on my actions, and I want to be judged on my—on how I—on how I conduct myself."[12] With Christian humility Bush stated he did not feel at all superior to his adversaries because of his religious faith, as it taught him to see the beam in his own eye instead of the mote in another's. Furthermore he wanted to be judged for his personality and program, not for his religious beliefs, even if they were more important for him than success in politics. "I am going to fight like heck and give this campaign my best shot, and I hope I will be the president," he said in an interview. "But should it not work out, I understand that there is a force greater than myself—and it gives me great comfort."[13]

Religion and Candidates

Most of the Americans did not at all object to the presidential candidates expressing their religious beliefs. A Gallup poll in December 1999 showed that 52 percent of the Americans were more likely to vote for a candidate who spoke of his personal relationship with Christ than for candidates who avoided doing so.[14]

In the 2000 elections, the Americans' attitude towards the relation between religion and politics seemed ambivalent, even though most of them were decidedly in favor of supporting the politicians who declared they were believers: 70 percent preferred a person with religious faith as president, even if this interested young people less, while half the voters did not like politicians and candidates who spoke too much about it.[15] The most important fact that emerged from the polls carried out during 2000 was the belief, shared by almost 70 percent of Americans, that religion was fundamental to preventing the nation's moral decadence, due to the crisis of the family, neglectful upbringing and lack of respect, spreading materialism, and the breakup of society. Eighty percent decidedly refused to believe that their society would be better if a greater number of Americans abandoned religious faith.

Many Americans thought that there could not be morality without religion, which they hoped could have a wider influence on people personally and on public life. Furthermore, 47 percent of Americans thought that if politicians had more religious faith, politics would improve, while 39 percent were skeptical, saying that it would not make any difference, and 11 percent stated that politicians with more religious zeal would even make politics worse. As regards the presidential elections, 54 percent said they would never vote for a candidate who declared he did not believe in God, and 52 percent said they would vote more willingly for a candidate who took comfort and strength from religion, while 58 percent believed it was wrong to take the candidates' religion as a criterion for their choice. However, most of those interviewed said they did not know what religion Bush and Gore belonged to. Moreover, 48 percent declared that the nation needed upright and honest politicians rather than religious ones, while 49 percent thought that this would be possible only if there were more religious politicians. To sum up, the same poll showed that most Americans, 74 percent of them, doubted that politicians who spoke too much about their religious faith were sincere, because they were only hunting for votes, although this was understandable, as the very nature of politics required being pragmatic.[16]

Whatever the Americans' attitude was towards the religious faith paraded by the politicians, one thing is certain: none of the presidential candidates could have won the elections without finding a religious language suitable to gain the votes of believers, who were the great majority of the electorate. Almost all the candidates, both in the Republican and the Democratic Party, involved God in their propaganda, declaring that their politics were inspired by their faith and that they considered God their guide. In the aforementioned debate of December 13 among the Republican candidates, God and Christ were mentioned more than 20 times altogether.[17]

An Electoral God

During the whole campaign, the presidential candidates made religion a subject of their speeches and interviews, so much so that many observers complained that their religious rhetoric was excessive. Faith is becoming an organizing principle of the first election of the third millennium, Howard Fineman commented in *Newsweek* on January 1, 2000.[18] The lay European press was even more surprised. The English daily *The Independent* remarked that it was not the religious faith that was disconcerting but the way the candidates presented it, like a slogan, giving the impression that there would be quite a difference between a White House closely linked to God and one engaged only in governing.[19]

Actually, the presence of God in the struggle for the White House was nothing new, and not even exceptional and unusual in the American tradition. Religion had never been absent from presidential competitions, as some noteworthy examples show.

Sydney E. Ahlstrom, historian of American religion, called the 1896 elections one of the great revealing events in the history of American religion, because the competition was between two candidates who personified American Protestantism: William Jennings Bryan, the forerunner of Christian fundamentalism, and the fervent Methodist William McKinley.[20] Religion was the dominating topic also in the 1928 elections, when the Protestants rallied against the Catholic candidate, and it was again in the 1960 elections, when for the first time a Catholic president, John F. Kennedy, was elected. Religious rhetoric was also abundant in the 1972 presidential competition between the Republican Richard Nixon and the Democrat George McGovern. President Nixon's tone was theological when he sang the praises of the American system, the American spirit, and faith in America.[21] The Democratic candidate presented his campaign as a religious crusade against evil, which he identified with the Nixon presidency, the most corrupt and immoral administration in history, and asked God for wisdom and knowledge to carry out the mission of raising up the nation, which risked plunging into decadence and losing the protection of Providence.[22]

Religion played an important part in the 1976 elections as well, with Jimmy Carter as the Democratic candidate against President Gerald Ford. *Journal of Church and State* remarked that religious problems and the relations between church and state were discussed much more in the 1976 elections than they had been since Kennedy was elected.[23] According to the magazine this was not surprising, both because the elections had taken place in an atmosphere of religious revival after a decade of war, racial conflicts, cultural uncertainty, and economic crisis, and because the candidates were the most religious couple of nominees from both parties since McKinley was elected in 1896.[24]

Jimmy Carter, a self-declared born-again Christian, was challenged in the 1980 elections by Ronald Reagan, who cleverly mixed religion and politics in his election campaign and managed to beat his rival, who was considered religious but inept. This victory came about because Reagan knew how to communicate a forceful patriotic message, extolling America's historical role in the world as a political and spiritual guide in the crusade against communist totalitarianism. Reagan was elected with the decisive votes of the Religious Right, which expected the new president to bring back a strong, traditionalist America, one capable of overcoming the aftereffects of Vietnam, of opposing the aggressive advance of Soviet imperialism, and of cancelling the humiliation suffered by Carter when Americans were confined in their embassy in Tehran, after Khomeini's theocratic revolution in 1979.

God continued to be present in presidential elections in the following years. During the 1992 campaign for reelection against his Democratic challenger Clinton, Bush the father said that nobody could be president of America without believing in God and prayer.[25] The president declared that America was still the most religious nation in the world, and its fundamental values were established by Almighty God. At the Republican Party convention, Bush made a speech after accepting his nomination, confirming his avowal of faith, saying that he believed America would always have a special place in God's heart, as long as he had a special place in Americans' hearts.[26]

William Safire wrote that never had the name of God been so frequently invoked, and never had America or any other nation been so constantly blessed, as during the 1992 presidential campaign.[27] The *Star Tribune* of Minneapolis made a similar comment, saying that faith was an element of the presidential campaign, and that sometimes that election campaign seemed like a Sunday religious meeting rather than a rational discussion of national problems.[28] Quoting the opinions of authoritative religious representatives, the daily severely criticized the president because he accused the Democrats of never mentioning three simple letters, GOD. The newspaper reproached Bush, who dressed God in Republican clothes, for thus giving a new slant to the traditional political custom in America of calling on faith to win the elections. The daily reported that the Reverend Martin E. Marty, a Lutheran theologian and historian of religion, did not like what the president said:

> I don't know a precedent of someone saying our party has God and yours doesn't. Presidents have always tied our nation to a God standard, but it has been bipartisan. To say one party has God and another doesn't, that's a novelty and it's a scary one.

Neither did the theologian James Skillen, director of an institute for evangelical politics in Washington, because, in his opinion, the president gave the impression that you had to be Republican to be a serious Christian.

Democrats for God

Actually the Democratic Party did not ignore God in the 1992 presidential campaign; on the contrary, for the first time in its history, it presented two candidates, Clinton and Gore, who were both professing Christians and belonged to the Southern Baptist Church. Clinton was not at all reluctant to speak of his religion. When the Democrats were accused of being in some way "Godless," Clinton reacted by accusing the president of deeply offending him and all those who shared his religious beliefs but also respected the American tradition of religious differences.[29] Clinton often spoke of his religious beliefs in his election speeches. At the beginning of the election campaign he stated: "I pray virtually every day, usually at night, and I read the Bible every week....I also believe in a lot of the old-fashioned things like the constancy of sin, the possibility of forgiveness [and] the reality of redemption":

> My faith tells me that all of us are sinners, and each of us has gone in our way and fallen short of the glory of God. Religious faith has permitted me to believe in my continuing possibility of becoming a better person every day. If I didn't believe in God, if I weren't in my view ... a Christian, if I didn't believe ultimately in the perfection of life after death, my life would have been that much different....That I have a deep faith in God and a sense of mission to try to do the right thing every day should be reassuring to the American People. But I don't expect to get marching orders from the fact that I was raised in the Baptist Church.[30]

Commenting on Clinton's performance in a television debate with Bush, an observer wrote that he had shown the empathy and self-assurance of a television evangelist.[31]

Clinton liked doing his election campaign in churches, so much so that he was nicknamed "Reverend Bill." The fact that he frequently used Protestant pulpits to propagandize was strongly criticized by the Catholic press.[32] The fundamentalists of the Christian Right, like Pat Robertson and Jerry Falwell, accused him of manipulating the Scriptures for political aims, because, at the Democratic Party's national convention, he embellished his speech accepting nomination with quotations from the Bible.[33] In fact, the Democratic candidate's speeches often took on a religious tone when he illustrated his political platform, beginning from the slogan he chose to explain his program, the "new covenant," stating, "America does not need a religious war ...It needs a reaffirmation of the values that are rooted in our religious faith," as he said at the Catholic University of Notre Dame.[34] Clinton called his campaign against Bush a "great crusade," to change the government and reestablish it on a sound footing, and to reaffirm the religious roots of American democracy.[35]

Not even Bush the son could have accused his Democratic rival Gore of ignoring God, of being insensitive and indifferent to religion, or of wanting to lessen the presence of religion in politics and public life. Quite on the contrary: the Democratic candidate could boast a religious faith just as fervent as his adversary's, and even a greater competence in the subject of Christianity, having cultivated theological studies when young.

A member of the Southern Baptist Church, Gore called himself a born-again Christian; he had dedicated his life to Jesus after fighting in Vietnam. The horrors of war led him to enroll in divinity school at Vanderbilt University after he returned home. Gore was interested in the relation between theology and science, and even though he did not finish his theological studies, he worked out his own evangelical concept of environmentalist Christianity, which spiritualized nature and considered protecting the environment a Christian duty. Religiously inspired environmentalism was an important aspect of his political platform, both as a senator and as vice president. In 1991 Gore organized a conference with representatives of the main American religions taking part, whose aim was to work out a strategy in defense of the environment. The result came three years later when the organization National Religious Partnership for the Environment was set up. His book, *Earth in the Balance,* published in 1992, extolled the spirituality of ecology as an expression of religiosity and was a great success. In 1996, when NASA reported that traces of microorganisms had been found on Mars, Gore organized a meeting of scientists and clergymen to discuss the possibility of life on Mars.[36]

During the 2000 presidential campaign, Gore spoke of his experience as a born-again Christian, stating that faith was the center of his life, his political philosophy, and that he made his own decisions always asking himself "What would Jesus do?"—a popular set phrase in America especially among young people, with the acronym "WWJD?" Gore said he was a firm supporter of the separation between church and state, but explained that "freedom *of* religion did not necessarily mean freedom *from* religion."[37]

Let's Regenerate the Nation

The real religious novelty in the 2000 presidential campaign was not Bush's answer to the question on his favorite philosopher, nor mobilizing God and Jesus in the presidential campaign: it was the choice of Senator Joseph Lieberman, a Jew belonging to the "modern Orthodox "group of American Judaism, as the

Democratic candidate for the vice presidency. It was a courageous decision: Lieberman was the first Jewish candidate for the vice presidency of the United States.

This was considered a historic event, because it was a further step towards real religious equality in America. It was a choice that brought down another barrier and opened the way to new opportunities, the African-American Reverend Jesse Jackson commented.[38] Even Jerry Falwell thought it was "marvelous" that a Democratic senator who took a break to pray three times a day during the sittings at the Senate, had been nominated. According to the English daily *The Financial Times,* Gore had deliberately placed religion at the center of his election campaign because asking for God's help in the election struggle against Bush was inevitable, considering that the Religious Right had been mobilized in favor of the Republican candidate. The polls gave Bush 51 percent of the born-again Christians' votes, compared to 31 percent for Gore. By choosing a moderate Orthodox Jew, born-again Gore wanted to send the religious electorate a strong signal: he intended to clearly mark his distance from the immoral shadow that had surrounded the last years of Clinton's presidency.[39]

Lieberman was one of the most respected persons in American politics, a conservative moralist who defended the integrity of traditional family values and, when speaking in the Senate, had deprecated Clinton's behavior. The English daily went on to say that by choosing Lieberman, Gore wanted a possible future president of the United States to be a man who had no intention of instilling his own religious beliefs in American politics but who meant to carry out a profound spiritual mission aimed at reviving moral values in the country.[40] Lieberman was a champion of national rebirth, and since the middle of the 1980s he had urged the Democrats to instill more religion in their politics in order to fight the immoral culture spread by Hollywood and which was corrupting America. In an interview on Pat Robertson's evangelical television program, the Democratic senator declared that America needed a new spiritual revival, and that was why he thought it was an encouraging sign that, after three decades, people of faith finally expressed their religious principles in politics. Lieberman pointed out that, since the origins of the American nation, the Great Awakenings had contributed to the progress of democracy, leading to the Declaration of Independence and the Declaration of Rights in the eighteenth century, to the abolition of slavery and to social reforms in the nineteenth century, and to the movement for civil rights in the twentieth century. Now a "fourth religious awakening" was necessary as an antidote to the violence, promiscuity, vulgarity, and the degeneration of family values.[41] Lieberman was firmly convinced of the necessity to give new vitality to the religious roots of American democracy.

In 2000 a book of his, *In Praise of Public Life,* was published, where he maintained that the Bible could be a source of inspiration for politicians to carry out their public functions.[42] That is why he criticized the direction taken by the Supreme Court which had fostered the removal of religion from the public sphere in the last few decades, relegating it to the private one and wrongly interpreting the principle of separating church and state. According to the vice presidency candidate, the founding fathers had worked out a constitution which, while wisely separating church from state, nevertheless guaranteed freedom *of* religion, not freedom *from* religion.[43] In September, Lieberman firmly repeated that more space for religion in public life was needed, and he urged the Americans to dedicate their nation and themselves to God once again.[44]

Wooing the White Evangelicals

So Bush was not the only one to involve religion in the presidential campaign. Nevertheless, his declaration that Christ was his favorite political philosopher caused a stir and contributed to heightening the religious tone of the whole presidential campaign. The declaration was received very favorably by traditionalist Christians, especially by evangelicals and born-again Christians, who saw Bush as the president they wanted at the White House. The conservative evangelicals made up quite a large part of the white religious population of the United States, with a high electoral potential which neither of the two candidates could ignore if he wanted to win.

Evangelical Protestantism is not the denomination of a church or a specific theological doctrine; it is an individual religious experience, a way of living Christianity based solely on the Bible, considered the authentic and infallible expression of divine will, where the principles required to lead one's own life can be found. Evangelical Christianity glorifies above all the figure of Christ, Savior and Redeemer of humanity through his sacrifice on the Cross, and its main aim is to save souls.

Born-again Christians belong to evangelical Protestantism with their own distinctive features. The expression "born again" does not mean the same thing for all those who use it, or for those who call themselves such. The expression entered politics in 1976 when Jimmy Carter was elected president, the first candidate who publicly professed he was "born again." Since then, the number of born-again Christians has continued to grow. Generally speaking, those who return to their faith through a personal spiritual experience which leads them "to be born again in Christ" and devote their lives to following his teachings, are considered or call themselves "born again." In the constantly changing kaleidoscope of American Christianity, born-again Christians are not a religious denomination but have their own distinctive way of understanding Christ's teachings. Born-again Christianity is a way of feeling and living religious faith as daily devotion to Christ— the Savior who ensures eternal life to those who acknowledge their own sins, are reborn in his faith, and follow the way he has shown them—without giving much importance to religious practices or churches.

A poll carried out in March 2001 revealed that the increase in born-again Christians, which passed from 31 percent in 1991 to 41 percent in 2001, coincided with a considerable drop in the numbers of members of traditional Protestant Churches and a decline in beliefs based on doctrinal theology, replaced by subjective theologies deriving from personal interpretations of the principles and values of Christianity. Furthermore, the survey showed that the spread of born-again Christianity in the decade 1991–2001 corresponded with a reduction in attendances in the churches, which dropped from 49 to 37 percent, while the number of Christians who did not belong to any church increased from 27 to 33 percent.[45] Some Protestant theologians complained of a real "collapse" in traditional Protestantism and that theological teaching had seriously diminished. The result was a spread of generic Christianity without solid doctrinal foundations and often the Holy Scriptures were little known: the number of those who read the Bible, in the decade from 1991 to 2001, dropped from 45 to 37 percent. These theologians were of the opinion that a profound change in popular religiosity was taking place, with a growing number of people who saw Christianity as a kind of deism.[46]

These facts can help to understand the importance of religious rhetoric in the 2000 election propaganda, spread by both Bush and Gore. Gore personally called himself a born-again Christian, while Bush preferred not to use this name, even though his personal experience of discovering faith in Christ again when he was about 40, was similar to the typical religiosity of born-again Christians. In any case, both candidates declaring their faith publicly was an impulsive act of conscience as well as political calculation, because neither of the two could have hoped to win without gaining the votes of the evangelicals and born-again Christians. In February 2000, the adult Americans who were considered born-again Christians made up an electoral body estimated at about sixty million people, most of whom were white.[47] In 2000 a group of scholars of the Pew Research Center, an important institute for research on religion in public life, observed that the conservatism of white evangelical Protestants was the most powerful religious force in the politics of that period.[48]

God's Right

It was important for Bush to highlight the religious aspect in order to conquer a very influential sector of the Republican electorate made up of the Religious Right, a vast and multicolored body of conservative Christians who had played a decisive part in the election of Republicans to the presidency and to Congress in the previous two decades.[49] By rallying supporters for the elections, the Religious Right contributed to Reagan's victory in 1980 and the election of Bush the father in 1988.[50]

The origins of the Religious Right date back to the origins of the United States. Its roots were in the Puritan movements which, from the birth of the republic, had fought against the decline of religious influence in public and political life, the laxity of customs, the spread of materialism, and against everything that, from time to time as American society developed, seemed to stray from the strictly traditional concept of religion and Christian morals, identified as the Puritan matrix of God's democracy. In the early decades of the twentieth century Protestant fundamentalism was born. It was committed not only to strictly

safeguarding the doctrinal principles of Christianity derived from a literal interpretation of the Bible, considered infallible, against the modernistic innovations
of the biblical exegesis, but also fighting to conserve Protestant religious
hegemony intact in American society.

Fundamentalism fostered or supported anti-Semitic and anti-Catholic
campaigns, led the Prohibition campaign, rallied supporters against introducing
evolutionary theories in school teaching, and opposed political candidates who
were not strictly Protestant and conservative. Many fundamentalists sympa-
thized with fascism and were also the founders and militants of the Ku Klux
Klan. During the 1930s, fundamentalism was defeated in almost all these campaigns, and this led to the decline of the movement, which retreated into the
strictly religious sphere, far from the political arena and from a society the fundamentalists saw as more and more corrupted by the advance of liberalism and
secularism, considered mortal enemies of religion. Another mortal enemy was
communism. From 1917 to when communist Russia ended, the fundamentalists
thought that it was the Antichrist embodied, and many of them, especially during
the Cold War, believed that the final battle between the forces of good and evil
was inevitable. Right from the beginning, millennarism was typical of the
Religious Right, with the belief in an apocalyptic catastrophe coupled with faith
in the providential destiny of the American nation as God's chosen people.

During the second half of the 1900s, the advance of liberalism and secularism in
culture, politics, and society was perceived by conservative Christians as a
progressive degeneration of the nation which had cut off its spiritual and religious
roots, plunging towards the total corruption and subversion of its moral foundations. During the 1970s, the Religious Right was composed mainly of white Protestants, evangelicals belonging to various religious denominations and
tendencies, ranging from fundamentalists to Pentecostal Protestants, from neoe-
vangelicals to charismatics, and from Baptists to Methodists. These groups formed
a galaxy in perpetual motion and were often divided and in controversy with each
other over theological issues. However, they all took the same direction against
modernism, rationalism, secular humanism, liberalism, communism, feminism,
the movement to legalize abortion, and the rights of homosexuals. They also
shared a fight to the bitter end in defense of the American nation's Christian origins, which they wanted to reassert, even going as far as proposing that the
Constitution be modified to introduce the principle that the United States was a
Christian nation. The decisions taken by the Supreme Court during the 1960s, from
legalizing abortion to forbidding prayer in public schools, were considered by the
Christian Right as the latest evil consequences of prevailing secular humanism,
which was both immoral and corrupting, bringing about a radical change in the
constitutional principle of separation between church and state. This was interpreted as excluding religion from public life and relegating it to the private sphere.

At the end of the 1970s a movement which rallied supporters politically and
focused on these subjects emerged in the Religious Right, which sided with the
Republican Party in order to restore the traditional Christian foundations of

God's democracy, not only regarding religion but also on a social and institutional level, opposing the intrusiveness of the federal government, defending private enterprise and capitalism, demanding that taxes be reduced, cutting federal subsidies for assistance to the poor, supporting the death penalty and the free possession of weapons, and encouraging an energetic unilateral foreign policy with strong armed forces, in order to affirm the international hegemony of the United States. The more conservative Religious Right opposed international organizations like the United Nations, considering them a kind of Antichrist. They did not want a new world order bringing peace through international agreements and treaties, and they enthusiastically supported Israel's cause against the Palestinians, convinced that the Jews would be justified by the apocalyptic prophecy if they totally reconquered the promised land.[51]

The political mobilization of the Religious Right came about by their creating and developing a widespread and close-knit network of universities, colleges, associations, publishers, study centers, and radio and television broadcasting companies, which became the basic structure which the conservatives and Christian traditionalists, the evangelicals and fundamentalists, had in common. One of the first organizations of the Religious Right was the Moral Majority, founded in 1979 by Jerry Falwell, which greatly contributed to supporting Reagan's nomination and victory but which dissolved 10 years later. It was followed by the more combative Christian Coalition, founded by Pat Robertson in 1988 to support his nomination for the Republican Party against Bush the father. Robertson said that his organization aimed at the election of a Republican majority in Congress in 1994 and the election of a conservative Republican president in 2000.[52] In the years when Clinton was president, strongly opposed by conservative Christians as the worst expression of the America they detested, the Religious Right and the Christian Coalition were very aggressive and contributed to getting a Republican majority elected in Congress in the 1994 elections, even though they did not succeed in preventing Clinton from being reelected two years later.

Choosing a Leader

Nevertheless, when the 2000 presidential election campaign began, the Religious Right seemed to be in retreat, discouraged, and breaking up. The Christian Coalition was suffering from internal conflicts and losing members and financing. The conservative magazine *National Review* published an article on the decline of the coalition titled "Slouching toward Irrelevance."[53] The Religious Right's long march to take its own man to the White House seemed to have stopped, and a retreat began in the face of liberal and secular America, embodied by Clinton. When he was reelected in 1996 and the campaign to have the president incriminated failed, the Religious Right was convinced that the political crusade for the nation's Christian revival had ended in defeat. A poll carried out by the magazine *Fortune* in the fall of 1999 in the political circles of

Washington, showed a drop in Christian Coalition's influence among the pressure groups of the capital, from the 7th to the 35th place.[54] In December, Paul Weyrich, one of the founders of the Moral Majority, wrote a letter which caused a great deal of comment in the Religious Right, saying that probably they had lost the cultural war, because their 30-year-long work had not been efficacious and there was no longer a "moral majority" in the country. Although he did not speak of surrender, Weyrich proposed that conservative Christians put themselves in quarantine against a hostile culture, abandoning politics to create alternative cultural institutions.[55] Two of Jerry Falwell's lieutenants, Cal Thomas and Ed Dobson, brought out a book titled *Blinded by Might,* which was much discussed by the Religious Right. They accused the evangelicals of letting themselves be tempted by the lure of political power, while it was their duty to withdraw from politics and return to their primary mission, saving souls. They did not question everybody's right and responsibility, whether a clergyman or not, to participate in politics, but thought that when the clergy and other church institutions did so, they ran the risk of compromising themselves and being seduced by the Sirens' song of temporal political power.[56]

The decision to change course and turn back was made at the beginning of 2000, when religion dominated the presidential campaign. If Bush the father was not reelected in 1992 because a part of the Religious Right had lost confidence in him, disappointed by his political conduct which had not satisfied the requests of the conservative Christians, Bush the son seemed to be the political leader so eagerly awaited by the Religious Right in order to start advancing again, succeed in reaching the White House, and regenerate America, taking it back to its original principles as a "Christian nation."

The rhetoric and agenda on the role of religion in politics of both Bush and Gore had some points in common, dear to the evangelicals and born-again Christians. For example, they agreed on supporting a greater influence of religion in public life and federal financial support for religious charity organizations and religious private schools. Above all they shared the commitment to regenerate the nation's morals through religion having a more active role in renewing and consolidating democracy. Nevertheless the Religious Right thought Bush was clearly a more congenial candidate, above all because they thought he had a strong character, solid moral principles, and was honest and pious, one who could really be a turning point to regenerate American politics after the scandalous Clinton presidency. A quarter of the voters coming out of the polling stations said that honesty was the most important factor that influenced their choice, and 80 percent of them voted for Bush.[57] He also had the influential support of Billy Graham, who publicly said he had prayed for Bush to win, so that God's will would be done. When speaking in public before Bush and his wife during the election campaign, the reverend declared that it was a crucial election in America's history. He believed that it would be a resounding victory and an enormous change in how the country would be governed, when entrusted to the right person. Furthermore he believed in Bush's integrity.[58]

The fact that 70 percent of the Religious Right voters chose in favor of the Republican candidate was decisive for his success. With young Bush at the White House, the Religious Right thought that God had answered their prayers, giving new impulse to their long and tortuous march towards the millennium, starting as outcasts to then reach the center of American politics.[59] Bush's first official act as president was to proclaim his inauguration day a national day of prayer and thanksgiving to God, to ask him to guide the nation and its government.[60] The second day of his presidency began with a religious service, in which Jewish, Christian, Christian Orthodox, and Catholic representatives took part, as well as other religions. It took place in Washington National Cathedral, an Episcopal cathedral which had become the most important temple of the American nation's ecumenical religious observances.

God in the White House

Bush's arrival at the White House was interpreted by many observers, especially in Europe, as a new event in presidential history, because he was so ostentatiously religious. On February 3, 2001, the French newspaper *Le Monde* commented, "A strong religious element has entered the White House with President Bush."[61] In fact, a great number of the most important members of the new government and administration, Jews, Catholics, evangelicals, white and black members, were clearly very religious.[62] Condoleezza Rice, daughter of an African-American preacher and nominated secretary of state, professed a very powerful faith in God. The wife of the White House chief of staff, Andrew Card, was a Methodist pastor. John Ashcroft, the U.S. Attorney General, was the son of an evangelical pastor and fervent Pentecostal. In 1999 he expounded his religious and political beliefs at Bob Jones University, one of South Carolina's universities, which has an anti-Catholic and racist tendency and is the main school of conservative fundamentalists. Ashcroft declared that alone among the nations America acknowledged that the origins of democracy were divine and eternal, not social and temporal. That was why America was different. Americans had no other king than Jesus.[63] Bush nominated Donald Evans, the evangelical friend who had led him back to reading the Bible when he was born again to faith, as U.S. Secretary of Commerce. Michael Gerson, the main writer of the president's speeches, was a devout evangelical. Also the atmosphere at the White House was pervaded with religiosity. Officials who worked there said that Bush's presidency had introduced an aura of devotion and prayer.[64] Bush began the morning by praying and every government meeting opened with a prayer. Furthermore, Bible study groups were set up in the White house among the administration members, and sometimes also the president took part. David Frum, a Jewish intellectual who worked for some time at the White House with the staff who wrote Bush's speeches, explained that "attendance at Bible study was, if not compulsory, not quite *uncompulsory* either."[65] Garry Wills compared Bush's White House to a whitened monastery.[66]

However, so much religiosity in the presidential residence was nothing new, nor was it right to consider the chance winner of the 2000 presidential campaign responsible for having brought God into the White House, whether it was worthwhile or blameworthy. This is because God entered the White House with the first president two centuries earlier and stayed there uninterruptedly, living together both with Republican and Democratic presidents, even though at times more discreetly and almost imperceptibly. *God in the White House* is the efficacious title of a book by Richard Hutcheson published in 1988, which shows how religion changed the American presidency in more recent times.[67] It was the Republican Dwight D. Eisenhower, who arrived at the White House on January 20, 1953 and stayed there until 1960, who was the first and so far the only president who included a prayer to Almighty God that he himself wrote, in his inauguration speech. He called himself the most intensely religious man he knew,[68] and religion at the White House immediately took on greater importance with his arrival. On August 17, 1954, the historian of religions William Lee Miller observed that the displays of religion in Washington had "become pretty thick."[69] On the morning of his inauguration before being sworn in, Eisenhower, together with the vice president Richard Nixon, members of the government and officials of the White House, attended a religious service in the national Presbyterian church to look for strength in prayer and in the Word of the Lord in order to face his enormous new responsibilities. A few days after being sworn in, the president was baptized and became a member of the same church. It was the first time in American history that the head of the state was baptized while in office.[70] In 1953 he introduced the ceremony of the National Prayer Breakfast into the White House, and this became a customary presidential ritual. In 1956 Eisenhower gave permission for an office to coordinate religious affairs to be set up in the White House, nominating the Congregationalist minister Frederic E. Fox to direct it.[71] Billy Graham's personal friendship with the president, who often invited him to the White House, helped him to emerge as the president's main consultant on religious matters. Eisenhower assigned the most important ministry, the position of secretary of state, to John Foster Dulles, a very religious and devout churchman and a determined supporter of America's mission in the world. He was above all the one who started off the anticommunist crusade in the 1950s. The president wanted the first meeting of his cabinet to begin with a prayer, a practice which continued throughout his administration. Furthermore, Eisenhower supported the annual "Back to God" campaign, backed by the American Legion. And it was during his presidency, in 1954, that the expression "In God We Trust" was adopted officially as the national motto, and in 1956 the expression "under God" was included in the "Pledge of Allegiance" to the American flag.

God was not driven out of the White House in the two following Democratic presidencies of John Kennedy and Lyndon B. Johnson, who followed Kennedy after he was assassinated in 1963. The election of Kennedy, the first Catholic president of the United States, symbolized the decline of Protestant hegemony faced with the growing religious pluralism of American society, which also influenced the role of religion in politics. Kennedy did not display marked religiosity in public during his brief presidency, maybe because he was the first Catholic president, but his rhetoric was generous with references to God and the divinely inspired mission of the United States.[72] Moreover, his presidency began in a period when religion seemed to retreat as secular liberalism advanced, and a generation less imbued with religion and more eager for new experiences was growing up. In 1973, Robert S. Alley, who was studying the relation between religion and the presidency, observed that the newly formed generation of the 1960s considered religion to be politics, economy, sociology, and so on, if it meant anything at all. Religion did not sell well. Americans were in a phase of religious recession.[73] Lyndon B. Johnson had the religious assistance of Graham at the White House, he assiduously took part in National Prayer Breakfasts, and called on God to help him in his crusade against poverty and for greater social equality:

> Above the pyramid on the great seal of the United States it says in Latin, "God has favored our undertaking." God will not favor everything that we do. It is rather our duty to divine his will. I cannot help but believe that He truly understands and that He really favors the undertaking that we begin here tonight.[74]

The profound crisis in society and America's power in the 1960s, together with the disastrous outcome of the Vietnam War and the advance of the Soviet empire, brought God back to the White House again during Richard M. Nixon's presidency, which began on January 20, 1969 and ended ingloriously in 1974 because of the Watergate scandal. Hutcheson wrote that the Nixon presidency began with "a flurry of religiosity."[75] There were five officiants of the religious service at the inaugural ceremony on January 20, 1969: besides the ever-present Graham, there was a Catholic archbishop, a Christian Orthodox archbishop, a rabbi, and a black bishop. The following Sunday, Nixon began to foster religious services in the White House, starting them off with a sermon by Graham, who was a personal friend of his and who had predicted in 1967: "I think it is your destiny to be President."[76] The religious services were held in the large East Room of the White House, turned into a "church" on Sundays. The most complicated and enigmatic president of the United States was nominated "Churchman of the Year" for his religious zeal by the institution Religious Heritage of America in 1970.[77]

After Nixon's "imperial presidency"[78] ended, God continued to have a prominent place at the White House. Hutcheson pointed out that each of the three then most-recent presidents—Ford, Carter, and Reagan—"had brought God into the White House in a unique way."

> Especially with born-again, Sunday School-teaching, Southern Baptist Jimmy Carter, and again with the antiabortion, pro-school prayer program of the new religious right which has been promoted so vigorously by Ronald Reagan, religion has affected the presidency in ways previously unknown in American history.

But seldom if ever before "in the history of this nation, based as it is on the separation of church and state, [had] religion played such a prominent role in the Oval Office" as during Carter's and Reagan's presidencies.[79] Born-again Carter was faithful to the principle of the separation between church and state, a cornerstone of the Baptist confession, even though there was a predominantly religious influence on his political conduct which inspired him to end American sovereignty over the Panama Canal and to foster the Camp David agreements between Israelis and Palestinians. He made use of his position not to glorify America but to urge the Americans to humbly acknowledge their errors and sins after over a decade of profound moral and political crisis, and to regenerate God's democracy, devoting themselves to the struggle against poverty and social injustice for the defense of civil rights.

Religion helped Carter gain the White House, but the prophetic tone of his presidency, admonishing rather than glorifying the nation, together with the unfortunate undertaking to free the Americans who were hostages of the theocratic Iranian regime, contributed to his losing the elections four years later. He left the presidential residence to the new tenant, the Republican Ronald Reagan, who was borne to the White House on the Christian Right's wave of political mobilization, announcing a traditionalist program and a strong-arm foreign policy.

God was installed in the White House with the clamor of a triumphal march when Reagan took office, and the new president glorified the greatness of an America determined to leave the drama of Vietnam behind it, as well as that of the inglorious, anticipated end of Nixon's presidency and the Carter presidency's humiliations, to return to being "a shining city on a hill," a model for humanity and the champion of freedom in the world. Someone who criticized Reagan wrote that although all the presidents of the United States, without exception, had shown how attached they were to the God of the Christian Bible, none of them had dared to associate God with his own political philosophy so obstinately as President Reagan.[80] Reagan was not a churchman, and even when he was president did not often go to church; perhaps he went even less than any other president. However, as someone who admired his religiosity wrote, rather than go to church himself, President Reagan brought the church to his presidency. Once installed in the Oval Office, there were signs and proof of his faith everywhere.[81] Reagan's presidency has been called an "ongoing spectacle of politicized religiosity."[82] His political rhetoric was endlessly dressed up in religious clothes, from extolling the American nation, blessed and protected by God, which was resuming its mission in the world after years of humiliation and frustration, to reasserting traditional religious values against secular humanism and the crusade against communism and the Soviet Union, "an evil empire."

God stayed at the White House during the four years that Bush the father was president, who, however, was very discreet in showing his religiosity publicly, and during the eight years of Clinton, who, on the contrary, frequently spoke of religion in churches and at political meetings, assiduously taking part in all the National Prayer Breakfasts and often meeting religious representatives and theologians of every confession, preferring above all Billy Graham who had recited the invocation at the inaugural ceremony of his presidency. Also Bible study groups were organized in Clinton's White House.[83] The president went to church regularly on Sundays, usually on foot and carrying a showy Bible and, according to some estimates, apparently often beat his successor to the White House for the number of times he mentioned the name of Jesus.

Therefore there was nothing exceptional about the presence of God at the White House when Bush the son arrived. However, the new president's lifestyle and way of governing were certainly new: serious, precise, disciplined, demanding as regards order and punctuality, sober clothes and behavior. Bush's style, rather than his show of religiosity, was symbolically the novelty of his government program to renew the nation morally through a greater influence of religion in politics and public life—just as he had asserted during the election campaign, accusing the Democratic presidency of helping to weaken the moral foundations of the American nation. Once at the White House, the new president firmly repeated that his political line would be inspired by his religious faith, although respecting the constitutional principle of the separation between church and state.

4

Moses of America

A "Higher Calling"

In the interviews Bush gave during the election campaign and also in his autobiography, published before September 11, he said he decided to stand for election to the presidency on January 1, 1999, two hours before the inauguration of his second mandate as governor of Texas.[1] He came to this decision after listening to a sermon by the pastor of a Methodist church in Austin. Bush recalled that the pastor deprecated the moral decadence of the United States, alluding to President Clinton's scandalous conduct, and said that the people needed sincerity and honesty in the government, because members of a government who deceived their wives would deceive their country. The pastor said that the Americans wanted honest members of government and needed guidance, leaders who were ethically and morally courageous. A compass was not enough to distinguish between good and evil. The Americans needed a government with the moral courage to do the right thing for the right reason. It was not always easy or convenient for leaders to make progress.

At this point, the pastor told the story of Moses, whom God had asked to lead his people towards the promised land. Moses put forward many reasons to avoid this task. But God did not listen to him, and finally Moses obeyed and led his people, wandering in the wilderness for 40 years, trusting in God for strength, guidance, and inspiration.[2] According to Kengor, on hearing this, George's mother turned to her son and said to him: "He's talking to you." Her son nodded. "I believe that God wants me to run for president," he said, when speaking to some evangelical friends after the inauguration.[3] "I can't explain it, but I sense my country is going to need me. Something is going to happen, and, at that time, my country is going to need me. I know it won't be easy, on me or my family, but God wants me to do it...My life will never be the same," he repeated when talking with another evangelical friend.[4] After his son was elected president, Bush the father also expressed belief that the victory was due to some providential design: "You ever heard the expression, 'The Lord works in mysterious way'?...If I'd had won that election in 1992, my oldest son would not be president of the United States of America....So, what more can a dad ask? I think the Lord works in mysterious ways."[5]

Bush the son thought the same thing. Arriving at the White House despite his controversial election, he thought, was a new sign that God had called him to carry out the task of leading God's democracy in the new century: "The twenty-first century must become the 'Century of Democracy,'" said the new president on July 12 when proclaiming the Captive Nation Week.[6] And 10 days later, when answering the salutation of John Paul II, who had urged America to be steadfast in respecting the most fundamental of human rights, the right to life, Bush answered: "We will always do our best to remember our calling," praising what the Pope said, as he had shown to the world not only the splendor of truth, but also the power of truth when overcoming evil and giving a new direction to history.[7]

Elementary Theology

Bush strongly insisted, both in public and privately, on his rediscovery of faith in Christ to explain the religious origin of his political vocation. He did not consider this rediscovery miraculous but a continuous journey towards salvation. Nevertheless, by the time he became president of the United States, his religious beliefs were firmly established.

Bush's religious faith is not the result of specific theological, fundamentalist, evangelical, or Methodist teaching. In 1994, when a journalist asked him why he attended a Methodist church although he had been brought up as an Episcopalian, Bush answered that he knew there were profound doctrinal differences between the two denominations, but that he did not know enough about it to explain what they were. On another occasion, he declared he was in favor of putting up the Ten Commandments in public offices in the "current version," showing that he did not know that Protestants, Catholics, and Jews have different versions of them. Bush's historical and theological ignorance is not surprising, because although American evangelicals claim their faith is inspired by God's Word, they seem to have little knowledge of the Bible: some surveys have revealed that only half of the evangelicals identify Jesus as the person who gave the Sermon from the Mount, and less than half can repeat at least five of the Ten Commandments from memory.[8]

Bush's religious faith is impervious to doubt, refractory to knowledge and critical reflection, and is based on elementary theology, shared by millions of evangelical and born-again Americans. He believes there is an omniscient, omnipotent God who is good, just, and merciful, the Creator of the universe, who watches over mankind with divine providence. He believes that Christ is the son of God who became man, free from sin; that he is the Savior and the

highest spiritual guide of those who want to win the battle against evil and gain
paradise, taking the Ten Commandments and the Beatitudes as principles to
direct and lead their lives. Bush believes that evil exists, but also that people
can avoid its temptations by trusting in the regenerating power of faith and grace.
He believes that prayer is morally efficacious as a spiritual dialogue with God, to
receive comfort and advice from it, and several times during his presidency, he
said he prayed daily because faith in Christ constantly inspired his life and
helped him to make his political decisions.

Bush is a Christian convinced that the Word of God revealed in the Bible is
infallible. That is why he is considered a fundamentalist, but he is not so in
the proper meaning of the term, even though both he and the fundamentalists
and all the Religious Right defend traditional family values and the sacrality
of marriage between men and women, condemn abortion and encourage absti-
nence against the use of contraceptives, and abhor secular humanism and refuse
evolutionism as a scientific theory alternative to the Bible's creationism. Nevertheless, differently from fundamentalist Christians and most of the evangelicals
for whom Christianity is the only true religion and proselytizing a duty, Bush
has shown an ecumenical attitude towards other religions, holding that they
can all be useful for the moral and social good of the nation, if understood and
practiced correctly. However, in the past, Bush had expressed a different theological opinion. In 1993 he happened to incautiously state that only those who
were Christian could go to paradise, and that for this reason Jews and believers
in other religions could not. Faced with protests from Jewish religious associations, Bush immediately made amends, and from then on followed Billy
Graham's warning "to never play God" by deciding who went and who did
not go to paradise.[9]

During the 2000 presidential campaign, Bush's ecumenical attitude became
more evident. He repeatedly stated that it was exactly his Christian faith which
had taught him to respect other religions. He had become convinced that people
could communicate with God following different religious ways: "It is very
important for people to not be haughty in their religion. And there's all kinds
of admonitions in the Bible; haughtiness, rightfulness is a sin in itself."[10] And
he said in an interview:

> I think that we're all God's children, and far be it from me, as a lowly sinner, trying
> to decide who gets to go to heaven and who doesn't, for example....And so to
> answer your question, there are great religions in the world, and it's important to
> recognize that there are great religions in the world. And there are many shared
> tenets of the great religions. "Love a neighbor like you'd like to be loved yourself."
> And there are some wonderful callings. I just happen to be a Christian.[11]

When addressing the Catholic electorate, which traditionally sided with the
Democratic Party, Bush borrowed the expression "culture of life" from John Paul II
to explain his opposition to abortion and experiments on embryonic cells. Also his
appeal to synagogues and mosques to carry out his program of "compassionate

conservatism" was ecumenical, approved of also by Muslim traditionalists, who gave him a considerable number of their votes in the 2000 elections.

The concept of life and the world that Bush derived from his elementary theology is based on a distinct division between good and evil, which he applies also to his concept of politics; in the same way he derived the fundamental aims of his government agenda—a greater role of religion in public life to inspire worthwhile politics for the public good, the idea of the sacrality of life right from conception, opposition to marriage between homosexuals, state financing for private schools and religious organizations that carry out charitable activities. This was the program of his political line when he was governor of Texas, and it was still his program when he became president of the United States.

God's Democracy

Bush's faith lacks originality, theologically speaking, and the same can also be said of his religious interpretation of democracy and the destiny of the United States, which derives from a long and consolidated tradition of American political culture.

Faith in American democracy was the main subject of Bush's inaugural address, after being sworn in on the same Bible on which his father had taken his oath. Bush spoke of national reconciliation to heal the wounds caused by his controversial nomination as president of the United States. He praised the peaceful transfer of power, typical of America but rare in history, thanking President Clinton for serving the nation and Vice President Gore "for a contest conducted with spirit, and ended with grace." Then, declaring he felt humbled before the task awaiting him, Bush called up America's epic history again: "the story of a new world that became a friend and liberator of the old. The story of a slave-holding society that became a servant of freedom. The story of a power that went into the world to protect but not possess, to defend but not to conquer." The American story was "the story of a flawed and erring people" united over generations by great and constant ideals, through which it was able to overcome its imperfections and correct its errors, pursuing the greatest of its ideals, that is, to carry out the American promise: that everyone deserves to have a chance, that nobody was born insignificant. The Americans had been called to carry out this promise in their lives and laws, Bush said, and even if America sometimes stopped or took too long, it had to follow its course. For most of the preceding century, America's faith in freedom and democracy had been like a rock in a stormy sea. Now it was like a seed in the wind that would take root in many nations. Bush added that faith in democracy was something more than America's creed; it was the innate hope of humanity, an ideal Americans pursued but which did not belong to them, a responsibility they bore and handed down.

In order to continue America's mission, Bush committed himself to building a single nation of justice and opportunity, fighting the divisions brought about by circumstances of birth, by social conditions, prejudices, and poverty.

He appealed to the ethics of Americans' individual responsibility and to the humanitarian spirit of the churches, synagogues, and mosques, calling on them to cooperate with the government in carrying out a compassionate policy of solidarity and help for all those who had been left behind, prefiguring a renewed nation of citizens, not subjects, responsible citizens, enterprising communities of services, and a nation of character.

The new president said he was confident of success in his undertaking, because "we are guided by a power larger than ourselves, who creates us equal in his image," and because the American nation was endowed with civility, courage, compassion, and character to defend and spread freedom. The destiny of freedom in the world depended on the success of America's mission, because if America did not lead the cause of freedom, this cause would remain without a leader. The United States had to strengthen its own defenses and make them superior to every challenge, because weakness encouraged challenges. America had to face the weapons of mass destruction to spare the new century other horrors. That is why the world role of America's power was reasserted as a bulwark of liberty, ready to intervene everywhere it was threatened, in any part of the world, thus warning the enemies of freedom and America not to make mistakes, because America continued to feel committed, by history and by its own choice, to achieve a balance of power in favor of liberty.

Bush ended his speech by pointing out that the author of the story he had evoked was not the American people:

> We are not this story's author, who fills time and eternity with his purpose. Yet his purpose is achieved in our duty; and our duty is fulfilled in service to one another.
>
> Never tiring, never yielding, never finishing, we renew that purpose today: to make our country more just and generous; to affirm the dignity of our lives and every life. This work continues. This story goes on. And an angel still rides in the whirlwind and directs this storm.[12]

Bush's inaugural address was received with favorable comments from all sides, both political and religious, even though, during the ceremony, there were demonstrations against the president who had "stolen the victory" and caused "the death of democracy."[13] A liberal editorialist of the *Washington Post,* who had voted for Gore, wrote that he now considered Bush a more suitable president than Gore to unite the country.[14] The magazine *Time* dedicated a cover to him, thus consecrating him as the protagonist of the year.

Pontiffs of America

By celebrating America as the land chosen by Divine Providence to achieve God's democracy, Bush continued a tradition of presidential rhetoric that dated back to George Washington and which had been constantly renewed by all the following presidents, especially on the occasion of their inaugural addresses.

The ceremony installing the new president periodically renewed the bond uniting America's people, as well as their symbolic bond with the highest institution of the republic, which was conferred sacrality by the ceremony itself. The theologian Michael Novak observed that, in the United States, the presidency was the nation's most important religious symbol,[15] and Inauguration Day the most solemn national ceremony. Arthur Schlesinger Jr. wrote that every four years since 1789, the austere ceremony suspended political passions to allow an interlude of national reunion.[16]

April 30, 1789 was Inauguration Day for the first presidency of Washington, when the final expression "So help me God" was added to the form of oath, repeated by all the successors. Since then, the inaugural ceremony has been a symbolic, collective rite dedicated to God by the American nation through its president's oath. Also the inaugural address is essentially a religious declaration, which expounds the fundamental beliefs American values are based on. It periodically renews and strengthens the fact that the nation reflects these values as well as the American people's commitment to conserve and apply them in their daily lives. Given this meaning, the presidents' inaugural speeches are the "holy scriptures" of American civil religion, together with the Declaration of Independence, the Constitution of the United States, and the Bill of Rights.[17]

With the passing of time, a kind of presidential theology of God's democracy has taken form through the inaugural addresses, and apparently the basic canon of this theology was already firmly established by the first presidents of the United States, who were also the first pontiffs of American religion. This presidential theology originated in a religious interpretation of America's history, its institutions, and its role in the world. Its roots lay in the Puritan tradition of the pilgrim fathers, convinced they had been chosen by God to build in the new world the promised land, the new Jerusalem, "a city on the hill," which was the image used by John Winthrop, the first governor of the Massachusetts colony. Before reaching America in 1630 on board the ship *Arabella,* he and the other Puritans signed a covenant with God, pledging themselves to remain united and build a community founded on divine law. The belief that Divine Providence benevolently watches over the destiny of the American nation especially, to which God entrusted the mission of being an example for all humanity as long as it was faithful to the covenant with God, also dates back to the times of the colonies. However, identifying "a city on the hill" and the American mission with republican democracy dates back to the founding of the United States.[18]

Presidential theology clearly bears the mark of the Protestant biblical archetype; nevertheless, the image of God has no explicitly Christian connotations in most of the inaugural addresses but is generally deist or theist. According to what Washington said, which was echoed by his successors on practically the same line, the God of presidential theology is "that Almighty Being who rules over the universe, who presides in the councils of nations," "the Great Author of every public and private good," "the Invisible Hand which conducts the affairs of men more than those of the United States," "the benign Parent of the Human Race," who has lavished conspicuous gifts on the United States—an independent nation that "seems to have been distinguished by some token of providential agency."

Americans are more responsible before God, towards whom they have more duties than any other nation, the most important duty of all being to pursue "the experiment entrusted to the Americans" and "the preservation of the sacred fire of liberty and the destiny of the republican model of government."

The first president warned the Americans that they had to stay united, above every particular diversity and hostility, in order to safeguard their republican freedom, because if "one side or local prejudices or attachments, separate views or party animosities prevailed" the government cannot "win the affections of its citizens and command respect of the world." To achieve this, the American nation had to be faithful to God, respecting the "pure and immutable principles of private morality," "the eternal rules of order and right which heaven itself has ordained"; and cultivating private and public virtues, without which the republic could not live freely and grant "the preservation of the sacred fire of liberty and the destiny of the republican model of government."[19]

John Adams and Thomas Jefferson, who were Washington's first successors, contributed to working out a set of rules for the republican virtues needed to form the moral character of a nation which was to be governed carefully, applying justice, moderation, and constancy, "under an overruling Providence which had so signally protected this country from the first," as Adams said in his inaugural address on March 4, 1797. He called on "that Being who is supreme over all, the Patron of Order, the Fountain of Justice, and the Protector in all ages of the world of virtuous liberty, to continue His blessing upon this nation and its government and give it all possible success and duration consistent with the ends of His providence."[20]

It was his successor, Jefferson, who worked out again and defined the "sacred history" and the "sacred principles" of republican theology in his two inaugural addresses on March 4, 1801 and March 4, 1805, in a period of troubled growth of the young republic. Contemplating the extraordinary event of the birth of a "rising nation, spread over a wide and fruitful land, traversing all the seas with the rich productions of their industry, engaged in commerce with nations who feel power and forget right, advancing rapidly to destinies beyond the reach of mortal eye," Jefferson was overcome by a feeling of pride and humility before "the magnitude of the undertaking" and the difficulty of steering "with safety the vessel on which we are all embarked amidst the conflicting elements of a troubled world," which assailed America itself.

The foundations of Jefferson's republican theology—"the creed of our political faith"—were the "sacred principle" of the equality of rights and laws, the majority's right to govern respecting the rights of the minority, and putting an end to political intolerance as had already been done with religious intolerance, both having caused bitter suffering and persecution. All this made up the essence of the American republic, "the world's best hope." Loyalty to the union and representative government guaranteed progress and prosperity for America, a country "kindly separated by nature and a wide ocean from the exterminating havoc of one quarter of the globe; too high-minded to endure the degradations of the others; possessing a chosen country, with room enough for our descendants to the thousandth and thousandth generation," and where the citizens can work and prosper wielding their power with equal rights, "enlightened by a benign religion, professed, indeed, and practiced in various forms, yet all of them inculcating honesty, truth, temperance, gratitude, and the love of man; acknowledging and adoring an overruling Providence, which by all its dispensations proves that it delights in the happiness of men here and his greater happiness hereafter."

In his second inaugural address, Jefferson repeated firmly that the American nation and republic were born from the providential design of "that Being in whose hands we are, who led our fathers, as Israel of old, from their native land and planted them in a country flowing with all the necessaries and comforts of life; who has covered our infancy with His providence and our riper years with His wisdom and power."[21]

In the following 200 years, the presidents, in their inaugural addresses as in all their proclamations and speeches celebrating American history and ideals, variously tempered the canon of the theology worked out by the first presidents. They kept its fundamental themes, emphasizing some in respect to others according to their personal political beliefs, and adapting them to the various situations and circumstances of their periods, in peace and war. The main theme, constantly shared by all, is the divine inspiration of American democracy, which right from the beginning made it the best hope on earth. All the presidents in their capacity as pontiffs of American religion have contributed to preserving the canon of republican theology, and modifying it more or less significantly according to their own personality and religiosity. However, it was above all in the second half of the twentieth century that the president of the United States took on a more important role, consequent to his greater governmental power deriving from America's increased power in the world.

During Bush's installation at the White House, he glorified America with religious rhetoric, using a tradition of republican theology set out by his predecessors and widely shared by the Americans. However, in the early months of Bush's presidency, it did not seem that carrying out his pontifical duties was efficacious in gaining a higher approval rating; on the contrary, polls made before September 11 revealed that his popularity was waning. Some observers wondered if that was also due to his excessive use of religious rhetoric and overdone traditionalist and conservative attitudes, which made the new president seem sanctimonious, a prisoner of the religious and fundamentalist right. Yet others thought he was a mediocre but astute politicker, who dressed up a cynical and unscrupulous political line in religious clothes, aiming solely at fostering the interests of the economic groups that had supported his candidacy and financed his electoral campaign.

Unpredictable Charisma

It is probably impossible to scan the depths of the human mind in search of unquestionable proof that the religious faith a person displays is sincere. This probability becomes certainty when dealing with a politician who continually speaks of religion, declaring that God inspires his life and politics. Nevertheless, a critical analysis of the part played by religion in the political conduct of the president, who found himself leading America at the beginning of the first century of the third millennium, can assume that his faith is sincere and is effectively the main source of inspiration of his political strategy. After all, recognizing that Bush's religious beliefs are sincere does not mean expressing a positive judgment on how he acts politically, and even less on how, as president of the United States, he mixes religion with politics to justify his decisions, especially when they influence the whole of humanity. On the contrary, those who oppose Bush most severely think that it is just the sincerity of his religious beliefs that gives rise to the dangerous aspects of his politics, like, for example, his unshakable conviction that whatever he does is always to achieve the good of the American nation and the whole of humanity, and that his political choices are right because they are in agreement with the designs of Providence. Or there is his obstinacy in persevering in any action he embarks on without letting himself be moved by doubts or criticism, especially in war undertakings, because he believes it is not only his political but also his religious duty, as president of the United States, to resort to any means to protect American democracy from the threat of evil, and to fight evil anywhere in the world to spread the divine gift of freedom to all humanity.

Conceding Bush's religious convictions are sincere, the most interesting factor to study is the role that religion and the intermingling of religion and politics have had in his policies since September 11, in order to judge whether his religious presidency is unusual in the context of American history, even an aberration from its course and tradition, or expresses a part of contemporary America. This part is very religious, conservative, and traditionalist, made up of people who found an efficacious interpreter in Bush, who was capable of leading them to the highest office of the United States, giving them the strength and energy necessary to influence the course of American, and therefore world history, at the beginning of the first century of the third millennium. Their ambitious intention was to reshape America and the world following their own principles and political and religious values. The most important problem for our survey is not so much Bush's personal religion, as rather the part religion has played in his political success, and above all the effect of his presidency on the civil religion of the Americans, in one of the most tragic periods of their history.

However Bush's religious faith is judged, his publicly displayed religion contributed to favoring his arrival at the White House. Furthermore, after September 11 it played a decisive part in making many Americans, and above all the Religious Right, see him as a charismatic leader, a president to whom Providence had entrusted the arduous task of leading the nation at a tragic moment of its history.[22]

It seems obvious that Bush is convinced he was called by Providence to lead God's democracy in the twenty-first century, to give history a new direction.

Nevertheless, right up to the terrorist attack of September 11, the aim of the mission to which he felt called was not clear even to Bush himself. During the first eight months of his presidency neither his personality nor his activity gave clear signs of any charisma. Before September 11, perhaps not even the most favorable observers could have noticed anything charismatic about him or the way he carried out his presidential functions. His first political decisions, like considerably cutting taxes, setting up a special office at the White House for financing religious organizations that carried out social assistance, taking the measures to limit abortion, and deciding not to finance research on new stem cells, were applauded by most of his religious electorate, even though his more traditionalist supporters were disappointed because the more clear cut and severer measures they had hoped for were not included. However, these decisions did not increase his popularity, which, on the contrary, tended to decline.

Bush's honeymoon with the Americans did not last long, and it did not increase trust in the new president, who was not at all proficient at speaking in public and communicating. Rather, some mistakes in pronunciation and rash declarations on foreign policy made the Americans begin to suspect they were led by an inexpressive, dull, and inept president. The new president's infrequent contacts with the public played against his popularity—up to the evening of the terrorist attack, Bush had never addressed the nation from the Oval Office, never granted a real press conference that was open and not established beforehand, and never displayed the stature of a real leader on any occasion important for the nation.

David Broder wrote in the *Washington Post* that three months after Bush's installation, he had not yet given Americans a clear idea of their new leader.[23] After all, Bush himself did not seem to spend much time trying to work out what his presidency stood for; in fact, before September 11, he spent over 40 percent of his first year as president on holiday or traveling.[24] The approval rating of his political conduct continued to decline, dropping to just over 50 percent at the end of June. Then, in the month following the September 11 terrorist attack, his approval rating rose to 87 percent, reaching 90 percent at the end of 2001 after bringing down the Taliban regime in Afghanistan. Indeed, although Bush was lost and bewildered on the first day of the attack, a new man emerged from the experience of September 11, transformed by the crisis—resolute, determined, capable of interpreting the nation's feelings, who knew how to comfort, guide, and lead the terrorized Americans, urging them to be united and strong to react to the trauma of the tragedy, and declaring war on those who had declared war on God's democracy.

5

Going to War, with God

The Revelation

After September 11, Bush carried out intense pastoral activity from the presidential pulpit to comfort the Americans, relieve their sorrow, calm their anger, and encourage their patriotism, promising to capture and punish the terrorists who had violated America.[1] He used the right symbolic gestures and was unexpectedly loquacious and very expressive, thanks to the valuable help of his speechwriters, who were experts in religious language. Furthermore, the president took on the task of explaining to the Americans the meaning of the September 11 tragedy, so he could announce the new responsibilities that awaited them, faced with the war that Islamic terrorists had declared on America. From September 2001 to May 2003, when Saddam Hussein's regime was overthrown in Iraq by America's armed intervention, many of the president's speeches and proclamations had a sort of pontifical function, which he carried out by drawing up his own theology of war. This explained the destiny of the United States, faced with a war between good and evil, in which, however, it was clear right from the start that America was on God's side.

September 11 showed the Americans that the United States was not invulnerable, although it was protected by two oceans and its unequaled military strength, and that there were ruthless enemies in the world who hated America, its civilization, and the values it represented for all humanity. When proclaiming September 14 a national day of prayer in memory of the victims of the terrorist attack, Bush said that America and the civilized world had been attacked by wicked people who had to be pursued and handed over to the law, and justice demanded that anyone who helped and harbored them be punished: "The enormity of their evil demands it. We will use all the resources of the United States and our cooperating friends and allies to pursue those responsible for this evil, until justice is done."[2] The United States was at war against a new enemy, which was not a state but a terrorist organization with followers all over the world, ready to sacrifice their lives as long as they inflicted the greatest damage and suffering on the might and people of the United States. The Islamic terrorists had no compunction about committing the most atrocious crimes in order to terrorize, humiliate, and destroy America, because it represented free government, freedom of religion, and the rights and equality of individuals in the world. However, Bush explained to the Americans, although the greatest power in the world had turned out to be vulnerable, another contrasting revelation had emerged from the terrorist attack: the greatness and goodness of the American character, the strength of its virtues of heroism, courage, solidarity, and love of its fellowmen. The president repeated on more than one occasion that these virtues had come out in the Americans who reacted against the terrorists on Flight 93, simply saying "Let's roll"; in the hundreds of firemen and policemen who died during rescue operations in the two towers at the World Trade Center, sacrificing their lives; in the thousands of rescuers who gave their blood and tireless work trying to save others. And these virtues had appeared in all the Americans, who responded to the terrorist attack by showing they were united, determined, and ready to fight against the evil enemy. September 11 revealed the strength of the "American creed," based on the faith in freedom and equality that united millions of people who were Americans by birth or choice:

> In this 226th year of our independence, we have seen that American patriotism is still a living faith. We love our country, only more when it is threatened. America is the most diverse nation on earth. Yet, in a moment we discovered again that we are a single people, we share the same allegiance, we live under the same flag— and when you strike one American, you strike us all.[3]

The terrorists had wanted to terrorize America, declared its president, but the country had found its unity and strength in the tragedy, and was ready to fight the new enemies of freedom and democracy in the twenty-first century as it had fought fascism, Nazism, and communism in the twentieth century, to defend God's democracy and spread its universal values throughout the world.

The Mission

On September 14, Bush announced the decision to fight the "war on terror." He did so when the National Day of Prayer was celebrated solemnly in the cathedral church of St. Peter and St. Paul in Washington, a church in Gothic style known also as Washington National Cathedral, the sixth largest church in the world. About 3,000 people attended the ceremony, among whom were four former presidents of the United States—Carter, Ford, Clinton, and Bush Sr.; the former vice president Al Gore; a host of four-star generals; hundreds of members of Congress, along with other officials; judges of the Supreme Court; CIA and FBI directors; governors; mayors; and dozens of firemen and policemen.[4]

The religious service was ecumenical—Billy Graham, two black ministers, a woman bishop, a rabbi, an imam, and a Catholic cardinal spoke first, before the president of the United States. Speaking from the pulpit, Bush was profoundly moved when he spoke of the victims of the terrorist attack, and he said that America's new mission at the beginning of the twenty-first century was the war against evil:

> Just three days removed from these events, Americans do not yet have the distance of history. But our responsibility to history is already clear: to answer these attacks and rid the world of evil. War has been waged against us by stealth and deceit and murder. This nation is peaceful, but fierce when stirred to anger. This conflict was begun on the timing and terms of others. It will end in a way, and at an hour, of our choosing.

In the terrible experience the Americans were living through, they had shown the world their national character: "Today, we felt what Franklin Roosevelt called the warm courage of national unity. This unity is a unity of faith, and every background. It has joined together political parties in both houses of Congress." It was revealed in the prayer services, the candlelit vigils, and the American flags waved proudly as a challenge: "In every generation, the world has produced enemies of human freedom. They have attacked America, because we are freedom's home and defender. And the commitment of our fathers is now the calling of our time."

After describing America's mission as a "war on terror," Bush explained to the Americans how to interpret God's presence in the inhuman tragedy that had struck the United States. The Americans were asking God in their prayers "to give us a sign that He is still here," but the signs of God, Bush said, echoing Abraham Lincoln, are "not always the ones we look for. We learn in tragedy that his purposes are not always our own. . . . This world He created is of a moral design. Grief and tragedy and hatred are only for a time. Goodness, remembrance, and love have no end. And the Lord of life holds all who die, and all who mourn."[5]

Bush ended his speech calling on God to bless and protect America at war, trusting in his love for the American people, because as "we have been assured, neither death nor life, nor angels nor principalities nor powers, nor things present nor things to come, nor height nor depth, can separate us from God's love. May He bless the souls of the departed. May He comfort our own. And may He always guide our country."

At the Nation's Church

The speech at the National Cathedral had extraordinary symbolic, political, religious, and military importance, not only for its content but especially for where it had been made. The ceremony marked the beginning of a process that sacralized the September 11 events and the new mission which the Americans were taking upon themselves before God, through their president, to free the world of evil. To understand the symbolic importance of the ceremony, it should be remembered that the purpose of the National Cathedral when it rose was to become the most important temple of the American religion. The idea of having a national church building dates back to when the new capital, Washington, was built. The first amendment of the Constitution of the United States forbade the United States government to establish a state church, in order to assert the principle of freedom of religion. Nevertheless, even though the founding fathers as a body refused to allow any religious confession the privilege of becoming the church of the nation, none of them imagined the republic without religion. When Washington left the presidency, he reminded his fellow citizens that of "all the dispositions and habits which lead to political prosperity, Religion and Morality are indispensable supports. In vain would that man claim the tribute of Patriotism, who should labour to subvert these great pillars of human happiness."[6] As far back as 1749, Benjamin Franklin maintained the need for a "Publick Religion, from its Usefulness to the Publick," generally defined according to the basic beliefs of illuminist deism, very similar to the "civil religion" proposed by Jean-Jacques Rousseau in his *Social Contract,* published in 1762.[7] There was a church dedicated to a special function among the plans of the architect Pierre Charles L'Enfant, when President Washington gave him the task of designing the general plan for the new seat of the United States government. L'Enfant wrote:

> This Church is intended for national purposes, such as public prayer, thanksgiving, funeral orations etc. and assigned to the special use of no particular Sect or denomination, but equally open to all. It will be likewise a proper shelter for such monuments as were voted by the last Continental Congress for those heroes who fell in the cause of liberty, and for such others as may hereafter be decreed by the voice of a grateful Nation.[8]

The nation's church was not built as the French architect imagined it, but about a century later; on January 6, 1893, Congress granted the Episcopal Church of the District of Columbia authorization to build a cathedral and a study institute on Mount Saint Alban, which towers above the whole area of the capital. The foundation stone was laid on September 29, 1907, with the bishop of London, President Theodore Roosevelt, and an immense crowd present. Little by little as the building grew, the cathedral became a place for national rites. It was still a church of the Episcopal diocese of Washington, but the first bishop of the cathedral wanted to keep faith with L'Enfant's original idea, letting it be a place of prayer open to everyone. During the Second World War, monthly religious services were held there for a people united in times of emergency, and the Chapel of the Holy Spirit became a temple of war for community commemoration ceremonies. In 1956 the tomb of President Wilson, the only president buried in the District of Columbia, was consecrated. In 1968 the Reverend Martin Luther King Jr. gave his last speech from the pulpit of the cathedral, and in the following year, thousands of people attended the funeral of President Eisenhower there.

In 1976, President Ford, the Queen of England, and the Bishop of Canterbury were present at the inauguration of the nave. In 1980 the cathedral was at an advanced stage of building and hosted a national thanksgiving ceremony for the liberation of the American hostages in Iran. In 1983, the African-American bishop of the cathedral confirmed its national, ecumenical character as the great symbol of the nation's religious heritage and foundation. The building was definitively brought to completion on September 30, 1990, during the presidency of Bush the father, who attended the consecration ceremony.[9] The president said that the cathedral was not only a church:

> We have constructed here this symbol of our nation's spiritual life, overlooking the center of our nation's secular life...a cathedral that's not just about faith but was also about a nation and its people: a cathedral where mosaics of the Great Seal of the United States and the State seals are set into the floors....It's a place where the history of the cathedral and the country are interwoven.[10]

Although it is still an Episcopal church, Washington National Cathedral has become the nation's church, without a formal congregation like other churches or places of worship. It is a national place of prayer, open to everyone and to all the faiths, the most important temple of American civil religion.

Besides the governmental coat of arms, the symbols of the cathedral, even in its predominantly biblical iconography, evoke American civil religion in its stained-glass windows, stone and wooden sculptures, and metal decorations, calling up the history of the United States—its struggles for independence and human rights, its wars, its achievements in the fields of religion, science, law, politics, medicine, and civic morals, and its great national heroes. An aisle of the church is dedicated to Washington, with a statue of him and Masonic symbols, including his small Masonic hammer, which bears the image of the Capitol impressed on one side and the church tower on the other. Another aisle is dedicated to Lincoln, with a bronze statue, and yet another is dedicated to the Confederate General Robert E. Lee. There is a chapel for the fallen, with the coats of arms of the five forces, dedicated to all the men and women who gave their lives in war for their country. A fragment of lunar rock brought back to earth by Apollo 11 is set in one of the stained-glass windows. Bush the son celebrated the ceremony of prayer in the cathedral on the day he was sworn in.

Religion or Nationalism?

The National Day of Prayer in memory of the victims of the terrorist attacks, celebrated in the most important temple of American religion, was carefully organized to be a demonstration of mourning, but above all a display of strength and the glorification of America.

President Bush looked after every detail personally, from the choice of those participating and the speakers to selecting the music, giving every aspect a significant symbolic meaning. The ceremony opened with the martial rite of saluting the flag. As well as hymns and a reading of the Beatitudes from the Gospel according to Matthew, the participants sang "America the Beautiful." The religious service, with readings from the Holy Scriptures, closed with "The Battle Hymn of the Republic," a poem composed by Julia Ward Howe at the beginning of the Civil War, abounding in warlike expressions and apocalyptic flashes announcing the arrival of the Lord, with his terrible shining sword, to the cry of "Glory! Glory! Hallelujah! His truth is marching on! God is marching on!" The poem has become perhaps the most popular hymn for wars and moral crusades among English-speaking peoples, as the historian Ernst Lee Tuveson wrote. The final lines sing to the glory of Christ, "hence, the close association of Christ's dying to make men 'holy,' and the call to 'make men free,' in the hymn."[11]

After the final prayer and benediction, the ceremony ended with the martial rite of the flag being carried out. With religion, politics, and the armed forces represented simultaneously, the ceremony symbolically staged the Americans' faith, cohesion, and strength, united around their president to defend God's democracy. There was the gist of the new theology of war in Bush's speech, which he explained in the following weeks to morally justify the military operations that were about to be launched against terrorism. Now war joined the fusion of religion and politics in Bush's theology. In the *Washington Post,* Bill Broadway, after consulting the comments of scholars and clergymen on the president's speech, wrote that the language was the rhetoric of war. However, the speech did not come from the Oval Office or Camp David, but from a place of worship, before the altar of a church. The sociologist Robert N. Bellah, famous for asserting in 1967 that an American civil religion existed, judged the speech "stunningly inappropriate, basically because it was a war talk." He described Bush's statement that America had the historical responsibility for freeing the world from evil as absolutely astonishing. Also Professor James F. Childress, lecturer in ethics, said he was disconcerted by this: "By talking about ridding the world of evil, he's moving into a crusade mentality, a holy war mentality. If you take that approach, you lose sense of the kind of constraints that are appropriate in seeking justice for the terrorist attacks." Cardinal Theodore E. McCarrick, head of the Catholic archdiocese of Washington, approved of Bush's speech, because he thought his reaction was suitable to such serious events and the Americans' mood, even though he added that a military response should be carried out according to the rules of a "just war." Archbishop Demetrios, head of the Greek Orthodox Church in America, made a similar comment. Margaret Shannon, the historian of Washington National Cathedral, pointed out that Bush was not the first president to make a political speech in the cathedral, because in 1998, during a memorial service for 12 Americans killed in the terrorist attacks against the American embassies in Tanzania and Kenya, President Clinton incited America "to find those responsible and bring them to justice; not to rest as long as terrorists plot to take innocent lives...For our larger struggle for hope over hatred...is a just one. And, with God's help, it will prevail."[12] Important Democratic senators such as Edward Kennedy and Joe Lieberman judged the speech positively.[13]

Also a Mennonite church pastor, Heidi Regier Kreider, appreciated the religious service, as a heartfelt memory of the victims and a meditation on the country's suffering, but she severely criticized the nationalist tone of the ceremony, pointing out that there were victims of other nations who endured terror every day, because of military occupations, the threat of bombs and mines, extreme poverty, hunger, and AIDS. She wondered if compassion for the suffering experienced on home ground would lead the Americans to understand the suffering of other peoples, too, making them charitable towards the others as well: "If God's blessing is reserved only for American victims of terrorism, then nationalism has replaced true compassion." This is why the pastor did not like the "religious and national symbols blurred together in subtle but powerful ways" during the ceremony in the cathedral. Images of the flag were shown while the young choir sang a psalm, and images of the Pentagon ripped open and the mass of ruins of the World Trade Center during the hymn "A Mighty Fortress Is Our God." All this called for a new debate among the Americans on the values and priorities of the country and on the relation between church and state, renewing loyalty to a God who loves all nations equally, and commitment towards the church that transcends all national borders. The pastor protested indirectly against interpreting the September 11 attack as a war between good and evil, and contested the idea that the United States was morally superior only because it had been attacked, pointing out that the buildings destroyed represented wealth and weapons, which in turn had produced poverty, death, and suffering in the world.[14]

The Mennonite pastor's voice, out of tune with the chorus of approval the president's speech received, anticipated other similar voices, which grew in number and volume when Bush turned sacralizing September 11 into a renewed sacralization of America, presenting it as a nation engaged in a war to free the world of evil, so as to spread democracy, which God had bestowed so generously on the Americans for them to give to all humanity, all over the world. However, during the months of the war in Afghanistan, these discordant voices were unheard in the patriotic clamor produced by the chorus of approval for the military operation, and for the president who had become the commander of the country at war.

Consecrating a Leader

Bush solemnly carried out his function as the most important pontiff of civil religion, celebrating the American victims with the ceremony in America's church, and was symbolically consecrated as leader of the nation at war. "Civil religion goes to war," commented Mark Silk, director of the Leonard E. Greenberg Center for the Study of Religion in Public Life: "If civil religion is about anything, it's about war and those who die in it."[15] Bush's symbolic consecration as leader was confirmed on the afternoon of September 14, when, after the ceremony at the National Cathedral, he went to New York to visit Ground Zero for the first time. His meeting with the firemen, the policemen, the rescuers, the workers, and the relatives of the victims was spontaneous and moving.

Bush was profoundly shocked when he saw the heap of rubble, but he managed to pull himself together and quickly became a sure and determined leader again, speaking to the crowd that cheered him and demanded justice, shouting "U-S-A, U-S-A, U-S-A." A speech was not on the agenda, but Bush climbed up on the rubble with a megaphone, helped by an elderly fireman, and spoke to the crowd from there with one arm around a fireman's shoulders. However, his voice did not carry and someone interrupted him saying, "We can't hear you." Bush shouted back: "Well, I can hear you. The rest of the world hears you. And the people who knocked these buildings down will hear all of us soon." The crowd answered their leader with one voice, proudly repeating the chant, "U-S-A, U-S-A, U-S-A."[16]

After the ceremony at the nation's church and meeting the crowd at Ground Zero, Bush felt he had acquired charisma and on September 20 stood before Congress to have it confirmed definitively by the people's representatives, in the name of America's new mission. "We have suffered great loss. And in our grief and anger we have found our mission and our moment," he said in his address that sketched the basic lines of the "war against terrorism." America had been attacked by the "enemies of freedom," and in a single day "night fell on a different world, a world where freedom itself is under attack," because the al Qaeda terrorists' "goal is remaking the world—and imposing its radical beliefs on people everywhere." They "kill not merely to end lives, but to disrupt and end a way of life." Behind al Qaeda's claimed religious calling, there was the legacy of "all the murderous ideologies of the twentieth century. By sacrificing human life to serve their radical visions—by abandoning every value except the will to power—they follow in the path of fascism, and Nazism, and totalitarianism. And they will follow that path all the way, to where it ends: in history's unmarked grave of discarded lies."[17] The ideal world that the terrorists wanted to create already had a concrete model in the Taliban regime in Afghanistan. Bush ordered the Taliban leaders to hand over all the al Qaeda chiefs hiding in their country to the U.S. authorities, to close every terrorist training camp, and consign all the terrorists with their supporters, giving America total access to all the terrorist camps in order to check that they had been made inoperative. The requests were not negotiable and had to be carried out immediately: "They will hand over the terrorists, or they will share their fate." The "war on terror" which America had decided to fight began against al Qaeda, Bush explained, "but it does not end there. It will not end until every terrorist group of global reach has been found, stopped and defeated." Consequently, the Americans should not expect a single decisive battle, "but a lengthy campaign, unlike any other we have ever seen," to drive the terrorists out wherever they were and punish the countries which gave them hospitality and protected them: "Every nation, in every region, now has a decision to make. Either you are with us, or you are with the terrorists. From this day forward, any nation that continues to harbor or support terrorism will be regarded by the United States as a hostile regime." It was up to America to lead the war on terror, not only because it had been attacked by the terrorists, but because it was the only country with the resources and strength to face the mortal challenge of terrorism against freedom:

> As long as the United States of America is determined and strong, this will not be an age of terror; this will be an age of liberty, here and across the world....Freedom and fear are at war. The advance of human freedom—the great achievement of our time, and the great hope of every time—now depends on us. Our nation—this generation—will lift a dark threat of violence from our people and our future. We will rally the world to this cause by our efforts, by our courage. We will not tire, we will not falter, and we will not fail.

The most symbolically important moment of Bush's speech to Congress and America on September 20 was when the president showed the badge of a policeman "who died at the World Trade Center trying to save others," and said that the victim's mother had given it to him in proud memory of her son:

> This is my reminder of lives that ended, and a task that does not end. I will not forget this wound to our country or those who inflicted it. I will not yield; I will not rest; I will not relent in waging this struggle for freedom and security for the American people. The course of this conflict is not known, yet its outcome is certain. Freedom and fear, justice and cruelty, have always been at war, and we know that God is not neutral between them.

In conclusion, Bush addressed God, calling on him so that "In all that lies before us, may God grand us wisdom, and may He watch over the United States of America."[18]

In this way, Bush successfully concluded his consecration as leader of the nation at war with a new symbolic gesture, in front of eighty million Americans who had followed his speech on television. The president, suspected of having stolen the victory for the White House, was thus fully legitimated by the Americans' representatives, who were sanctioned by law, and by a vast public consensus. After his speech to Congress, 81 percent of the Americans declared that they highly approved of the president, and 73 percent stated that the president had made them better understand how the terrorists should be fought.[19] In October, Bush's approval rating rose to 87 percent and in May of the following year it was still quite high (75 percent).[20] The Democratic representatives at Congress gathered around the flag on the Capitol steps with the Republicans, singing "God Bless America," and rapidly approved all the laws, almost unanimously and first of all the USA PATRIOT Act, which Bush proposed to ensure protection of the Americans, and to carry out the war on terror.[21]

Presidential Ecumenism

The war on terror began on October 7 with the attack in Afghanistan, announced in a speech by Bush to the nation, where he repeated what he had already said on September 20—it would be a long war, no country could consider itself neutral, and the aim was described in the slogan of the war itself, which summed up America's mission: "The name of today's military operation is Enduring Freedom. We defend not only our precious freedoms, but also the freedom of people everywhere to live and raise their children free from fear."[22] When describing the kind of war declared against Islamic terrorism and its aims, Bush carefully avoided making it seem like a war against Islam and the Arabs. He immediately retracted the unfortunate word "crusade" that he had used on September 16.[23] In the following days, the president repeatedly drove home that the Americans were not to consider the Islamic religion responsible for what had happened, and he publicly condemned the serious episodes of intolerance and aggression against Arabs or people presumed to be, including some cases of murder. After September 11, the government, and Bush himself, did everything they could to prevent anti-Islamic violence from spreading. Bush had himself photographed while reading the Koran, which he called holy, saying it taught the value and importance of charity, mercy, and peace; he visited mosques, invited Islamic religious representatives to the White House, and had dinners for Ramadan there.[24] Also the fact that Imam Muzammil Siddiqi, president of the Islamic Society of North America, was among those invited to pray in the National Cathedral was not only paying homage to American religious pluralism, but was also ranking evidence of respect for Islam, a religion of peace, as Bush called it when speaking both to the Islamic world and non-Islamic Americans, urging them not to confuse the Islamic religion with the terrorists' politicized Islamism. "The face of terror is not the true faith of Islam. That's not what Islam is all about. Islam is peace. These terrorists don't represent peace. They represent evil and war."[25] At the Washington Islamic Center, where Bush went on September 17 to express his solidarity towards the American followers of Islam and condemn anti-Islamic acts of intolerance and violence by some Americans, he said, "they represent the worst of humankind, and they should be ashamed of that kind of behavior," and urged the Americans to respect the millions of their Arab and Muslim fellow citizens, to honor the values they had in common. "This is a great country because we share the same values of respect and dignity and human worth."[26] In his September 20 speech to Congress, the president addressed Muslims all over the world to express the Americans' respect for their faith: "We respect your faith. It's practiced freely by many millions of Americans, and by millions more in countries that America counts as friends. Its teachings are good and peaceful, and those who commit evil in the name of Allah blaspheme the name of Allah." A week later, when meeting representatives of the Islamic community at the White House, Bush reminded them "that the imam led the service at National Cathedral," and that he told "the nation more than once that ours is a war against evil, against extremists, that the teachings of Islam are the teachings of peace and good." He also wanted "to assure my fellow Americans that when you pledge allegiance to the flag, with your hand on your heart, you pledge just as hard to the flag as I do." Then the president concluded, "I'm proud of Muslim leaders across America who have risen up and who have not only insisted that America be strong, but that America keep the values intact that have made us so unique and different—the values of respect, the values of freedom of worship the way we see it. And I also appreciate the prayers to the universal God."[27]

Nonecumenical Christians

Showing respect for Islam was a genuine expression of Bush's religious ecumenism in line with that of American religion, besides being a political gesture addressed to the Islamic world to drive home that the war on terror was not a war against Islam. Furthermore, Bush's attitude toward, and statements about, Islam and Muslim Americans contributed to calming anti-Arab and anti-Islamic feelings among the Americans, who knew little about the Islamic religion. According to a survey published on December 6, 2001 by the Pew Research Center, only 27 percent of Americans over 65 years old said they knew something about Islam, compared to 44 percent of Americans younger than 30. Among those who said they knew something about Islam, 73 percent were favorably inclined towards Muslim Americans, an attitude shared by only 53 percent of those who knew little or nothing about them. Broadly speaking, the Americans' opinion of American Muslims had improved: those who were favorable rose from 45 percent in March 2001 to 59 percent at the end of the year. Knowing about Islam also influenced the Americans' opinion of the terrorists' motives— 49 percent thought that the terrorists' main motives were political, while 30 percent gave more importance to their religious beliefs, especially those who knew little or nothing about Islam.[28]

Bush's favorable approach to Islam and American Muslims influenced above all the attitude of conservative republicans: the number of those who considered American Muslims favorably increased from 29 percent in March 2001 to 64 percent in December. This trend was constant also in the following months, while criticism of Islam, no longer clearly distinguished from the terrorist Islamic fundamentalists, began to grow among the population. A Pew Research Center survey published on March 20, 2002 showed that only 27 percent of the Americans, compared to 31 percent in the previous year, thought that Christianity and Islamism had something in common, while the percentage of those who thought Islam was very different rose from 51 to 57 percent—among evangelicals this was 78 percent.[29]

During 2002 and 2003, some prominent but more conservative and fundamentalist personages of the Christian evangelical Right, who were close to the president but did not at all share his opinion of and attitude towards Islam, openly and heatedly expressed their disagreement. "We don't believe Islam needs validating at the highest level of American government. A lot of people think Bush has bent too far over backward to say nice things about Muslims," said David Crowe, director of Restore America, a political organization of conservative Christians.[30] In a television interview, Franklin Graham, Billy's son, called Islam "a very evil and wicked religion." Jerry Vines, formerly president of the

Southern Baptist Convention, said that Muhammad was "a demon-possessed pedophile." Pat Robertson called the prophet "an absolutely wild-eyed fanatic," "a robber and a brigand," maintaining that Islamic terrorists were nothing but faithful interpreters of the Koran, which continually incites its followers to go to war against the infidels.[31] The fundamentalist evangelicals considered it their missionary duty to convert Muslims to Christianity, taking the real faith to Islamic countries. They believed that the "war on terror" should be a crusade to evangelize the Arab world. Although the president was urged to openly take a position on these nonecumenical, religious conservatives who were all his supporters, he preferred not to, leaving his spokespeople to repeat that he respected Islam.[32] Even though Bush did not openly criticize his religious anti-Islamic friends' point of view, he continued to publicly call Islam a religion of peace, not to be identified with terrorist radicalism. On the first anniversary of September 11, Bush was careful to forestall anti-Islamic feelings. At a meeting with some American-Muslim leaders at the Afghanistan embassy, he said that "All Americans must recognize that the face of terror is not the...face of Islam. Islam is a faith that brings comfort to a billion people around the world. It's a faith that has made brothers and sisters of every race. It's a faith based upon love, not hate."[33] In December 2002, during the Turkish Prime Minister Tayyip Erdogan's visit, Bush said to him: "You believe in the Almighty, and I believe in the Almighty. That's why we'll be great partners."[34] Also the liberal press appreciated the president's conduct towards Islam. On March 10, 2003, Howard Fineman acknowledged that Bush had done his utmost to reassure Muslims that he admired their religion.[35] On June 10, 2003 in the *New York Times,* Nicholas Kristof wrote that Bush had shown he was really capable as a moral leader after September 11 when he praised Islam as a "religion of peace," making it clear that his administration did not intend to demonize it.[36]

God Wants Him

On the eve of a new war, the Americans had found a leader in one of the most tragic moments of their history, and he had been given charisma—which confirmed his calling, explained his mission, and assigned him to lead the country at war. The born-again Christian who had become president saw the design of Providence clearly: he had been called to the United States presidency in order to lead the Americans in the new mission, a long war against world terrorism to defend God's democracy and spread its values throughout the world. At a crucial moment after September 11, the president wanted the advice and comfort of clergymen and scholars of religion. On September 20, a few hours before his speech to Congress and the nation, he invited a group of representatives of different religious communities to the White House: all the Protestant confessions, Catholic, Orthodox, Jewish, Sikh, Hindu, Buddhist, and Muslim. Also Jean Bethke Elshtain, a lecturer in political and social ethics at the Theological University of Chicago, was invited to this ecumenical meeting. Bush spoke and prayed with them for over an hour, and asked them to pray for him in such a difficult moment. Elshtain urged him, as president, to exercise his role as "civic educator," to "explain things to the American people; teach patience to an impatient people; the need to sacrifice to a people unused to sacrifice." The meeting ended with everyone singing "God Bless America." The invitation could have seemed suspiciously like propaganda, but Elshtain wrote: "All of us were aware we had participated in an extraordinary event....It was clear that the President wanted counsel; that he sought prayer; that he also hoped to reassure us that he understood the issues involved."[37] When Bush had to make serious decisions, he always looked for comfort and advice directly from God, whom he consulted inwardly by praying and reading the Bible every day. Sometimes he confided that he felt God's presence in those tragic moments. On Palm Sunday in 2002, while he was aboard Air Force One, Bush organized an informal religious service. "I did feel the presence of God amongst my friends on Air Force One," he said later.[38] Those who worked closest with him at the White House witnessed and helped create their president's charismatic transfiguration, enhanced by his faith in God, and contributed to boosting it by confirming it publicly. One of the president's close assistants, Tim Goeglein, told *World Magazine,* a conservative Christian publication, "I think President Bush is God's man at this hour, and I say this with a great sense of humility."[39] After Saddam Hussein's regime was overthrown, General William Boykin, an important official in the Department of Defense tasked with hunting down bin Laden, spoke in a church, in uniform, and said that Bush was at the White House even if the majority of Americans had not voted for him: "Now ask yourself why is this man in the White House? The majority of Americans did not vote for him. Why is he there? And I tell you this morning he's in the White House because God put him there for such a time as this. God put him there to lead not only this nation but to lead the world, in such a time as this."[40] The president quite agreed and nodded when his assistants told him that God had wanted him at the White House. After Bush spoke to Congress on September 20, Michael Gerson called him after watching the speech on television and said, "Mr. President, when I saw you on television, I thought—God wanted you there," at which the president thanked him and answered, "He wants us all there, Gerson."[41] When speaking with the president after visiting Ground Zero, the Reverend Gerald Kieschnik, president of the Lutheran Church–Missouri Synod, told him that he had not only a civil but "a divine calling," because he had been called to serve God at such a grave time. "I accept the responsibility," was Bush's answer. One of Bush's friends who often visited the White House said: "The President really feels that this is his mission."[42] Pointing out a portrait of Abraham Lincoln to a group of religious leaders who had been invited to pray with him in the Oval Office, Bush told them that the portrait was a constant reminder of his mission: to spread freedom and unite the nation.[43]

After September 11, in a few days Bush managed to complete his charismatic transfiguration and become identified as president with the new American mission, which was consecrated by the sacrifice of the September 11 victims, blessed by divine benevolence, and confirmed by the people. At the same time, Bush exalted the pontifical function inherent in the figure of the president, not only by carrying out the pastoral duties of compassion and consolation, but above all by taking on the role of supreme theologian of American religion, interpreting and explaining to the Americans the meaning of September 11 in the context of the providential mission of God's democracy. Bush managed to monopolize the interpretation of the September 11 tragedy in the space of a few weeks, using an extremely efficacious language that mixed politics and religion. He personally took on the task of working it out, giving both a religious and a political explanation that was intended to be a clear-cut answer to all those in America—theologians, clergymen, intellectuals, and politicians—who asked the Americans to do some soul-searching to understand why there was so much anti-American hatred and what part American imperial power played in arousing it. Bush considered such attitudes as almost the same as betraying America, because they brought up issues that questioned America's innate goodness and its cause, and could undermine the Americans' faith in their country and institutions by insinuating that the United States was in some way responsible for the attack it had suffered, indirectly caused by its politics of power or even by its national sins in God's regard. By glorifying America, called by history to fight for freedom in the world once again, Bush indirectly conferred sacrality on America itself, as God's Democracy. At the same time he tried to ward off doubts about the reasons for the terrorist attack and the hatred that had inspired it, about God's attitude faced with the massacre of thousands of innocent people, the loss of invulnerability, and the destiny of America in a world that had suddenly turned out to be cruel and hostile.

6

Sacred Imperial America

The "Axis of Evil"

On January 29, 2002, when President Bush used the expression "axis of evil" in his state of the union speech, referring to North Korea, Iran, and Iraq, people were either surprised, irritated, or concerned. The expression was considered just another unfortunate gaffe by the president, like the word "crusade," used initially but subsequently eliminated from his rhetoric. However, "axis of evil" was not a mindless error. Actually, it was carefully chosen by the president's speech-writers, to announce to the world that war had been declared on terrorism.[1]

In fact the basic aim of Bush's war theology, formulated right after September 11, was the demonization of Islamic terrorism and the regimes he thought supported it. At first on September 11, right after he had received news of the attack on America while visiting an elementary school in Florida, Bush defined the attacks in a television interview as "cowardly acts."[2] The next day he said again that they were "heinous acts of violence" against the people of the United States and freedom, by "'faceless cowards' who would be hunted down, captured and punished."[3] Then, almost immediately, the image of the enemy began to have the impersonal connotations of evil. In this way, the war inevitably took on a religious nature. "We are at the beginning of what I consider a very long battle against evil. We are not fighting a nation or a religion, we are fighting evil."[4] On September 13 Bush said that terrorists were "evil doers" and proclaimed a nationwide day of prayer for the victims of September 11.[5] The following day in the National Cathedral, Bush continued to demonize the enemy, identifying it in a nonpersonified way with evil, depicted as a reality, a sacred entity, which the terrorists worshiped and served. On October 11, when attending a memorial service for the victims of the attack on the Pentagon, Bush described the al Qaeda terrorists as the "instruments of evil" who, devoted to the "cult of evil," rejected the limits posed by laws, morality, and religion. They had no home in any country, no culture or faith; they lived in the dark corners of the earth. "Behind them is a cult of evil which seeks to harm the innocent and thrives on human suffering. Theirs is the worst kind of cruelty, the cruelty that is fed, not weakened, by tears. Theirs is the worst kind of violence, pure malice, while daring to claim the authority of God. We cannot fully understand the designs and power of evil. It is enough to know that evil, like goodness, exists. And in the terrorists, evil has found a willing servant."[6] Since the tragic events of September 11, Bush said again on January 29, 2002, speaking about the "axis of evil," the Americans had learned an undisputable truth, that evil was real and had to be fought. The mission against evil was in the hands of the American nation, which had "a great opportunity during this time of war to lead the world toward the values that will bring lasting peace."[7]

The president's Manichaean simplicity was extremely well received with members of the Religious Right to whom he was speaking. Also, in order to understand Bush's religious rhetoric and its effectiveness in gaining consensus for his politics, it is necessary to take a look at tradition in America. In fact, as historian Robert Fuller demonstrated, demonization of the enemy as the incarnation of evil was not new to American history but had occurred many times in the past, especially when America was involved in a war against an external enemy or felt threatened by an internal one. In every war America had always believed it was acting in the name of God and was protected by him against the evil forces identified with the devil or, according to apocalyptic thought, with the Antichrist.[8] Demonization of the Indians by the Puritans was justification for their genocide.[9] During the War of Independence evil was represented by England, the new pharaoh who wanted to keep the people of Israel[10] in slavery. Then, during the early years of the republic, evil was identified with the factions that threatened the nation's unity and with the expansionist greed of old, reactionary, corrupt, warmongering, ostentatiously pious, and despotic Europe, as well as papal theocracy. Subsequently the dangers of evil came from the old world and were identified with Catholic and Jewish immigrants.[11] During the Civil War, northerners and southerners demonized each other, each side linking its own cause with that of God. Meanwhile, without claiming to know what God's intentions were, Republican President Abraham Lincoln meditated on the tragedy of an "almost chosen" people who read the same Bible and worshipped the same God only to tear each other apart in a fratricidal war.[12] And evil powers summarized all aspects of the external enemy during the two world wars.[13] Democrat President Wilson said that America's mission in the First World War was to put the design of Providence into effect and fight to free the world of evil in order to make it a safe place for democracy. The Americans were not fighting for power, but "the spiritual purpose of redemption that rests in the heart of mankind." They were the crusaders of a free nation and had sacrificed their lives for an ideal. "The noble army of Americans who have saved the world," proclaimed Wilson at the end of the war.[14] Twenty years later America was fighting a new crusade in the name of God against the evil powers, "to preserve our Republic, our religion and our civilization, and to set free a suffering humanity," as Franklin D. Roosevelt, the Democratic president, said in a radio broadcast on June 6, 1944, eve of the allies' landing in Normandy.[15] Then, during the long years of the Cold War the Soviet Union and communism were the incarnation of evil; for 50 years, led by Democratic or Republican presidents, America felt it was mobilized to defend the free world, western civilization, and religion against a godless and materialistic Russian totalitarianism that was trying to conquer and enslave the world.

Demonization of the Soviet Union reached its apex when President Reagan described it as the "evil empire" while making a speech before the National Association of Evangelicals on March 8, 1983. The Republican president praised the American democracy, which was blessed by God because the American people had faith in Divine Providence. Reagan condemned secularism because it distanced the nation from God, and he urged the Americans to reassert the traditional religious values on which the republic had been founded, so as to continue to enjoy divine protection.[16]

When the "evil empire" disappeared, America was without a visible external enemy for a while. Some announced that America had finally won the battle against evil in the world, because the world had understood that there was no other way to be saved than to follow the American model, founded on the liberty and equality of people, the parliamentary system, capitalism, and the free market. However, even after the disappearance of the "evil empire" America continued to feel committed to defending freedom in the world for all of humanity, thus carrying out the mission entrusted it by God in the covenant with the founding fathers.

By the end of the twentieth century, the hostility of evil towards God's democracy had migrated from Russia to the Middle East and was represented by Saddam Hussein, against whom President George Bush senior waged a war, in the name of God, to free the Muslim country Kuwait, attacked and invaded by the Iraqi dictator.[17] After that and since September 11, evil has been personified in Islamic terrorists and Osama bin Laden. This has led to a new war waged by America to defend freedom in the name of God. President Bush told the press on September 12 after a meeting with the National Security Council, "This will be a colossal battle against evil, but good will triumph."[18]

A Born-Again America

Bush countered the demonization of the terrorist enemy with the sacralization of an "innocent" America, working for the good of the country's people and of all humanity. The president's war theology saw America as the incarnation of liberty, goodness, and justice. Although its history is studded with sins and wrongdoing like slavery, America had been able to cleanse itself and pursue the mission assigned by Providence. While there were still bad spots and shadows before September 11 due to the relaxation of morals and customs, the cathartic experience of that day cancelled them, and the inborn goodness of the nation emerged renewed and reinvigorated: "And something even more profound is happening across our country," said Bush on November 8, 2001 as the American attack in Afghanistan got underway:

> The enormity of this tragedy has caused many Americans to focus on the things that have not changed—the things that matter most in life: our faith, our love for family and friends, our commitment to our country and to our freedoms and to our principles. In my inaugural address I asked our citizens to serve their nation, beginning with their neighbors. This fall, I had planned a new initiative called Communities of Character, designed to spark a rebirth of citizenship and character and service. The events of September the 11th have caused that initiative to happen on its own, in ways we could never have imagined....Through this tragedy, we are renewing and reclaiming our strong American values.

Bush added that the terrorist attack had changed America:

> Tonight, many thousands of children are tragically learning to live without one of their parents. And the rest of us are learning to live in a world that seems very different than it was on September the 10th. The moment the second plane hit the second building—when we knew it was a terrorist attack—many felt that our lives would never be the same. What we couldn't be sure of then—and what the terrorists never expected—was that America would emerge stronger, with renewed spirit of pride and patriotism....During the last two months, we have shown the world America is a great nation....We are a different country than we were on September the 10th—sadder and less innocent; stronger and more united; and in the face of ongoing threats, determined and courageous.[19]

On the first anniversary of the September 11 terrorist attack on the World Trade Center, in view of the by-now certain war against Iraq, President Bush put forth the basic theories of his war theology in an article published by the *New York Times* and, that same evening, in a speech at Ellis Island, gateway to the "American dream" for millions of immigrants greeted by the Statue of Liberty. In the article, Bush wrote that the attack had revealed the enemy's cruelty and the spirit of the American nation, but it had "brought new clarity to America's role in the world." While tragic, the attack had given the Americans the opportunity to use their "position of unparalleled strength and influence" to create "a balance of world power that favors human freedom," to build "an atmosphere of international order and openness in which progress and liberty can flourish in many nations," and "to extend the benefits of freedom and progress to nations that lack them." For this reason the American people and government were determined to answer the challenge posed by a changing world, to defend the values on which their nation had been founded, refusing to "ignore or appease the aggression and brutality of evil men." The president added that terrorism had not only challenged the world, it had clarified some fundamental values for which, he threatened, every nation "now faces a choice between lawful change or chaotic violence...;

between the celebration of death in suicide and murder and the defense of life and its dignity." As for the United States, the article concluded, it "welcomes its responsibility to lead in this great mission."[20] "Our generation has now heard history's call and we will answer it," said Bush that evening on Ellis Island. The Americans had tragically discovered they were vulnerable and that they had very determined enemies, but they had also rediscovered the spirit and greatness of America. The spirit showed up in the passengers who had rebelled, even as they died, to save other lives; in the rescue squads that climbed the stairs leading to dangerous areas; and in the citizens who everywhere were compassionate and supportive of each other. According to Bush, the greatest difference between the Americans and their enemies was that the former respected life "because every life is the gift of a Creator who intended us to live in liberty and equality," while the latter did not value life at all. For that reason, with "the resolve of a great nation and a great democracy," in "the ruins of two towers, under a flag unfurled at the Pentagon, at the funeral of the lost we made a sacred promise to ourselves and the world: We will not relent until justice is done and our nation is secure. What our enemies have begun, we will finish."

Once the decision to go to war was confirmed, President Bush spoke to the Americans as if speaking for God. He explained that even though no one knows what the future might have in store, their duty was perfectly clear:

We cannot know all that lies ahead. Yet we do know that God has placed us together in this moment, to grieve together, to stand together, to serve each other and our country. And the duty we have been given—defending America and our freedom—is also a privilege we share. We're prepared for this journey. And our prayer tonight is that God will see us through, and keep us worthy.

At the end of his speech President Bush praised America, saying with biblical fervor that it embodied the principles of divine origin because it was a gift of God, and of universal values because they belong to all of humanity:

Ours is the cause of human dignity: freedom guided by conscience, and guarded by peace. This ideal of America is the hope of all mankind. That hope drew millions to this harbor. That hope still lights our way. And the light shines in the darkness. And the darkness will not overcome it.[21]

By glorifying the spirit of the Americans, regenerated after the September 11 tragedy, Bush seemed to want to extend to the collectivity his own experience as a "reborn" Christian through the discovery of faith. The brutality of what happened on September 11 brought about a collective "rebirth" among the Americans, because it enabled them to rediscover faith in America, its values and principles. Thus Bush transfigured America into a sort of abstract, universal, and sacred entity; a powerful, charitable, savior, redeemer of individuals and peoples—the empire of "good" called into battle to defend "good" in the war against "evil."

The celebration of America's moral rebirth after the tragic events of September 11 was a rhetorical motif in line with the pastoral function Bush carried out, comforting and encouraging the Americans to overcome the trauma of the terrorist attack by uniting against the new enemy. He knew how to stir the innermost emotions of the American people at a time when they did put up a good show, with a renewed sense of collective solidarity, harmony, and national unity. Such was the patriotic impetus that it cancelled, in a second, the issues that had divided the nation during the past 10 years, with divisions so deep that there was even talk of "America's disunion," worsened by the results of the 2000 presidential elections.

From Disunion to Reunion

The president's presentation of a reborn America is all the more significant in its rhetorical and political efficacy if we consider that, despite its position as an incomparable imperialist power, when it was attacked by the terrorists, it was still in the middle of the national identity crisis it had been suffering since the Vietnam War years, as Arthur M. Schlesinger noted in 1969.[22] A few years later in 1975, Robert N. Bellah, in his dramatically titled book *The Broken Covenant*, accused American society of betraying its civil religion and becoming egoistic and merciless. According to Bellah, the widespread importance given to personal satisfaction, supported by utilitarianism, had weakened the ethics of obligation towards others preached by republicanism, thus diffusing "a deepening cynicism about the established social, economic and political institutions of society" as well as the "erosion of moral and religious understandings."[23] Five years later, historian James O. Robertson analyzed the concern spreading among Americans about their declining national identity, a decline which had occurred because the ideals and values on which the country was founded were no longer valid.[24] In March 1984 the influential journal *Harper's Magazine* organized a conference to debate the issue "Does America Still Exist?"[25] This widespread sense of moral malaise in America had not been cured by the strong doses of nationalism administered during the Reagan and Bush senior eras, when a series of military ventures in Grenada, Panama, Nicaragua, and lastly the successful 1991 Gulf War, were undertaken to reestablish the prestige of America as an imperialist power.

Furthermore, starting from the end of the 1970s, American society began to come apart due to the "struggle for America's soul,"[26] as sociologist Robert Wuthnow defined it. The struggle was fought between conservatives and liberals and t resulted in a "great fracture in American religion,"[27] because it originated from the confrontation between different interpretations of the Bible, different types of moral concepts, and different spiritual concepts, after a period of very intense secularization of that society and its customs. According to sociologist James D. Hunter, it was a "culture war"[28] engaged by traditionalist Christians, fundamentalists, and conservative evangelicals. They launched a crusade against the moral degeneration of America by an "invisible enemy threatening our society,"[29] as fundamentalist Reverend Tim LaHaye said. He was supported by Reverend Falwell, who added, "Satan has mobilized his forces to destroy America....God needed voices raised to save America from inward moral decay."[30] The anti-secularism crusade led to the political mobilization of the Religious Right against a coalition of evil forces that were destroying the nation—secular humanism, liberalism, relativism, progressivism, postmodernism, feminism, homosexuality the spread of a permissive and hedonist culture, pornography, violence, legalization of abortion, separation of church and state, elimination of religious symbols and practices from public places and government offices, and many other evils that jeopardized the moral fiber of the nation.

When President Reagan won the election in 1980, it seemed that "America's rebirth" was about to begin: the dark night of the nation's soul had passed; the identity crisis the nation had suffered for 10 or 15 years was over, wrote Jeane Kirkpatrick, exponent of the neoconservative intellectuals.[31] Yet, even during the Reagan administration in the mid-1980s, the Religious Right evoked the fate of the Roman empire when predicting the imminent end of America if it did not go back to being a Christian republic as it was originally.[32] America was "a nation adrift" because of the "most ferocious assaults on Christian faith and morals; first on the part of the intellectual community; and then on the part of the government," stated Senator Jesse Helms in 1986. Every day he prayed for the "rebirth of the spiritual values that made us a nation in the first place...when, once again, the United States rededicates itself to the cause of freedom under God's law."[33]

The pessimistic view of America's moral health was not only perceived by conservative Republicans, but also by religious, intellectual, and political Democrats, although the diagnoses and identification of the causes were different. In the mid-1980s, Robert N. Bellah and a group of sociologists, philosophers, and theologians debated the cultural and moral transformation of Americans. They queried "how to preserve or create a morally coherent life," necessary to support a free republic at a time when individualism, that is, the search for individual satisfaction—while in itself an integral part of the American spirit and society—tended to be exaggerated and thus rule over the other essential ingredient of the American tradition, communitarianism, without which the very survival of freedom was in danger.[34] Arthur Schlesinger wrote in 1991 that the national identity was threatened by relativism and multiculturalism that jeopardized the moral heritage common to Americans, endangering the very survival of a national unity: "A struggle to redefine the national identity is taking place. It is taking place in many arenas—in our politics, our voluntary organizations, our churches, our language—and in no arena more crucial than our system of education." American life was being corroded by the "cult of ethnicity," as opposed to the cult of a common American identity founded on universal values capable of transcending the many races, ethnic groups, cultures, religions, and languages which make up the exceptional "nation of nations" that was the United States.[35] In a review President Clinton praised the book *The Culture of Disbelief,* by Stephen L. Carter, which denounced the negative effects of the "trivializing" of religion by politicians who thus deprived religion of its moral vigor. Carter proposed a revision of the interpretation of the separation between church and state, sanctioned by the first amendment, to reestablish a greater osmosis between religion and politics on the American scene.[36] That same year President Clinton's wife, Hillary, in a speech at the University of Texas, complained that America suffered from a "sleeping sickness of the soul," because individuals did not feel they were part of a larger community and could no longer understand the significance of an individual versus a collective life.[37] Five years later a survey found that 76 percent of Americans thought the values and moral convictions of the United States were in crisis.[38] "America is having an identity crisis," stated political expert Eldon J. Eisenach, in 2000, and the crisis manifested itself in many aspects—from multiculturalism to the redefining of the importance of a national history, to philosophical debates on individualism versus communitarianism, to intellectual disputes over national identity and the fate of America. Eisenach added that it was an individual crisis as well as a national one, due to a lack of moral direction, and one in which religion was directly involved because of the central position religion had in American history.[39] Many American intellectuals said that the growth of affluence, welfare, and power in the 1980s and 1990s was accompanied by a greater impoverishment of the national conscience. America suffered "spiritual hunger in an age of plenty," said psychologist David G. Myers in 2000.[40] Eight years before that Al Gore had already said the same, affirming that most Americans "are hungry for a deeper connection between politics and moral values; many would say 'spiritual values.'"[41] One year later, in his inaugural speech, President Clinton celebrated "the mystery of American renewal," advising the Americans to think about their own failures in a society where there was still widespread unemployment, poverty, degradation, and fear:

> A spring reborn in the world's oldest democracy, that brings forth the vision and courage to reinvent America....
> Our democracy must be not only the envy of the world but the engine of our own renewal. There is nothing wrong with America that cannot be cured by what is right with America.
> So today, we pledge an end to the era of deadlock and drift—and a new season of America renewal has begun.[42]

The Religious Right undertook a very aggressive campaign against President Clinton, accused of being the prime example of corruption and moral decadence in America. Thus the "culture war" was rekindled by conservative and traditionalist evangelicals in the hopes of gaining religious and political hegemony. The polemics demonizing liberal America were extremely violent. In 1997 Frederick Clarkson, liberal essayist, wrote that there was a raging struggle in America between "theocracy and democracy," in which the American democratic system was at stake.[43]

One of the consequences of the national identity crisis and sense of moral decadence, said political expert Robert Putnam in 1995, was the decline of the communitarian spirit as the founding element of the democracy. Putnam cited as emblematic of this crisis the fact that, while the number of Americans who went bowling had increased by 10 percent in recent years, playing in bowling leagues had dropped by 40 percent: "bowling alone" was symbolic of the progressive atomization of American society.[44]

However, six years later, after the terrorist attack, the very same Putnam was comforted in seeing the Americans lined up to volunteer at emergency squads and to donate blood, determined to deal with terrorism and overcome fear, united around the flag; the trend of the last decades towards disunion seemed to have come to a halt with the dramatic events of that tragic September 11, he wrote in February 2002.[45] Following the terrorist attack the Americans had rediscovered their patriotic spirit, showing greater confidence in the institutions and in collective solidarity over and above political divisions, a greater interest in the common good, greater social involvement, and a greater desire to participate and collaborate. Of course, Putnam warned, this sudden, unexpected change of outlook could not be considered proof of a renewed, everlasting civic sense, but it could be an important premise that should not be allowed to vanish, because it might generate a new "great generation," like the American generation which straddled the Second World War, advocating widespread political and social renewal. Similar considerations were made on the first anniversary of the September 11 attacks by sociologist Amitai Etzioni, one of the major champions of a new American communitarianism. According to Etzioni the Americans were showing a greater interest in the public good. They were less materialistic, more concerned with their families and the community, as well as being more spiritual.[46] This renewed community spirit was the result of the intense patriotic feeling that developed after September 11. In October 2001, the University of Chicago did a study on the Americans' reaction to the terrorist attack. It recorded a patriotic effervescence unequaled in the past 50 years: 97 percent of the Americans were extremely proud of their country, and 85 percent considered it the best in the world. The most significant fact that emerged regarding the reasons for such patriotic pride was that 80 percent of the Americans considered the armed forces paramount, an increase of 32 points compared to a similar study done in 1996. This was followed by science and technology, 75 percent (26 points more); American history, 68 percent (21 points more); the workings of democracy, 61 percent (34 points more); economic advances, 60 percent (32 points more); the arts and literature, 56 percent (28 points more); and lastly, political influence in the world, 39 percent (19 points more). Of the Americans 77 percent (27 points more) had great confidence in the armed forces; 52 percent (38 points more) in the federal government; 47 percent (19 points more) in religious organizations; 44 percent (15 points more) in banks and financial institutions; 43 percent (31 points more) in Congress.[47] It was evident from these data that, after the terrorist attack, the Americans were more patriotic, had increased faith in the federal government, and, above all, were proud of and put their total faith in their military strength. Compared to previous years, the increased confidence in the institutions clearly surpassed confidence in the church.

Manifest Destiny

Between January 2002 when he spoke of the "axis of evil" and May 2003 when Saddam Hussein's regime was toppled, Bush continued to act as the pontiff of American religion. The themes were the same as those he treated right after the terrorist attack and repeated with few variations—in style rather than content—during the attack on Iraq as well as during the 2004 presidential campaign, and after his reelection: the glorification of a strong and united America, ready to obey history's call to continue its mission—with God's help, defending and spreading democracy throughout the world and combating its enemies.

Apart from the president's religious inspiration, when he inferred that the "war on terror" had an apocalyptic connotation, the theological definition of the war as an all-out conflict between good and evil morally legitimized the United States' new imperialist strategy based on the "preemptive war" doctrine. This doctrine was devised by the neoconservatives in the Republican administration on the basis of considerations they felt were genuinely realistic, that is, to claim that America had the right to take military action when and where it thought necessary, in order to prevent new terrorist attacks, defend the security of the United States, and preserve its supremacy as a world power. The "preemptive warfare" doctrine was anticipated by Bush on October 26, 2001; at that time "the first battle in the war of terrorism" had already begun with the attack on Afghanistan. "We are now interested in preventing attack. We're now interested in finding those who may attack America, and arrest them before they do."[48]

The theological justification for the war on terror was revealed by the president with greater emphasis at the end of the victorious military campaign in Afghanistan, when he decided to bring down Saddam Hussein's regime, suspected of supporting al Qaeda terrorists and producing weapons of mass destruction ready for use against America and its main ally in the Middle East, the state of Israel. Subsequently the suspicions were to prove unfounded, and the evidence put forward by the Republican administration to make them appear well-founded, nonexistent. However, for the president, none of this invalidated at all the new strategy for national security and the theological interpretation of the "war on terror," transformed into a war to export democracy to the Middle East. The sacralization of America as the universal model of democracy—because it was conceived and put into effect by divine plan and was, for that reason, to be considered good and undisputable—enabled Bush to re-propose a new version of the myth of America as the "benevolent empire." After the attack by evil forces, America was forced to undertake a long war against a new enemy in order to continue the mission assigned the nation by God. The September 11 tragedy, the president kept saying, had brutally awakened the Americans from the illusion that they lived in a world which had banished or removed evil, but at the same time, had revealed and confirmed America's inborn goodness. In essence, it was an innocent nation because it did not pursue particular ambitions or interests but rather acted for the good of all, to defend the divine gift of freedom throughout the world.

The myth of the "innocent nation" evoked by Bush was an integral part of American religion. This myth had its roots in the origin of the United States and had accompanied its expansion up to the twentieth century, despite serious contradictions, such as slavery, extermination of the Indians, racial discrimination, and segregation. The myth was reinforced by American intervention in the First World War and, above all, in the Second World War, the "just war," *par excellence,* fought by the United States against evil.[49] Notwithstanding the serious jolts it received due to the "dirty Vietnam War" and the disgraceful end of the Nixon administration, the myth of the "innocent nation" received new impulse when Reagan became president. Attenuated by Clinton, who urged the Americans to examine their consciences in order to regenerate the country, the myth was then brought back by Bush following September 11. The Religious Right, convinced that it was the genuine expression of the "innocent nation," supported Bush and mobilization to combat the internal and external dangers of evil powers. The "innocent nation" was traumatized by the terrorist attack not only because it suffered the loss of so many innocent lives, but also because it had discovered that it had enemies in this world whose hatred went so deep that it was lethal. The explanation given by Bush was that they hated America's goodness and innocence. In a press conference on October 12, 2001 he said that it was surprising there was so little understanding of what the country was as to make people hate it. It was hard to understand, he said, because he knew how good the country was.[50] According to Bush the holiness of the American mission originated from this goodness, which committed the United States to act even by means of armed intervention to make the world a better place, taking America as its model.

In so doing, Bush was moving in the wake of another truly American mythical tradition, the myth of "manifest destiny," or belief in America's missionary role as the model of redemption for humanity.[51] Even if the expression "manifest destiny" was coined only in 1845, the myth connected with it, observed sociologist Roberta Coles, derived from the original myths of American religion: the myth of a morally superior nation chosen by God, whose duty it was to redeem the continent and perhaps the world, thus justifying the expansion of America's geographical and political borders. Experts have identified two different versions of the myth of mission and the myth of manifest destiny. The former views *mission by example* for humanity, with the continuous improvement of the nation's democratic experiment because, as God's chosen country, it feels committed to always acting in conformity with the divine commandments, never assuming attitudes of arrogant superiority with respect to other nations, instead proposing itself as the model to follow by virtue of its behavior. The latter sees *mission by intervention* by America, in the world to rescue peoples whose tyrannical regimes prevent them from enjoying their natural rights and the freedom God gave to all men. Therefore, according to this version, American military intervention is a moral obligation, the result of being the nation chosen by God to defend and spread freedom throughout the world. Coles specifies, however, that historically this distinction has often created confusion and the two versions have been mixed up in various military interventions carried out in the world by the United States, as was the case recently with the 1991 Gulf War and the air raid on Serbia in 1998.[52]

In George W. Bush's military interventionism after September 11, the myth of mission and of manifest destiny continued to play a vital role as part of American politics, but with an important new aspect: unlike other past experiences, America itself had been attacked this time. The new element generated a new version of the myth of manifest destiny, which through Bush's theology became what one may define as the doctrine of *mission by preemptive, self-defensive warfare.* This involved not only the need to defend God's democracy by conducting a preemptive war against eventual threats from anti-American regimes, but it also imposed the obligation to make God's democracy secure, spreading the American democratic model worldwide, peacefully if possible, militarily if necessary. In the past other American presidents had believed they were being guided by God when undertaking the responsibility of the United States entering into war. However, unlike Bush, probably none of them had been so determined in attributing to their own religious experience and faith in God their firmness in making decisions and implementing them, convinced that they were on the right path because it corresponded to God's will and the designs of Providence.

An Imperial War

The glorification of the American character, and the sacralization of America as the universal God-given democracy, were refashioned by Bush through the new perspective of the war on terrorism, where politics and religion were mixed in order to determine America's new imperialist policy for the twenty-first century. The policy was explicitly formulated by the government on September 17, 2002 in a document called "The National Security Strategy of the United States of America."

Although neither Bush nor anyone in his administration used words like "empire," adversaries of the president's war theology did not think the viewpoint of American foreign policy, as stated in the document on national security, could be described any other way. As Bush wrote in the introduction, it was founded on the statement that today, "the United States enjoys a position of unparalleled military strength and great economic and political influence" that was to be used to guarantee freedom and peace in the world. The first commitment, however, was to fight terrorist threats: "The war against terrorism of global reach is a global enterprise of uncertain duration."[53] According to Robert N. Bellah, the document on national security clearly described a new American empire when it stated that America laid claim to "absolute military supremacy" in order "to rid the world of evil." "Apparently what even God has not succeeded in doing, America will accomplish,"[54] commented Bellah ironically. In an article on American-style imperialism, written on the eve of the attack on Iraq,[55] Bellah stated that on principle he was not against the use of America's military forces to combat the enemies of freedom, as was the case in the Gulf War and the bombing of Serbia. He was not even against an imperialist role for America, provided it created a "benign empire" capable of changing the world by using itself as a good example—like "a city on a hill"—rather than using the force of weapons, in which case America would act alone and adopt an imperialist strategy. However, observed Bellah, the United States was not prepared for this and could not sustain it for any length of time without radically modifying American democracy itself:

> Our greatest need, in our hour of imperial eminence, is moderation. Our greatest danger, in our present moralistic and belligerent mood, is taking on responsibilities we cannot and will not fulfill....
> A nation that is in many ways falling apart at home can't be the only player on the world stage. We need to build a society—and a world—in which it will be clear that we need one another, that we will bear one another's burdens.[56]

Even more radical was the condemnation of the new American strategy by religious pacifists, such as the British theologian Michael Northcott. He not only opposed Bush's war policy and his religious rhetoric, just as he had for the same reason deplored Clinton's foreign policy, but he indicted the fundamental myths of American religion, from the myth of the chosen people to the myth of the manifest destiny to the apocalyptic myth of the war between good and evil which had accompanied American foreign policy for two centuries. These myths had functioned like a "sacred ideology that has cloaked the expansionary tendencies of America's ruling elites," thus contributing to "the sacralization of American Empire."[57]

These arguments, however, did not convince the majority of the Americans who, instead, seemed to share the basic reasoning of the president's war theology. In February 2003 a large majority of Americans, 66 percent, favored the use of military strength against Iraq, provided the United States was backed by its closest allies.[58] In March 2003, 77 percent of the Americans considered the war morally justifiable in some cases. This was slightly lower than in November 2001, when the percentage was 83 percent. The war against Saddam Hussein was considered morally just by 85 percent of evangelicals, 62 percent of Catholics and liberal Protestants, and 36 percent of African-American Protestants, whereas the nonreligious groups were clearly divided, half for and half against.[59] Also, Bush's religious language was approved of by 62 percent of the Americans, and 52 percent found it comforting to know that his political decisions were influenced by his religious faith; this percentage rose to 78 percent among white evangelicals.[60]

There was another unusual aspect to the Americans' religious attitude after September 11: their relationship with God. The Americans were virtually unanimous, 91 percent, in rejecting the interpretation of September 11 as a sign that God no longer protected the United States. Furthermore, 48 percent believed that God had given their country special protection for most of its history. Of these,

71 percent were white evangelicals, that is, the largest and most faithful following of the Republican Party and of President Bush.[61] A year after the terrorist attack, on the eve of a new battle in the war against terrorism, these Americans had no doubt as to whose side God was on in the era of terrorism: God was with America, mystically united in invoking "God Bless America," which rang out everywhere in the United States after September 11. Flying everywhere was "Old Glory," the Stars and Stripes—the most popular symbol of the reawakening of civil religion in America following the terrorist attack.

"Old Glory"—Icon of America

Perhaps no other nation worships and glorifies its flag as the Americans do. Some say this cult is even totemic.[62] Samuel P. Huntington wrote, "The Stars and Stripes has the status of a religious icon and is a more central symbol of national identity for Americans than their flags are for peoples of other nations."[63] The national flag flies outside offices and all public places, schools, homes, shops; it is on postcards, posters, tee shirts, and souvenirs of all kinds. It stands alone or with other symbols of American religion, such as the Statue of Liberty, the American eagle, and the Twin Towers—before and after their disappearance. It is flown on every occasion and watches over every ceremony. It flies over stadiums and stands in churches. Moreover, the flag wraps around and accompanies the nation's heroes on their last journey, to be folded up religiously and given to their families as a mystical symbol of the permanent union between the victim, the family, and the nation. The Americans have dedicated a special holiday to it, Flag Day, on June 14, in remembrance of the day in 1777 when the Continental Congress adopted the Stars and Stripes as the flag of the United States.

The "religion of 'Old Glory,'" seen as the symbol of the religious beliefs that led to the founding of the United States,[64] has its origin in the American revolution, but its institutionalization came after the Civil War. Since the end of the nineteenth century, school children have been required to start the day off reciting the "Pledge of Allegiance," written in 1892 by Christian-socialist and patriot Francis Bellamy. It was a promise of faithfulness to "the Flag of the United States of America, and to the Republic for which it stands, one Nation, indivisible, with liberty and justice for all." Students who refused to recite the pledge were expelled until a U.S. Supreme Court ruling in 1943 acknowledged the right to remain silent. The experience of the First and Second World Wars gave new vitality to the cult of the flag. In 1919 William Guthrie wrote that devotion to the flag was the one unifying religious symbol in a society of many religions, because it represented the idea and ideal of America and could guarantee the nation's unity.[65] In 1942 Milo Milton Quaife affirmed that "Old Glory" "is our most sacred political symbol." For this reason "it is more than a brilliant banner; it is a prayer, a poem, and a prophecy. It is a prayer for the perpetuation of the principles of freedom; the poem of a people's history; a prophecy of greater and grander achievements."[66] The photo of a group of American soldiers, raising an American flag so that it waved on Mount Suribachi, Iwo Jima, on February 23, 1945, became the symbol of the United States' victory in its crusade against evil during the Second World War. The group in the photo, taken as a model for a monument in Washington, D.C., represented the American hero: "the common man—working in concert with his neighbors—triumphant. The very faceless-ness of the heroes sanctified a common cause. The raisers were not individuals, acting for their own, private motives: they were just American boys, and they made war on behalf of all Americans."[67] In 1954 during the Eisenhower administration, the sacredness of the flag was accentuated, linking it with God symbolically. The "Pledge of Allegiance" was modified to read, "one Nation, under God." Burning or offending the flag was considered an "act of desecra-tion," and this for many years, from the Vietnam War to the end of the last century, gave rise to never-ending, heated constitutional debates.[68] In some states profanation of the flag was punishable by criminal law. At one time such gestures were more frequent, so a movement developed to protect the sacredness of the flag. For years this movement, backed by the American Flag Association and some other traditional patriotic associations, has tried to make legislators introduce a constitutional amendment sanctioning the flag's sacredness, but the principle of freedom of speech has prevailed so far. The "crusade against symbolic desecration"[69] of the flag was taken up by the Republican Party and the Religious Right in their cultural war. In 1989 there was a nationwide protest in favor of the flag's sacredness, when the Supreme Court rejected a statute proposed by Texas to punish profanation of "Old Glory" with imprisonment. The court ruled that such a punishment violated freedom of speech, a principle guaranteed by the first amendment to the Constitution. The Republican Party took the matter up as part of its political platform. During the administration of President Bush senior, Congress passed the Federal Flag Protection Act, which condemned anyone who deliberately ripped, stamped on, or burned the Ameri-can flag to payment of a fine or one year in prison or both.[70] The new law for pro-tection of the flag sparked a series of demonstrations and, in several cities as well as on the steps of the Capitol, the flag was burned as a provocation. The follow-ing year the Supreme Court, in a five to four vote, criticized the law, stating that punishing profanation of the flag weakens that very freedom which makes this emblem so sacred and worthy of veneration.[71] However, the movement against profanation of the flag did not give up and a new attempt was made in Congress in 1995 to introduce an amendment in defense of its sacredness. The proposal did not pass, by a narrow margin.

On June 7, 2001 President George W. Bush announced the introduction of Flag Day and National Flag Week, recalling that during the darkest hours of the Second World War the Americans had seen in "Old Glory" the ideals "worthy of the ultimate sacrifice in order to defeat tyranny." He called on Amer-icans to gather together to honor America and recite the "Pledge of Allegiance" in public.[72]

We do not know how many followed the president's entreaty then, but after the terrorist attack no exhortation was necessary to reawaken veneration for "Old Glory" in the Americans. When some firemen raised the flag over the shambles at Ground Zero, it became symbolic of the nation's will to rally against the aggression. Photos of the event were soon famous like the photo of Iwo Jima, and the scene has been represented in many sculptures of different sizes and variously modified. In some, the Statue of Liberty appears to rise above the flag, while towards the front the firemen appear to be deep in thought or kneeling in prayer. The Ground Zero flag was preserved like a holy relic and was given to the U.S. Marines by the fire department, to be raised over the Kandahar airport in Afghanistan after the Taliban regime was defeated. Susan Willis wrote that "Old Glory" expresses a form of patriotism elevated to a religious level, like the Sacred Shroud in Turin.[73]

After the terrorist attack there was a real boom in the sale of flags. In September 2000, Wal-Mart sold 26,000 flags, whereas in the first three days after September 11 it sold 450,000, until they were out of stock. A month later, flags were still coming off the shelves quickly. The companies making flags for Wal-Mart produced an average of 30,000 flags per week, but they had to increase production up to 100,000 per week. Many newspapers published the flag as an insert.[74] Above all, American-Arabs and other ethnic groups of oriental origin rushed to buy an "Old Glory," because they feared they might be mistaken for Arabs, and because they wanted to prove their patriotic feelings. They also wanted to avoid being attacked by white Americans hunting for terrorists or itching for a vendetta against fundamentalist suspects. The Sikh and Hindu communities distributed red, white, and blue turbans.

After September 11 "Old Glory" was displayed everywhere, in different sizes and shapes, from badges to tattoos, in front of houses and on cars. It was symbolic of the tribute being paid to the victims, of faith in the nation, national pride, and the country's way of challenging the enemy. "Why the flags? 'They give me a sense of telling the victims that I care about their pain, that I actually feel it,' my friend said. 'It's also showing support for this country, which I love and which I feel is in a terrible crisis, I want to—I need to—show that I'm part of the effort to stop all of it. If America can't crush these guys, no one can,'" said a New Yorker standing near the World Trade Center. He also explained that even if he had always been patriotic he had never displayed the flag.[75]

Flag worshipping was solemnly confirmed by the nation's representatives. On October 12, 2001 the secretary of education urged 107,000 public and private, elementary and secondary schools to simultaneously recite the "Pledge of Allegiance."[76] When on June 26, 2002, a western state's court of appeal ruled in a suit brought by an atheist parent that reciting the "Pledge of Allegiance" at school was unconstitutional because it contained the phrase "under God," Democratic and Republican congressmen alike, after voting a resolution against the ruling, made a sensational demonstration by gathering on the steps of the Capitol to recite, all together, the formula of loyalty to the flag. Hillary Clinton defined the ruling "outrageous"; the spokesman for President Bush called it "ridiculous," and the president immediately began a battle to defend the integrity and sacredness of the flag as expressed in the phrase "under God." According to a survey by the *Washington Post,* 84 percent of Americans favored keeping the phrase "under God" in the "Pledge of Allegiance." Three years later the Supreme Court solved the matter, declaring that since the atheist parent was divorced he did not have the authority to intervene in matters regarding his daughter, who was in the custody of the mother. In 2002, every day about sixty million children in the United States recited the pledge of loyalty to the flag.[77]

At the time of the tragedy, "Old Glory" was symbolic of a renewed union within the national community. "The flags were physical evidence of the sudden and dramatic rise in salience of national identity for Americans compared to their other identities," observed Huntington.[78] *Rally 'round the flag* was the cry that helped many Americans to overcome the trauma caused by the attack and to feel united in dealing with the enemy. They rallied around their president as they had in the past when the nation felt it was threatened by an external enemy.[79] United around the flag, the Americans went from being a *community of sorrow* to being a *community of faith,* ready to become a *community at war.*

The renewed cult of "Old Glory" was the most evident, popular demonstration of the newborn American civil religion resulting from the September 11 events. Through President Bush's war theology September 11 helped reconfirm America's sacredness as the "good empire," called on once again by history to fight against evil forces in order to save God's democracy. Consecration of September 11, as one of the fundamental events in the "sacred history" of the American people, began immediately after the attack and continued with great intensity and coherence up to the commemoration of the first anniversary. The official ceremony on September 11, 2002 was one of the most important in the history of American religion, because, like few other past events, it gave America an aura of holiness at a time when it was at its most powerful; that time became the era of the "war on terror."

7

The Great Awakening

A Mournful Dawn

It was two o'clock in the morning in New York that September 11, 2002 when groups of bagpipers in their ceremonial kilts, the flag flying from their instruments, began to form the slow, solemn procession headed to Ground Zero. They came from the city's five boroughs to commemorate the terrorist attack on this first anniversary. Along the route the city was waking up, lights were turning on, and a silent, compassionate people, holding candles and waving the American flag, stood and watched the procession go by. The bagpipes played songs dear to the American nation, like "Yankee Doodle Dandy," "America the Beautiful," "A Nation Once Again." In the United States and all over the world, the nations that a year ago had shared the Americans' sorrow were getting ready to commemorate the innocent victims of the terrorist attack by observing a minute of silence at 8:46 A.M., when the first airplane hit the south tower of the World Trade Center.

President Bush proclaimed September 11 Patriot Day in memory of those who had perished in the attacks and to remind everyone that it is "our collective obligation to ensure that justice is done, that freedom prevails, and that the principles upon which our Nation was founded endure."[1] The official commemoration ceremonies had already begun on September 6 when the senators and representatives held a special session of Congress in New York at Federal Hall, near Ground Zero. This was the first session in the city after 200 years, and it was held to show that the nation was united against terrorism and determined not to let similar attacks ever happen again. Besides being a tribute to the victims and the city, the meeting was of great symbolic value in the "sacred history" of American religion, because New York was the first capital city of the United States. It was the place where the first Congress met—precisely at Federal Hall—where the Bill of Rights was written and where the first president was sworn in on April 30, 1789.

On the day of the commemoration, the most imposing ceremonies were planned for where the terrorist attacks had taken place—Ground Zero, the Pentagon, and in the field in Pennsylvania where one of the hijacked planes crashed. Other ceremonies planned all over the United States "[would] bring reality to the *Pledge of Allegiance* assertion of America as 'one nation...indivisible.'"[2] The press announced that the commemoration ceremonies would be the widest-ranging collective celebrations ever in American history—a fundamental point in time in the effort to overcome the trauma of the tragedy suffered, wrote the *Gotham Gazette* on September 9. "What I'm trying to do," said New York Mayor Michael R. Bloomberg on the eve of September 11, 2002, regarding the commemoration ceremonies, "is that in the morning, we will look back and remember who they were and why they died. And in the evening, come out of it looking forward and say 'O.K., we're going to go forward.'"[3] During the year that had passed, there had been many different initiatives to commemorate September 11, from television documentaries to photograph exhibits, from museum exhibitions to the publication of more than 700 books, and 150 more were expected in the fall. In fact, it was referred to as the most documented tragedy in the history of mankind. Furthermore, as Amu Harmon noted, on the first anniversary many people had raised a virtual monument on the internet in memory of the victims, with their words of condolence, comfort, and hope.[4] And other collective monuments, consisting of messages, poems, drawings, invocations, prayers, and photos of the victims, sprang up spontaneously the day after the tragedy in Union Square and Washington Square, in many streets and subway stations, which became places of worship for many. In these temporary sacred places a suffering community tried to rediscover its own closeness, solidarity between the living and the dead, through a message that appeared everywhere: "We Will Never Forget."[5] Photos and brief biographies of the victims were published in a special insert of the *New York Times.*

However, a year after the tragedy, public opinion seemed divided in its attitude towards the memory of September 11: even if the phrase that September 11 had "changed everything forever" had become a sort of national slogan, less than half the Americans thought that September 11 should be made a national holiday like Memorial Day or Labor Day.[6] During the year there had also been much controversy about the future utilization of the empty area where the World Trade Center had once stood—64,748 square meters of very valuable land—and on how to dedicate a monument there to the memory of the victims. Sacred and profane were mixed in a never-ending diatribe about the reconstruction plans, followed by criticism from artists and town planners, a clashing of interests and ambitious rivalry.[7] Former mayor Giuliani wanted to turn the whole site into a remembrance park, consecrated by the death of thousands of victims, many of whom had been dissolved on that spot, making it a perennially symbolic cemetery. By July the entity in charge of rebuilding the World Trade Center had already drawn up six plans, each proposing different combinations of monuments and commercial buildings. While the city was getting ready to commemorate the first anniversary of the terrorist attack, observed Eileen Davis Hudson on September 9, its citizens and politicians continued to discuss the plans to rebuild the World Trade Center. It was not easy to foresee a final decision because the families were also involved.[8] However, the controversies stopped in respectful silence on that first anniversary to be celebrated at Ground Zero, where all the blueprints provided for a "sacred space" in memory of America's tragic experience.[9]

"Ground zero" is the term used to describe the epicenter of a total ruin where everything has been destroyed, which is what happened to the people who perished there without leaving any trace of themselves. On the first anniversary there were still about 20,000 unidentified human remains at Memorial Garden, where they were preserved. Gary Laderman, professor of religion, observed that perhaps one of the most unusual and expressive aspects of the anniversary was the great importance given to the material remains of the World Trade Center, to the remains of the collapsed buildings mixed with destroyed bodies and, for this reason, transformed into sacred ruins.[10] For almost a year during the work to remove the debris, Ground Zero was an enormous "mass grave" already tinged with religious devotion.[11] The sight of the pile of smoking ruins aroused a sensation of holy terror—a mixed feeling of terror, reverence, wonder, awakened by a holy or sublime experience, an intense religious emotion, as the philosopher Jean-Pierre Dupuy recalled after going there in December 2001.[12] The ruins of the World Trade Center, commented theologian Kathleen McManus, mark what has become and will always be a "sacred ground."[13]

Sacred Ground in America

The sun had not yet risen when the procession of bagpipers reached Ground Zero. It was met by a huge crowd that had gathered to pay tribute to the memory of the victims. Similar ceremonies were taking place at the same time in every city of the United States, despite the threat of terrorist attacks. The government had raised the nation's state of alert several days prior to the anniversary, following a sudden television announcement by Attorney General Ashcroft that broke into the usual programs.[14]

One year from the attack, where the World Trade Center once stood there was only a vast cement pit—known as "the Pit." With all the debris removed the bottom had been leveled to form an esplanade. The only access was the ramp used by the trucks that took away the debris. The pit was surrounded by a railing to keep the public out. An American flag flew over Ground Zero together with a banner that said, "We Will Never Forget." To one side of the pit a roughly hewn cross in tarnished steel stood out. It was made of cut-off girders found among the ruins of the Twin Towers. Behind the cross a large heart, in the colors of the American flag, was painted on the facade of a building overlooking Ground Zero, and a multitude of waving American flags—the stars and stripes of all sizes and shapes—encircled the pit. In the middle of the esplanade at Ground Zero there was the "Circle of Honor" dedicated to the victims. Their deaths had already made this a holy shrine, which the commemoration of September 11 consigned officially to American religion.

Religion originates from a sense of sacredness and death. Places where death reigns supreme are holy places. Religious populations believe the land inhabited by a divinity to be sacred. The American Indians held their land to be sacred, and America was a sacred land for the Puritans who landed in the new world, convinced they had reached the promised land, endowed to the new people of Israel by God in order to create a new Jerusalem, "a city on a hill," a lighthouse and example of virtue for all of humanity. The myth of the new Jerusalem, one of the fundamental myths in American religion handed down to future generations of Americans, was the vision of the new world as the land reserved for those people who were to accomplish God's democracy.[15] And the founding fathers considered the birth of the republic of the United States sacred, a "sacred experiment" in the free government of a new nation that would indicate to the rest of humanity the way to regeneration.

Modern nationalism is a secular religion resulting from the sacralization of the country and which, in that name, consecrates events, places, and heroes that make up its "sacred history." Perhaps no other nation has bestowed a religious nature on its own collective identity as the United States has, interpreting its history as a continuous epiphany of Providence through the "manifest destiny" of the American nation.[16] Like other modern nations, America was founded on an inherent link between religion and politics. Although it (America) sanctioned the principle of separation between church and state, this foundation was accompanied by the creation of places consecrated to the celebration of America's "spiritual history" and the commemoration of events, heroes, and victims who, over generations, have contributed to the nation's vitality, prosperity, and greatness. An event is sanctified when the place that reminds people of that event is given a positive and long-lasting meaning for the collectivity—for example, a continuous lesson in heroism or a sacrifice for the community. The place to be consecrated is sanctified by a rite which separates it from the surrounding environment so as to dedicate it to an event, a martyr, a hero, or a group of victims. The place is thus transformed into a symbol so that future generations will remember a virtuous action or sacrifice, or will be guarded against events which should be prevented.

The Living and the Dead

A national community's conscience consists of continuity between the dead and the living, and this is perpetuated through rites and symbols which every so often recall the past in the present. In 1959 W. Lloyd Warner, pioneer in the field of American symbolism, wrote, "human culture is the symbolic organization of the remembered experiences of the dead in the past as newly felt and understood by the living members of the collectivity."[17] In every instance of modern nationalism sacred grounds are fundamental, in order to create and feed the collective sentiment of being a national community, and to confer on the nation an eternal dimension, which transcends the lives of the individuals that make it up, flowing into the generations, and which, at the same time, gives each life an everlasting meaning and value through the commemoration and celebration of the nation's memory. The places sanctified as national shrines, in particular, battlefields, cemeteries, and war monuments, are an integral part of the symbolic process in creating a national conscience: they transform the memory of the dead into a permanent period of the collective life and, therefore, somehow tend to hide or remove the event of death from the nation's collective life, which becomes perpetual in time. The United States has always venerated greatly its holy grounds as places where the sense of national community is preserved and transmitted, particularly when these grounds are dedicated to war victims. Warner demonstrated that the cemeteries were central to American community celebrations and that the main occasion encouraging a sense of community was Memorial Day, the day dedicated to commemorating war victims.

His considerations still seem to be thought valid by a nation that was involved in the principal conflicts of the twentieth century. "No generation of Americans has managed to avoid fighting a major war," wrote G. Kurt Piehler, military historian: "How we have remembered these conflicts has played a crucial role in shaping the American national identity over time. Most significantly, we used memorials and rituals to define who is a good citizen."[18] Tragedy and violence have disseminated sacred places all over the United States; these places are mainly dedicated to the memory of battles and death.[19] Some experts consider this an important aspect of American civil religion which, as has been observed, "explains the uniformity of American death rites, and enables us to discuss them in general terms. Paradoxically, it is a death-centered religion."[20] This was confirmed by the thousands of commemoration ceremonies all over the United States on September 11, evidence of a "specific and deep-rooted feature of the nation's life," as Laderman wrote:

> the use of communal rituals to create social solidarity by invoking those who have died. For, despite the conventional wisdom about America as a death-denying culture, our history is riddled with examples of obsessive interest in, if not downright cultic activity surrounding, the bones of the dead.[21]

As in all forms of patriotism, commemoration of war victims has a preeminent role in American religion: one of its most important sacred places is the cemetery at Gettysburg, where from July 1–3, 1863 a bloody Civil War battle raged. The transformation of the battlefield into a sanctuary came about on November 19, 1863 when Abraham Lincoln pronounced his famous address. That address became one of the sacred texts of American civil religion, an extraordinary model of synthesis, effectiveness, and beautiful public speech. In his address the president stated regarding the battlefield that the "brave men, living and dead, who struggled here have consecrated it far above our poor power to add or detract," and he ended asking the American people to honor the fallen, thus confirming their devotion to the cause for which they had died and the task they had left to be accomplished: "that we here highly resolve that these dead shall not have died in vain; that the nation under God shall have a new birth of freedom, and that government of the people, by the people, for the people shall not perish from the earth."[22]

Sacralizing September 11

There were no memorable speeches made by politicians at Ground Zero on that first anniversary. The ceremony began at 8:45 A.M. when the mayor of New York said a few words in memory of the victims. At 8:46 there was a minute of silence in observance of the exact time when the first plane had hit the World Trade Center. After that the governor of New York, George E. Pataki, read Lincoln's Gettysburg address. Former mayor of New York Giuliani then began reading out the names of the 2,801 victims who died in the two planes and the collapse of the towers. The *New York Times* commented, "a litany of names, whose very syllables, reverberating with so many different ethnicities and religions, conjured up the multiplicity of this country, its multifarious dreams."[23] Each name was spoken slowly to emphasize the single individual in the commemoration of a group of victims. It was a personal tribute to each person from the national community, which thereby committed itself to never forget them.[24] The reading of names, which went on for about three hours, was accompanied by music from a cello and the whistling of the wind, which swept up clouds of dust, dispersing them as if they were ashes. Readers included Hillary Clinton, Robert De Niro, Secretary of State Colin Powell, members of the victims' families, firemen, and policemen. The reading was interrupted by minutes of silence at 9:03, when the second plane hit the other tower; at 9:59, when the first tower collapsed; and at 10:29, when the second tower came down, at which time all the church bells in New York tolled. When the reading of the names ended, the governor of New Jersey read the Declaration of Independence. The victims' family members, who had come from all over the United States and the world, then descended the ramp leading into the pit and the "Circle of Honor." Here they placed flowers and built rudimental altars with tiny pieces of stone, and stood in meditation and prayer. It was the first time family members were allowed into the place where their dear ones had perished. Some gathered pieces of stone, others a handful of the dust from the pit to put in bottles as a symbolic relic.[25] Families that had not been able to recover some remains of their loved ones were given urns containing dust from Ground Zero.[26]

President Bush visited Ground Zero in the afternoon, after having attended the ceremonies at the Pentagon and in the field in Pennsylvania, and laid a wreath in the "Circle of Honor." He did not make a speech but spent over an hour in emotionally moving conversations with the victims' family members.[27] That evening in Battery Park, not far from Ground Zero, in front of the "Sphere," a ruined sculpture that had once adorned the World Trade Center Plaza, the mayor of New York lit an eternal flame in memory of the victims. Then he read Franklin D. Roosevelt's speech on the "four freedoms"—freedom of speech, of religion, from fear, and from need, pronounced in January 1941.

The reading of previous presidential speeches all belonging to times of war evoked only indirectly the war on terror, while the lack of speeches by politicians confirmed the intention to consider the ceremony at Ground Zero only a civil one, to commemorate victims who were ordinary people, who had perished while carrying out their daily jobs. Remembered for their simple humanity, they were representative of the nation. Probably the decision to avoid direct reference to the "war on terror" depended on the negative attitude expressed towards the president's warmongering or belligerent initiatives by many of the victims' family members, who had set up an organization to try to find alternatives to war and to work towards ending such a violent cycle.[28] Some of them had written to the president immediately after the tragedy to state their aversion to any kind of armed revenge, because the victim also would have been against this solution: "Our government is heading in the direction of violent revenge, with the prospect of sons, daughters, parents, and friends in distant lands dying, suffering and nursing further grievances against us. It is not the way to go. It will not avenge our son's death. Not in our son's name," wrote the parents of a young man who died at the World Trade Center.[29] It is significant that the president did not say anything, but made his commemoration speeches elsewhere that day, where the reasons for the war could not but prevail.

The "war on terror" was the main theme at the ceremony to commemorate the victims of the attack on the Pentagon, where the reconstruction of the destroyed wing had already been completed. It was decided not to set aside any "sacred area" at the site of the attack—which became the Phoenix Project Site, symbolic of America's ability to recover. "Some of the relatives of the 184 people killed a year ago say they are disconcerted by the speed of the process, but not surprised to see such a rapid response in a military culture trained to deal with tragedy," commented John Tierney in the *New York Times*, evidently alluding to the war on terror. Secretary of Defense Donald H. Rumsfeld said, "We're here today to honor those who died in this place and to rededicate ourselves to the cause for which they gave their lives, the cause of human liberty. In a sense, we meet on a battlefield." And Bush added, paraphrasing the Gospel, "We fight for the dignity of life against fanatics who feel no shame in murder.... We fight to protect the innocent so that the lawless and the merciless will not inherit the earth."[30]

The *New York Times* editorialist Michiko Kakutani scolded the politicians who took part in the ceremonies at Ground Zero for abdicating their responsibility to create a vision, a state of mind, set a direction, and express ordinary feelings of sorrow or hope as required of leaders by history at such an important time. They had missed the important opportunity to describe the events of September 11 for history by means of their own speeches and, instead, chose to read speeches given in war contexts, which seemed inappropriate for the particular, unusual tragedy of September 11. America was no longer a nation taking its first steps, as it was at the time of the Declaration of Independence; the victims of the World Trade Center were civilians devoted to their own daily lives and not soldiers fighting in a fratricidal civil war, unlike the dead at Gettysburg; and, lastly, the future of America today was not comparable to the future of America in January 1941 when, as Roosevelt said, the future of America was seriously in danger.[31]

Such criticism, however, did not take into consideration the relevance that the texts read had as sacred scriptures of American civil religion. Because they were connected with wartime, they contributed to the sanctification of September 11 through the transfiguration of the victims into the heroes, martyrs, and saints of American religion. According to Laderman, this was another peculiar characteristic of the anniversary:

> the rhetorical effort to transform innocent, unsuspecting civilians into national heroes who sacrificed their lives—implicitly comparing them with American soldiers who died fighting for the country in wars past. This popular strategy aimed at reassuring the united nation that these deaths were not meaningless, and that American justice will prevail.[32]

The 40 passengers who rebelled against the hijackers were consecrated at Shanksville as the first "soldier citizens"[33] in the "war on terror," whereas all the other people who perished became martyrs unknowingly, slain by the enemies of freedom and a civilized world. The firemen and policemen who died while performing rescue operations had already been spontaneously consecrated by public sentiment as heroes and saints, the incarnation and symbol of America's good, courageous, and unselfish nature. The heroism of the New York City Fire Department has become the heart-throbbing symbol of Ground Zero, said theologian McManus.[34] Postcards and posters showed images of firemen and policemen being received in heaven among the angels. New York fire stations became the destination for pilgrimages so visitors could pay tribute to the memory of the dead. In this way the commemoration of the first anniversary completed the sanctification process of September 11 that had begun on the very day of the tragedy, to be incorporated into the "sacred history" of American religion.

The people who died on September 11 were ordinary people of different races, religions, and professions, who represented in their experience the realization of the "American dream": their consecration contributed to the sacralization of America as God's democracy, an exceptional experiment in free government, accomplished by the "nation of nations," the only nation in history founded on a freely chosen creed, shared by people from all over the world, committed to defending and spreading democracy throughout the world. When he proclaimed September 11 the nation's Patriot Day, the president of the United States said, "We are a people dedicated to the triumph of freedom and democracy over evil and tyranny."[35]

There was no religious service at Ground Zero during the commemoration, but a solemn function was held in Washington, D.C., in the National Cathedral, officiated by the Anglican archbishop of South Africa, Desmond Tutu. The ceremony was attended by Attorney General John Ashcroft and the ambassadors of more than 30 nations that had lost some of their citizens in the terrorist attacks on September 11. Those citizens were also represented by their national flags, which arrived in a procession headed by a bagpiper. Prayers were recited by ministers of the Hindu, Buddhist, Muslim, Jewish, Lutheran, Baptist, Presbyterian, Sikh, Catholic, Methodist and Greek-Orthodox religions. The function was interrupted four times at the hours when the planes had crashed. Religious services were held all over America as part of the commemoration of September 11.

That night, from Ground Zero, two powerful searchlights projected on the sky the lighted outline of the two towers that had disappeared, a luminous tribute that was a testimony of life.

God in America: One Year Later

The impact of the terrorist attacks on the religious conscience of American believers was very great, and their behavior in the days following showed it because there was an extraordinary turnout in churches, synagogues, mosques, temples, and other places of worship. The Pew Forum on Religion and Public Life, an independent research center dedicated to promoting a deeper understanding of the role played by religion in forming the ideas and institutions of American society, conducted an investigation into the religious scene in the United States after September 11. The outcome showed that religion had more influence on lifestyle in America than in previous 10-year periods, even if the overall, ever-changing kaleidoscope of religions was not modified by the effect of the attacks on the American conscience. A poll carried out in December 2001 to find out how important religion was in people's lives listed the Americans still at the top worldwide, compared to other wealthy nations. In America 59 percent of the population stated that religion played a very important role. This percentage was double that of Canada, and far greater than that of Japan (12 percent) and the European countries (33 percent in Great Britain, 27 percent in Italy, 21 percent in Germany, and 17 percent in France).[36] Furthermore, a Gallup poll in December 2001 found that the index of attendance at religious ceremonies had risen to 47 percent, up compared to 40 percent, the average attendance since the period of the Second World War.[37] According to *The Christian Science Monitor*[38] in a December 7, 2001 article, this was the first time in almost 50 years that a considerable majority of Americans admitted that religion had increased its influence on public life. It was, however, a personal type of religion, an individual type, emotional more than doctrinal; often it did not belong to the traditional confessions and institutional places of worship, and so it corresponded to the growing diversity of American religions, making the changing pattern of a new religious America so unique.[39]

Impressed by the sudden growth in church attendance and intensified devoutness in America following September 11, the most important exponents of traditional and fundamentalist evangelicalism stated triumphantly that America was more religious once again. Jerry Falwell predicted that the Americans were about to devote themselves to God at long last, and Pat Robertson announced that there was occurring one of the greatest spiritual awakenings in the history of America.[40] The general American phrase "Great Awakening" indicates the Protestant evangelical movements, born of a renewed faith and religious enthusiasm, to preach individual and collective moral regeneration through a more rigorous observance of the Scriptures in private and public life. In the history of America these movements had preceded and influenced decisive changes in politics. The first Great Awakening, in the mid-eighteenth century, had prepared the structure of American patriotism on the eve of the War of Independence; a second Great Awakening which developed during the early decades of the nineteenth century had accentuated the evangelical nature of American Protestantism and its democratization, and it contributed to America's westward expansion with its missionary ardor to evangelize; at the end of the nineteenth century there was talk of a Third Awakening with the spread of millenarian movements. During the last 10 years of the twentieth century, theologians and clergymen thought that America was about to experience another Great Awakening.[41] In 1998 Robert W. Fogel, winner of the Nobel Prize in Economics, maintained that the United States was about to embark on a Fourth Great Awakening, a new religious revival animated by rebellion against corruption in contemporary society.[42]

The intensification of devoutness in America after the September 11 tragedy seemed to confirm this forecast. However, a year later it was apparent that September 11 had not brought about a lasting change in the Americans' religious conduct. In October 2001, 18 percent of Americans declared they participated in religious services more assiduously after September 11, but in May 2002 the percentage had dropped to 8 percent. During 2002 only 11 percent of Americans sought the advice of a minister, priest, or some form of religious guidance, according to a survey by the University of Chicago. In the churches pews were empty, while the offices of psychologists were crowded. Drinking and the use of tranquilizers increased while, at the same time, religious practices declined.[43] Places of worship did not benefit from the surge of religious fever caused by the September 11 catastrophe. Where the Catholics were concerned, this may also have resulted from the pedophilia scandals among American priests and the ecclesiastical hierarchies' attempts to hide them, because their reputation had been damaged. There was also a drop in the number of Americans who stated that religion was very important in their lives. It went from 64 percent during the weeks immediately following September 11 to 56 percent in May 2002, back to the pre-attack level. Even more significant, according to a poll by the Barna Research Group, was the fact that the percentage of Americans who believed that moral truth was absolute fell from 38 percent in January 2000 to 22 percent the following fall, despite the president's sermon on the all-out war between good and evil.[44] Furthermore, polls conducted during 2002 showed significant changes in attitude towards the role of religion in public life.[45] According to a Pew Forum survey, in March the number of Americans convinced that the influence of religion on public life was growing had dropped from 78 percent in the previous November to 37 percent, just as it had been the year before the terrorist attacks. However, 58 percent believed that religious faith was at the bottom of America's success, and 83 percent of white Protestant evangelicals thought that religion was the quintessence of America's strength. As for the influence of religion world-wide, 80 percent considered this positive, but 51 percent felt that September 11 was proof that there was little religion in the world. Regarding the role played by religion in most of the wars and conflicts, 65 percent said it was very impor-tant, and they also maintained, with an implied reference to Islam, that "some religions are more inclined than others towards violence."[46]

During 2002 hostility towards Islam increased, particularly among conservative evangelicals who did not share the president's ecumenism. The following year the percentage of Americans who thought Islam was more likely than other religions to support violence rose from 25 percent in March 2002 to 44 percent in July 2002.[47] The changes in attitude towards Islam, however, did not modify the favorable attitude of most Americans towards their Muslim fellow citizens. Also there was no strain on the conviction that many religions can lead to eternal life, shared by three quarters of Americans, including 50 percent of white evangelicals, against 18 percent who believed this was true only in their own religion. More-over, even if the majority thought that religion was at the basis of American soci-ety, 84 percent felt that a person could be a good citizen without professing a religious faith, and 53 percent did not think it necessary to believe in God in order to believe in good moral values. These data indicated, as E. J. Dionne Jr., co-director of the Pew Forum observed, that most Americans were able to recon-cile profound religious beliefs with tolerance, and this was also proof that religious beliefs were compatible with liberal democracy.[48]

What Kind of Awakening?

Although there was a decline in attendance at religious services one year after the attack, data regarding the Americans' social attitudes confirmed the persist-ence of a greater sense of devoutness and desire for community, together with a more positive consideration of religion as a source of comfort. At the same time, 40 percent of Americans confirmed that the September 11 tragedy had strength-ened their religious faith.[49] This was not just a "Great Awakening" in the tradi-tional sense, but a religious-type awakening that occurred as a result of September 11. It was the awakening of a civil religion evidenced by a renewed worshipping of the flag and a burst of patriotic sentiment and nationalist pride, all of which contributed to the widespread support of President Bush from a united nation. He, in turn, cleverly used his own devoutness, his Christian ecumenism, and his vision of America as being sacred, to develop a new version of American civil religion, notably modeled after the ideology of the Religious Right.

There was much talk about civil religion in America during the second half of the twentieth century, particularly in 1967, after the publication of an essay called "Civil Religion in America," by Robert N. Bellah. He took the concept formulated by Jean-Jacques Rousseau, using it to define the religious aspects of American politics, distinct and independent of the churches, as being a series of beliefs, symbols, and rites relative to things sacred and institutionalized within the collectivity. According to Bellah, American civil religion was an authentic interpretation of a transcendental, universal religious reality seen or revealed in the historical experience of the American people.[50] For more than two decades historians, sociologists, and theologians debated whether the civil religion analyzed by Bellah existed or not. And in 1975, 10 years after his famous article, faced with the crisis of American society and its conscience at the time of the Vietnam War and the Watergate scandal, Bellah stated, "Today, the American civil religion is like an, empty, broken shell."[51]

Actually, in the years that followed, civil religion continued to exist in both public and political life in America and even experienced periods of new vitality during the Reagan, George Bush senior, and Clinton administrations. All of their references to God, to the American mission, and to the destiny of America testified of the existence of civil religion, as did the rites and symbols that celebrated God's democracy, sacralizing America. During the administration of President Clinton, a master at exercising the role of pontiff of American religion, there was much debate about the nature of civil religion relative to its Protestant matrix, at a time when Protestant churches were losing many of their followers. According to a study conducted in 1994 by the *Star Tribune* of Minneapolis, Minnesota, the experts interviewed maintained that the principal denominations had lost millions of members. However, they were still quite jubilant because the Protestant values—emphasis on the individual, the work ethic, the need for the government to concern itself with its people's lives, the need to strengthen the principle of public morality, diffidence regarding hierarchy—had become fundamental values for American society. According to political expert John Green, civil religion is reasserting itself in America. It is as old as the Mayflower, not exactly Christian, but it derives profoundly from Protestant beliefs and morality, above all in the need to base life on religion. The Protestant matrix had influenced the way in which religion was constantly entwined with life in America, to the point where other religious confessions that had arrived in the United States had become Americanized and had, therefore, been influenced to a certain extent by Protestantism. The Roman Catholics are Americanized, and the divisions between Catholics and Protestants are becoming less evident; they both agree on many values and social matters. In Minnesota, Protestants and Catholics practice civil religion in many areas, observed the author of the study. She also stated that American civil religion appears to be Protestant; it feels and acts Protestant, but actually it is not Protestant—it is American.[52]

At the beginning of the twenty-first century the focus was once again turned to civil religion. In April 2000 the Reverend Welton Gaddy, president of the Interfaith Alliance, an interconfessional liberal organization, stated that American civil religion was a reality, a cultural and political phenomenon more than a spiritual one, but nevertheless influential in forming the American national identity. He explained that civil religion made an important contribution if it offered values which foster unity among groups of different faiths, without compromising the specific diversity of their respective religious traditions; whereas, a civil religion that has as its requisites conformity and homogeneity can damage both the nation and its religious traditions.[53] According to several commentators, President Bush's first inaugural speech was an example of positive civil religion. Religion expert Charles Henderson especially appreciated the way Bush had evoked God without any particular confessional inflection, expressing the best of American civil religion in his inaugural speech. He also said that the fundamental principles of this civil religion transcended confessional identity and were sufficiently ample to include Christians, Jews, and Muslims, and millions of other citizens not affiliated with an organized religion. In this regard, Henderson added, civil religion has worked during the course of American history as a unifying factor rather than a dividing one, because it has been defined as all-embracing, thus inclusive of all those who are marginalized, forgotten, or spurned. According to Henderson, by invoking this aspect of the "national creed," which pledges to care for those who linger behind because that is the will of "a power larger than ourselves, who created us equal in his image," and again when, speaking of the "nation's grand story of courage," the president commented, "We are not this story's author, who fills time and eternity with his purpose. Yet his purpose is achieved in our duty; and our duty is fulfilled in service to one another,"[54] Bush had expressed the better part of civil religion's Christian principles in his inaugural address. Similar comments came from Barry Hankins, historian on the relationship between church and state. On January 24, 2001 he wrote that the president's speech was full of references to American civil religion. He was referring not only to the religious metaphors used by the president, but also to his presentation of America as the country of a newly chosen people determined not by blood ties or ethnic group, rather by a series of transcendental ideals, and destined to play an important role in the history of man.[55]

American Civil Religion: A New Birth

Despite these comments that showed that civil religion was constantly a part of American politics, it was certainly true that until September 11 "American civil religion had been a sort of joke which, in times of political pessimism, was associated with the Vietnam War and the Watergate scandal, although there was a brief revival when the country celebrated the centennial of its independence," as anthropologist Michael Angrosino remarked in 2002. In the decades that followed, testimony to an increasingly harsh division between political groups, civil religion was not considered an important part of the national frame of mind, and, in fact, the theories on an inevitable secularization, at the time prevalent among social scientists with positivist and Marxist backgrounds, postulated a growing indifference towards religion, including civil religion. However, noted Angrosino, sometimes in a secular society, worried people can find comfort and meaning in civil religion—for the same reasons, sentiments, and combinations as induce people in traditional societies to turn to religion in the traditional sense.[56] And this is what happened on September 11, when the devastation caused by the terrorist attacks compelled the Americans to react to the trauma of terror, seeking moral strength in religion and patriotism. The state of mind illustrated by historian Richard Slotkin, relative to the situation in America following September 11, clearly describes the circumstances which led to the rebirth of civil religion:

> When a society suffers a profound trauma, an event that upsets its fundamental ideas about what can and should happen and challenges the authority of its basic values, its people look to their myths for precedents, invoking past experience—embodied in their myths—as a way of getting a handle on crisis.[57]

In February 2002, the Pew Forum on Religion and Public Life organized a debate among experts on religion, theologians, and exponents of different religions, on the topic of post-September 11 civil religion. The meeting dealt with the extraordinary nationwide spread of patriotism imbued with religiosity, to the tune of "God Bless America."[58] All of this, according to Melissa Rogers, director of the center, shows once again that in times of crisis there is a revival of civil religion, intended as Bellah describes it, and that is, intended as an interpretation of the American experience in the light of a supreme, universal reality. In the years that were to follow, there was more and more talk of civil religion as a real phenomenon that was gaining vitality and importance in American politics. Wilfred M. McClay, historian of American culture, recalled that before September 11 the Americans had become increasingly disenchanted with civil religion, particularly as a consequence of the Vietnam War. Contributing to this disenchantment was the "culture war" against President Clinton conducted by the Religious Right. They maintained that he showed religious devotion in public while acting in a morally scandalous way in private. The president seemed to be proof that American civil religion was not only false, but seriously dangerous. And the future of civil religion could not have looked bleaker when the 2000 presidential election revealed a nation that was deeply divided with a dubiously legitimate president. Then came the September 11 attacks, which decidedly inverted the trend. The rebirth of civil religion became immediately evident in the unanimous protest that arose against the fundamentalist reverends who saw the signs of divine punishment in the event. As Wilfred McClay commented, it was certainly surprising how quickly an ailing civil religion acquired new life, especially through the many improvised religious services that took place all over the country, instinctively mixing civil and religious rites, as demonstrated by the presence of "Old Glory" in churches and all places of worship.[59] *The Dallas Morning News* wrote that the American flag had replaced the cross as the most evident symbol in many churches throughout the country.[60]

This was the most obvious demonstration of civil religion's rebirth. Even more so, according to many observers, was the rebirth of civil religion in the president's rhetoric after September 11 and in the show of religious patriotism by Congress. President Bush's speech before Congress on September 20 was described by the evangelical journal *Christianity Today* as a moving patriotic sermon, the right kind of civil religion which encourages us to be the best citizens wherever God wants.[61] In December 2001, when commenting on Congress's decision to allow the use of the Capitol's rotunda for its prayer meetings, Robert Benne, director of the Center for Religion and Society at Roanoke College in Virginia, noted that the presence of civil religion demonstrated the uselessness of actions to ban religious symbols and language from public areas; civil religion has existed since the birth of the republic and has continued to be present in all of the major events of civil life, emerging with unusual strength during a national crisis. According to Benne, this was apparent in the hymn "God Bless America," in which also American Muslims could ask God to bless America, because civil religion carefully avoided any specific reference to the Jewish or Christian religions:

> The American Civil Religion is the common denominator religion of a religious country with the First Amendment. When there is no established church or religion, and yet there is a great deal of religious vitality in the country, the Civil Religion is an inevitable result. A religious people want a transcendent dimension to the great moments of national life and the Civil Religion is the vehicle for that.

Civil religion, Benne added, could be "both trivial and dangerous if it is used merely to give a religious gloss to national ambitions. But if there is a serious effort to connect America with both divine blessing and guidance, as 'God Bless America' does, Civil Religion can be noble and necessary. And it won't disappear."[62]

Another example of civil religion's rebirth, "in the noble sense," was provided by the winter Olympics held in Salt Lake City in February 2002. An imposing ceremony was dedicated to the American flag from Ground Zero, placed next to the flags of more than 80 nations. As the *Star Tribune* commented, once again the American nation has seen "the expression of one of this country's cherished values, its 'civil religion'":

> Ever since Sept. 11 the United States has seen a resurgence of sensitivity to and expressions of civil religion—we value service, cooperation, equality of justice and opportunity, respect for diversity and national symbols and ideas. And we have a sense that this nation is divinely ordained.[63]

The rebirth of civil religion after September 11 did not seem to be contingent upon the fact that people were flocking to the churches. In fact, three years later there were still important signs of its vitality. Throngs of visitors continued to crowd Ground Zero as a place of pilgrimage and a profound emotional experience even though all signs of the disaster had been removed. "It has become a shrine, a holy place, and has thereby become assimilated into the American civil religion. Yet the single most moving, the most powerful and immediately understandable symbol, is the famous cross-shaped girders that were pulled out of the wreckage and have been raised as a cross," remarked McClay. And he added:

> What, one wonders, does this object mean to the people viewing it, many of whom, one presumes, are not Christian and not even American? Was it a piece of nationalist kitsch or a sentimental relic? Or was it a powerful witness to the redemptive value of suffering—and thereby, a signpost pointing toward the core of the Christian story? Or did it subordinate the Christian story to the American one, and thus traduce its Christian meaning?[64]

Such questions highlighted the ambiguity of the symbol which summed up much of what is good and much of what is dangerous in civil religion. As noted by McClay, apart from these doubts, the events of September 11 confirmed what the most experienced scholars of society already knew, and that is that "the impulse to create and live inside of a civil religion is an irrepressible human impulse, and that this is just as true in the age of nation-state," which in itself "is something more than just a secular institution. Because it must sometimes call upon its citizens for acts of sacrifice and self-overcoming, and not only in time of war, it must be able to draw on spiritual resources," deep bonds and honored memories of the past, and visions of history's trend in order to suitably carry out its function, because without "such feelings, no nation can long endure, let alone wage a long and difficult struggle."

"Pontifex et Imperator"

It is unlikely that President Bush was aware of the studies on civil religion and its function as a unifying factor within a collectivity, particularly during a time of crisis. As a matter of fact, he was probably uninterested in the phenomenon, secure in his Christian evangelical faith and convinced that his patriotic rhetoric was coherent with his religious convictions. In an interview with *Christianity Today* on November 12, 2001, religion sociologist Peter Berger said that Bush had not founded a new civil religion but had expanded its recognition and the inclusion of other religions, such as Islam and the east and south Asian religions. Consequently he had demonstrated an extraordinary ability in promoting pluralism, particularly if we consider what happened to the American Japanese after Pearl Harbor.[65]

Whatever Bush's personal feelings towards civil religion were, he contributed greatly to its rebirth after September 11, carrying out the task of American religion's *Pontifex Maximus* with greater commitment than any of his predecessors. He used the whole set of American myths, from the myth of the chosen people blessed by God to the myth of the virtuous empire and that of manifest destiny. All were re-proposed by Bush in his war theology. At the same time, in his ecumenical manner Bush renewed the syncretism of civil religion, that is, its tendency to combine and cohabit with other religions in the name of a generic God, constantly evoked and invoked in "God Bless America" by the Americans, regardless of their personal religious confessions. However, the most important aspect of civil religion, as it was reformulated in Bush's theology, was the accentuated sacralization of America, which embodied, better than any other nation in the world, the universal values of liberty, endowed by God to all men. For this reason, according to Bush, it was America's duty to spread these values worldwide and fight their enemies even if that meant resorting to a preventive war. According to Mark Silk, religion historian, Bush's speech in Washington National Cathedral, given two days after the terrorist attacks, was a typical example of civil religion.[66] By reconfirming the sacredness of America as God's democracy, Bush was able to justify morally and legally the preventive war against the regime of Saddam Hussein. Even after the justifications founded on the presumed existence of mass-destruction weapons in Iraq and on the assumption that Saddam was linked to Osama bin Laden were revealed to be groundless, Bush maintained that the war on terror was the continuation of the American mission to spread the liberty endowed by God throughout the world, not only to Americans, but to all of humanity. In so doing, Bush used the traditional myths of American religion to describe his version of a "just war," following criteria that were totally different from the Christian concepts that both Protestants and Catholics invoked to contrast the preventive war against Iraq, thought to be neither legitimate nor moral. This reiterated the dispute between nationalism and Christianity, typical of all conflicts where Caesar's arguments clashed with those of Christ. However, in the case of the preventive war, this dispute became more dramatic because the president was a Christian who had declared that his faith was the inspiration for his politics, and who continued to invoke God to give a universal and moral dimension to the new doctrine of the "war on terror."

This doctrine played an important role in the development of Bush's civil religion, resulting in what was called "messianic militarism,"[67] symbolically condensed in his double presidential function as *Pontifex Maximus* of American religion and commander in chief of the nation at war, *Pontifex et Imperator*. It is well known that the model Bush openly declared to be inspired by after September 11, as commander in chief of the nation, was Winston Churchill. However, in the history of America there have been other bellicose presidents anxious to carry out the manifest destiny and civilizing mission of America, and Bush could have referred to them as they had more in common with him. There was, for example, James Polk who waged war with Mexico in 1846 to annex California,[68] or William McKinley who was perhaps more like Bush because of his religious devotion, which he expressed in politics. McKinley declared war on Spain in 1898 and conquered the Philippines, all in the name of God and for the glory of Christianity, after spending several nights in prayer asking for advice and guidance from the Almighty.[69]

In any case, the "messianic militarism" was a new aspect in Bush's civil religion, made more evident also by the symbolism linked to the places where he chose to give important speeches regarding the "war on terror." For example, the speech announcing the preventive war doctrine was given by Bush on June 1, 2002 to students at West Point, the military academy; the announcement that Saddam Hussein's regime had been toppled was made on May 1, 2003, three months into the war, on board the aircraft carrier *Abraham Lincoln,* where he arrived piloting the plane. The president was wearing a pilot's uniform, he was surrounded by soldiers, and in the background there was a banner which said "Mission Accomplished." In many other public appearances the president stood beside symbols of military power as if to constantly remind the Americans they were at war, that the war was endless, and that, in him, the Americans had a chief who was resolute, decided, devoted, and entirely dedicated to defending America, armed with his faith in God. Bush's military symbolism was clear-cut, observed *Time* in the May 5, 2003 issue, predicting that from then to the presidential elections in November 2004 Bush would mix military images with the rhetoric of tax cuts, so that the Americans would not forget that they were at war, abroad and at home, and also when he talked about domestic matters there would be the shadow of cannons behind him. Flanked by airplanes and cannons, Bush would tell voters that in this new world, with the threat of terrorism all around America, changing presidents would be dangerous.[70]

The importance of Bush's contribution to the rebirth of civil religion is demonstrated by the sudden intensification of observers' interest in his religion, precisely at a time when the war against Iraq was being prepared. It is significant that in the editor's note of a special issue on "Bush and God," published on March 10, 2003, the editor of *Newsweek* manifested surprise that the press up to then had not paid greater attention to the president's religious beliefs and, in fact, the research engine LexisNexis at that time recorded only 23 articles on the subject.[71] From that moment on to his reelection in 2005, religion was a constant topic in everything written about the president and his politics. It was the object of passionate defense and drastic criticism. Meanwhile, and as a result of the Bush presidency, there has been growing controversy in America over the relationship between religion and politics, in which civil religion has acquired new meaning and importance.

—— 8 ——

The Golden Calf

A Religious and Ecumenical Nationalism

The rebirth of civil religion after September 11 coincided with the rebirth of American messianic nationalism. The fact that these two phenomena coincided led people to think about American religion once again, associating it with the Bush administration's "new imperial strategy."[1]

The Americans are one of the world's most nationalist peoples, perhaps the most nationalist among Western countries, and certainly much more so than many European peoples, noted Mixin Pei, head of department at the Carnegie Endowment for International Peace, when analyzing the paradoxes of American nationalism in 2003. Surveys show that Americans are prouder of their nation than any other of the Western democracies. In 2000, 72 percent of Americans declared they were very proud of their nationality, compared with 49 percent of the British, 40 percent of the French, and 39 percent of the Italians. Yet, observed Mixin Pei, America does not sincerely consider itself nationalistic. For this reason, despite the strong nationalist feeling which permeates American society, the architects of American politics have considerable difficulty in understanding the power of nationalism in other societies.[2] The incomprehension is probably due to the difference between American nationalism and other nationalistic tendencies, particularly European ones. While these were based on their historic tradition as collective entities established by ethnic identity and originating from a remote past, American nationalism, which arose out of the War of Independence and resulted in the birth of the United States, is founded on an ecumenical creed. This means that American nationalism is based on a system of values and ideals, shared by a population which set itself up as an independent and sovereign state—not by claiming a centuries-old ethnic or historic identity, but by claiming a civic and political one stemming from a freely undersigned social covenant. This covenant transformed the cultural and ethnical identity of the English colonists into a new nation of free and equal citizens, a nation where anyone from anywhere in the world, regardless of ethnical group or religion, can be given access provided they pledge allegiance to the Constitution.[3] This is why the Americans do not consider themselves "nationalist" and why they speak of patriotism more than nationalism to describe their national ideology; and it is why they claim that, compared with other nationalist tendencies, theirs is a universal vocation that derives from the universality of the "American creed." This is also why, since the founding of the United States, the Americans have considered themselves a nation of "new men," regenerated in a new world, morally superior to the nations of an older, corrupt Europe and not tainted by the egoism, exclusiveness, and aggressiveness of European nationalism. Nevertheless, if nationalism is the modern ideology which establishes the superiority of the sovereign nation in its own state, and which elevates it as an eternal sacred entity to which the community of citizens owes devotion and faithfulness, the Americans have to be described as nationalist, albeit with their own historic and cultural peculiarities, defined as "Americanisms." One of these peculiarities is the religious element in American nationalism that has its roots in Puritanism and that today is still evident in its fundamental myths, from the myth of the chosen people to that of the "innocent nation" and of "manifest destiny." As the British Catholic writer Gilbert K. Chesterton commented in 1922, America is "a nation with the soul of a church," because it is the only nation in the world founded on a creed, expressed with dogmatic, theological clarity in the Declaration of Independence.[4]

Religiousness stemming from Protestantism has been a fundamental component of American nationalism for a long time.[5] However, over the years, thanks also to the assertion of the principle separating church and state, American nationalism has acquired its own autonomous religious significance, becoming independent of traditional religion and assuming the characteristics of a civil religion as defined by Robert N. Bellah.[6] This is true because it connects the American nation directly with God (not described according to any specific religious confession), and also because it confers sacredness on the American experience, its values, and institutions.

Even the traditional religions are symbolically loyal to the American civil religion when they display "Old Glory" in their places of worship and their believers invoke "God Bless America" and sing patriotic hymns.

This religious feature of American nationalism was highlighted in 1955 by sociologist Will Herberg, a professor of Judaic studies, who called attention to the existence of a "civic religion" that sanctified America by cohabiting with the principal biblical religions—Protestantism, Catholicism, and Judaism—but dominated them as the proper American national religion. Herberg cited a significant episode about this. In 1954 Ignazio Silone was asked what, in his opinion, was the most important date in world history, and the writer answered "December 25th of the year zero"; some time later about 30 eminent Americans were asked to list the

100 most important events in history: the first was the discovery of America in 1492, while the birth of Christ was 14th, next to the Wright brothers' first flight.[7] American civic religion, which Herberg referred to in different ways—"the American way of life," "Americanism," "American religion"—was founded on "an institutional and ideological pluralism" and on "the stable coexistence of three equi-legitimate religious communities grounded in common culture religion of America,"[8] but was strongly tempted to "identify the American cause with the cause of God."[9] According to Herberg, the identification of nation with religion was almost inevitable in the American situation, where religion was often considered a way to belong to a group. The rudest version of this identification was "a kind of national messianism which sees it as the vocation of America to bring the American way of life, compounded almost equally of democracy and free enterprise, to every corner of the globe," while in the "more mitigated versions, it sees God as the champion of America, endorsing American purposes, and sustaining American might." Herberg added that it was easy to pass unintentionally from the merging of religion and nation to the direct exploitation of religion for economic and political ends.[10]

In time, American religion became more ecumenical, welcoming new religions from Islam to the oriental faiths, under its dome dominated by "Old Glory." The height of this process came after September 11, when everywhere in the United States the faithful of all creeds united in prayer, singing "God Bless America."

President Bush participated directly in America's religious awakening after September 11, accentuating both the ecumenical and nationalistic aspects, thus celebrating the universality and eternity of American values:

> In America's ideal of freedom, the public interest depends on private character—on integrity, and tolerance toward others, and the rule of conscience in our own lives. Self-government relies, in the end, on the government of the self. That edifice of character is built in families, supported by communities with standards, and sustained in our national life by the truths of Sinai, the Sermon on the Mount, the words of the Koran, and the varied faiths of our people. Americans move forward in every generation by reaffirming all that is good and true that came before—ideals of justice and conduct that are the same yesterday, today, and forever.[11]

At the same time, Bush used his "war theology" to promote a review and update of the manifest destiny myth with a stronger missionary intimation, adapting it to his administration's new international strategy. After September 11 American religion and United States foreign policy influenced each other reciprocally: on the one hand American religion was unable to morally legitimize preventive war in the name of the missionary vocation of God's democracy. On the other hand, the Bush administration's foreign policy influenced the transformation of American religion, developing within it a militaristic missionary tendency which strengthened the alliance between the Religious Right, the Republican Party, and the neoconservatives, united in asserting the restoration of traditional values by bringing down the "wall of separation" between church and state, and strengthening America's uncontested supremacy in the world in the twenty-first century.

Imperial Theology

President Bush and the executive branch of his administration have always denied that America is an imperialist power, while the neoconservatives who inspired Bush's foreign policy have never hesitated to speak of an imperialist America. "If people want to say we're an imperial power, fine,"[12] William Kristol, chair of Project for a New American Century, a neoconservative group, stated in 1996. The neoconservatives not only did not hesitate to speak of an American empire, but they wanted America to be conscious that it was an imperialist power and to act accordingly, taking advantage of its predominant position and the supremacy it had gained with the end of the Soviet empire, and using any means to prevent the rise of a new world power or coalition of powers that could rival the United States. This, for the neoconservatives and the President, was not imperialism, but a civilizing mission to spread the values of God's democracy and the free market throughout the world. According to historian Anatol Lieven, like the European imperialists of the past, many Americans really believe that the interests and ambitions of America coincide with "good," civilization, progress, and the interests of humanity in general.[13] However, the populations of countries hostile towards the United States think differently, as do most of the populations of many allied countries. They have seen in the Bush administration's unilateral, warlike policy the expression of an "arrogant empire,"[14] which also claims that America is morally legitimized by divine mission to wage preventive warfare in the interest and good of humanity.

"Who would deny that America is an imperial power," asked James Chace in 2002. The question posed by the international relations expert evoked a similar one asked by Arthur Schlesinger Jr. more than a decade earlier.[15] Chace thought it was extremely appropriate to describe a world power like America as being imperialist, because it reacted to a terrorist attack by declaring, unilaterally, a preventive war against the regimes of other countries considered the incarnation of evil; because it has stationed its military might in many countries throughout the world; because it has spent more on armaments than the other 15 most industrialized countries put together, that is, a sum equal to 40 percent of the military expenses of the rest of the world; and because, at the same time, its productive activity has been the main driving force of the world economy. The imperialist logic that inspired and justified American expansion in the past and has continued to justify it since the terrorist attacks is the desire for absolute security, combined with the "messianic complex" of a nation which considers itself morally superior to other nations because it is the living legacy of good, the perfect example of virtue, and a model for all of humanity.[16] Among the Religious Right there is a certain apocalyptic tendency to interpret the current events from a millenarist viewpoint. Over 40 percent of the Americans believe that the biblical prophesies forecast the real occurrence of historical events; millions of Americans interpreted the September 11 attacks according to millenarist beliefs. As Paul Boyer recalled, already during the first Gulf War, Saddam Hussein was considered by many apocalyptic-minded Americans to be the Antichrist. And this apocalyptic image of the Iraqi tyrant reappeared during the second Gulf War, also seen as a further sign that the biblical prophesies were coming true.[17] The apocalyptic-minded members of the Religious Right agreed with President Bush's foreign policy, because they support military might (just as they support, along with Bush, the death penalty and the freedom to carry firearms), and they consider the United Nations a satanic instrument to impose a worldwide anti-American order. They also support Israel and the Israeli settlements in the Palestinian territories because, according to the apocalyptic prophesy, repossession of the Holy Land by the Jews announces the coming of the kingdom of Christ (and the Jews' conversion to Christianity) and, above all, because they believe that America was chosen by God to carry out the universal mission of spreading democracy. This is why Bush's war theology has received the consensus of a large majority of conservative Christians, traditionalist evangelicals, and fundamentalists. After September 11, wrote the evangelical journal *Christianity Today,* Bush's viewpoint of foreign policy has become coherent with and strongly tied to his Christian convictions, which coincide with those of other traditionalist Protestant, Catholic, and Jewish believers. The apocalyptic members of the Christian Right see the prelude to the coming of the kingdom of God on earth in the assertion of America's global supremacy.[18] Even if it is unlikely that similar apocalyptic viewpoints influenced the president's political choices, according to the liberal review *The American Prospect,* apocalyptic millenarianism is not unknown among the members of the Republican administration, "a coalition of religious and secular millenarians," who agree that America's common enemies must be fought, even if for different reasons:

> For many fundamentalists involved in Republican politics, the United Nations and other instruments of "world government" are literally satanic. For the almost entirely secular neoconservatives who provide most of the intellectual direction for this administration, the United Nations, the European Union, the International Criminal Court and kindred institutions are all obstacles to the emergence of unchallenged American hegemony. The neos don't view the coming American empire as God's kingdom, of course; they see it—better yet—as their own.[19]

Whatever the reasons, fundamentalists and neoconservatives are convinced that America should use its military might to impose its supremacy on the world. And the conservative evangelicals, who believe that America is a chosen nation, think the same. Being chosen, stated the Reverend Richard Cizik, vice president of the National Association of Evangelicals, "is not a privilege, but a duty. No one else in the world today has the moral might and military stature of the United States."[20]

Our God Is Not Mars

Even though millions of American Christians approved President Bush's war policy, much of the Christian clergy and many theologians voiced their disapproval. As happened after September 11, there were also many different, contrasting opinions as to what God would say about the war in Iraq. During a television debate on CNN to discuss the topic "What would Jesus say about the war in Iraq?" it was evident that there was a clear-cut divide between the Catholics and Protestants who opposed the war, and the evangelicals who supported it, although both sides defended their positions in the name of Christian teachings; the former quoted the Sermon on the Mount as a hymn to peace, the latter cited the evangelical references to the use of the sword to justify war.[21] Richard Land, eminent exponent of the Southern Baptist Convention, said, "As Christians, we must pray for our enemies, and we cannot seek personal vengeance." However, he also added: "Sadly, the resort to armed conflict is the price human beings must periodically pay for the right to live in a moral universe."[22] The Southern Baptist Convention was the only Protestant organization to approve the war in Iraq while all the other confessions, including the Catholics, condemned preventive war, judging it in contrast with the criteria of a "just war," according to the Christian doctrines of Saint Augustine and Saint Thomas, which considered war the "last resort" in the resolution of conflicts.[23] The principle exponents of the Methodist Church, to which the president and vice president belong, published a "prophetic epistle" on April 5, 2003 to persuade "our brother George W. Bush" to repent.[24] But the president did not listen to these voices and refused to receive a delegation of the dissident churches, who wanted to express their concern about the war, according to the March 10, 2003 issue of the *New York Times*.[25] The only religious exponent Bush agreed to receive was the emissary of Pope John Paul II, Cardinal Pio Laghi, who delivered a message against the war from the pope.[26] The message had no effect. As religion historian Sebastian Fath observed, "the Churches are preaching in the desert in Bush's America."[27]

For the first time since the Vietnam War, the American churches were openly and unanimously against a war. Right after September 11, numerous Catholic priests, Protestant ministers, theologians, and intellectuals manifested their reluctance to respond to terrorism with war. An ecumenical declaration, undersigned by almost 4,000 Christians, Jews, and Muslims was made public on September 14, 2001. While it approved punishment of the criminals who had carried out the terrorist attacks, it called for renouncing any kind of violent retaliation: "We must not allow this terror to drive us away from being the people God has called us to be."[28] The strongest opposition came from the Christian pacifists, headed by Stanley Hauerwas, who was proclaimed "theologian of the year" in 2001 by *Time*. In a dispute with the journal *First Things*, edited by the Catholic reverend and theologian Richard John Neuhaus, who approved of the war in Iraq, Hauerwas maintained that one could not be a Christian without being a pacifist.[29] Belief in Christ, said Catholic and Protestant theologians, was never compatible with violence and could never admit to the use of violence to react to violence, because that would mean there was no end to the spiral of hate, while Christianity is founded on love of your neighbor and forgiveness. Others condemned the religious rhetoric of a war against the "axis of evil" to "rid the world from evil," because it suggested a bellicose and Manichaean viewpoint and mirrored the outlook of Islamic terrorists. "A very good reason that it should be a last resort is that war drives everyone to and everything to extremes," commented *Theology Today*:

> If indeed we are engaged in a "war against terror," against diabolic forces, then all the world's weapons of mass destruction will never topple them—though the worst demons of our nature could someday commandeer them. According to the church's creed, victory in *that* war belongs only to Jesus Christ, who claimed initial skirmishes in his own wilderness, broke sin's back at Golgotha, and will put paid to all that is yet unredeemed under the aegis of Death.[30]

To the Christians who supported the war in the name of Jesus, singing "God Bless America", Donald B. Kraybill, professor of Anabaptist studies, objected that "As God's highest and final revelation, Jesus disclosed an uncommon kind of God":

> This God doesn't fight. Most gods relish conquest and military victory. This God is willing to suffer and die. This God contends that evil can be overcome by good. This is not a god of chariots and swords, but a God of stables and donkeys, who willingly suffers and dies on a cross. Suffering and forgiveness are his answer to evil.[31]

Anger and desire for revenge are human sentiments, understandable reactions to the inhumanity of violence, but precisely for this reason, observed the theologians who were against the war, Christians should know how to react by allowing Christ's teachings to prevail over natural instinct. According to Donald W. Shriver, president of the Union Theological Seminary of New York, September 11 was "a test to see how capable American Christians were to express moral judgment without resorting to the instinct of revenge, to demonstrate empathy for their enemies without approving of their crimes, and in the end to find a way to make peace with them by forgiving them."[32] Other religious exponents directly criticized President Bush's war theology and his use of religious rhetoric to legitimize his policy-making. It made no sense to declare that God was our ally in the war against terror, observed Andrew M. Greeley, priest and sociologist, referring to the president's affirmation that God was not neutral:

> You may be able to create a God who will lead us into battle, the God who will bless America on demand. But when you put that God in an American uniform, you'll find out that you have created him in our own image and likeness and that this God is not God at all, but a blasphemous idol.
>
> The real God is mysterious. If he weren't a mystery, he wouldn't be God. We cannot fit him into our categories, our plans, our programs, our ideologies, our wars of revenge. God is not the Roman god Mars. He is not a God of battle.[33]

Bush and God

One of the main topics for discussion during the war in Iraq, and also greatly highlighted during the 2004 presidential campaign, has been the president's religion. Many articles and television inquiries emphasizing the greatly diverging points of view on the subject have been devoted to the question of "Bush and God."[34] Many critics who targeted the mixing of nationalistic, militaristic, and messianic tendencies in the president's rhetoric to justify the war felt that the objective was really only to satisfy strategic interests and the energy problem. The president, like some of his predecessors, did not hesitate to use theological expressions to justify the empire, maintained Chalmers Johnson, author of a book on the costs and consequences of the American empire.[35] According to Lee Quinby, a professor of American studies, Bush's rhetoric consisted of a "Holy Trinity" of militarism, masculinity, and messianic zeal, and it followed the logic of apocalyptic thought, which has a religious basis but has been secularized in military style. Meanwhile, Chip Berlet, expert on Christian right-wing activist groups, maintained that Bush was beginning to think along the lines of the Christian evangelical activists' apocalyptic theory, because he seemed to share the viewpoint that the world was experiencing a gigantic struggle between good and evil which would end in a final clash. People with this concept often run dangerous risks because they think they are carrying out God's will. On the other hand, Frederick Clarkson, expert on the radical right, insisted that the president used such expressions only for political purposes, to address his activist base who think they are about to experience the biblical "end of time."[36]

These statements created doubts about the sincerity of Bush's religious convictions and led people to think that his continuous reference to God and paraphrasing of the Scriptures was only a political expedient to legitimize his actions. For many of his critics both in the United States and in Europe, Bush is not a true believer but a timeserver, who shrouded his cynical politics in religious rhetoric; for others, he is an ostentatiously pious person who, not being very intelligent, is a prisoner of the religious and fundamentalist right and maneuvered by the neoconservatives. Fath thinks that Bush's devoutness is sincere, but that it does not influence his politics very much because the president is a political predator, accustomed to the media, whose actions are more inspired by pragmatism than the Christian evangelicalism he professes and displays.[37] According to Federico Rampini, correspondent from the United States, Bush is "not a mystic or one possessed, but convinced that religion 'works' and that is enough for him to remain faithful to it."[38] According to Christopher Hitchens, on the other hand, the president is not a fanatic or a person who uses religious rhetoric only as a cynical tactic. He considers his religion a confirmation or an encouragement. He does not think he is a prophet. He prefers being a fatalist, saying that everything is in God's hands.[39] In turn, Bill Keller, editorialist for the *New York Times,* says that Bush is not a religious zealot, a fundamentalist, a timeserver, but a believer whose devoutness gives him self-confidence and comforts him that his actions are correct, although it is difficult to assess how and how much of his religion influences his policy-making.[40]

During the war in Iraq the prevailing opinion among the president's critics has been that Bush's devoutness is sincere, but this has led many to consider it dangerous, because it gives him the "blinding certainty" that his choices are in accordance with God's will and the mission that Providence has entrusted to the American people.[41] According to Ron Suskind, author of a book on the White House under Bush, the conviction that he is always instinctively in the right and on God's side has made the president indifferent to any doubt, annoyed by any criticism, and hostile towards dissent.[42] Carl Mirra, professor of American studies, does not blame the president for revitalizing the myth of the chosen people, because in doing so he is acting like a parent who assures his children that they will triumph because God protects and favors them; instead, what is disturbing in Bush, according to Mirra, is the president's personal conviction that the war on terror is a sign of his mission and the destiny of the nation, and that he is like a modern Moses who must shoulder the task of leading oppressed populations to freedom.[43] Presbyterian Reverend Fritz Ritsch has defined Bush's rhetoric as a fanatical form of nationalism baptized using Christian words.[44] Very severe criticism has also come from the supporters of the separation between state and church. They criticize the president's religious rhetoric as well as his legislation in favor of federal aid for religious charitable organizations. Welton Gaddy, president of the liberal organization Interfaith Alliance, observed that very often Bush seemed to be serving the nation as its religious head rather than its political chief.[45]

> The President of the United States is the political leader of the nation, not its religious leader. Just as religion should not be a test for any political candidate for public office, religion should not be a tool of any political leader in a public office. In no way should the President of the United States politicize religion, or by the use of religious language from one particular religious tradition, alienate citizens from other traditions or no tradition.[46]

The use of religious expressions by the president "to buttress his ongoing assault on the wall of separation between Church and State is inappropriate, appalling and dangerous," said Barry W. Lynn, director of Americans United for Separation of Church and State. Lynn described Bush's religious rhetoric as "uncivil religion" because it tends to make his Christian right-wing supporters believe that he has been sent by God to lead the nation.[47] In fact, many conservative Christians saw Bush as a providential messenger, and so they approved his warmongering policies despite the obvious contradictions with the teachings of Jesus. When Saddam Hussein's regime was toppled, religion historian Randall Balmer said that Bush's popularity showed that despite all the rhetoric about America being a Christian nation, the Americans, including the evangelicals, had little tolerance for a foreign policy based on the principles of the New Testament.[48]

In the opinion of Martin Marty, minister and theologian, the problem of Bush's relationship with God is not his sincerity, but his obvious conviction that he is carrying out God's will.[49] That the president invokes the Almighty, added Kenneth L. Woodward, is not surprising, but the danger in invoking God for political or military purposes lies in the presumption that God is on our side.[50] Former senator and 1972 Democratic presidential candidate George McGovern speaks sarcastically of Bush's claim to act with divine consensus, saying "if God guided him into an invasion of Iraq, He sent a different message to the Pope, the Conference of Catholic Bishops, the National Council of Protestant Churches, and many distinguished rabbis—all of whom believe the invasion and bombardment of Iraq is against God's will":

> I most certainly do not see God at work in the slaughter and destruction now unfolding in Iraq or in the war plans now being developed for additional American invasions of other lands. The hand of the Devil? Perhaps. But how can I suggest that a fellow Methodist with a good Methodist wife is getting guidance from the Devil?[51]

There was no sarcasm in what the lay philosopher Peter Singer had to say about Bush and his religion. He thought the president's religious convictions should be taken seriously because, as he wrote in 2004, not only was Bush the president of the United States, but he was its most eminent moralist.[52] Singer accused Bush of having violated the principle of the separation of church and state, using the presidency as an ideological and partisan-political means to further the Christian Right, and to consolidate the Republican Party's strength by implementing policies that contrasted with his professed Christian principles.[53] From the presidential pulpit Bush spoke of morality and not only politics; he expressed his opinion on ethical and religious matters; he discussed God and religious beliefs with foreign heads of state; he continuously repeated that his political diary was inspired by his religious faith and by a clear understanding of the distinction between good and evil—therefore, observed the philosopher, it was perfectly legitimate to judge the president's actions according to the religious and ethical principles that he himself professed. Following an analysis of his internal and foreign policies, Singer reached the conclusion that, in the light of Christian principles, such policies were a "conspicuous failure."[54]

A year later, the Reverend Jim Wallis came to the same conclusions. Wallis, one of the main exponents of liberal Protestant evangelicalism, has perhaps been President Bush's principal antagonist in the field of religion. He is a Baptist church minister, preacher, professor, journalist, writer, and founder of the organization Sojourners, which is involved in promoting social justice, spiritual rebirth, and peace in the world; and he not only preaches, he also practices his religious convictions with social commitment. Wallis has lived in poor, violent districts; he has promoted initiatives to fight poverty and social injustice, and in 30 years of civil battles he has been put in jail some 20 times. His criticism of the Bush administration's internal and foreign policies can be found in his book *God's Politics,* published at the beginning of 2005.[55] It received widespread consensus, if we consider that the book, which is a long-winded tome, was at the top of the *New York Times* bestseller list for weeks, while at the same time the author was meeting with crowds of readers all over the United States. According to Wallis, Bush's internal and foreign policies were the opposite of authentic politics blessed by God, which should try to remedy social injustice, help the poor, protect the environment, and promote international relations to achieve peace without resorting to war, whereas Bush's politics have mainly benefited the rich, increased the number of poor, contributed to the devastation of the environment, jeopardized the search for peace—and he entered into a preventive war whose outcome was unpredictable, isolating America in an increasingly hostile world where even its traditional allies distanced themselves. Wallis felt that the most dangerous aspect of Bush's religion was the religious legitimization of the new imperial policy because the president was convinced that he was making the right choices, thanks to his faith in God. Wallis did not doubt the president's religious sincerity, but he considered his theology a bad theology, because by claiming that America had the divine task of liberating the world of evil, he confused the nation, the Church, and God, and he undertook actions that clearly contrasted with Christian theology. Among the worst consequences of Bush's "imperial theology" was not only the preventive war, but also the torturing of Iraqi prisoners by American soldiers in the Abu Ghraib prison, revealed in 2004 when photos of the sadist scenes were published. The practice of torture on the part of American soldiers during the war in Iraq, observed Wallis, posed serious theological queries, particularly when the commander in chief of this war speaks so often of his Christian beliefs. In fact, Christian theology teaches that brutality is the "predictable consequence of domination, the inevitable result of empire, and an enduring part of the cycle of violence." The president was directly implicated in what happened at Abu Ghraib because, wrote Wallis, when the White House promulgates "an official theology of a righteous empire in which 'they' are evil and 'we' are good," this "contributes to an atmosphere that makes abuse more likely." Thus, the "theology of empire" generates the "theology of torture."[56] This brought the nature and function of American civil religion under discussion once again.

A Double-Edged Sword

The religious matrix of American nationalism, claimed by Bush, comes from the merger of Christianity with patriotism, which to varying degrees is still largely present in the political culture of the United States, in both the left and the right. The trials the American people experienced and the building of their nation have been equally influential in creating a theology with typically American characteristics.[57] These twofold characteristics in the symbiosis between religion and politics in the United States—which can be summarized according to the formula used in 1937 by the theologian H. Richard Niebuhr, "the Kingdom of God in America"[58]—helps us to better understand the renewed interest of academics and the current affairs press in civil religion after September 11. Today civil religion is widely acknowledged both as an existing religious phenomenon, written up in manuals and encyclopedias devoted to religion in the United States,[59] and as an important aspect of American politics even before September 11.[60] However, American followers of the Christian faiths (that is, the creed of the majority of the population and also the president's) have contrasting opinions relative to civil religion. Some accept it because they take it to be a form of patriotism inspired by Christian teachings, useful to increase sensibility towards the common good, and therefore they also accepted favorably the revival of national sentiment after September 11. They felt it had contributed to invigorating the fusion between religion and politics, symbolically represented by the widespread presence of "Old Glory" in churches and at religious services. After the terrorist attack *Christianity Today* wrote that the time had come to put the American flag back in the churches. The publication recalled that the flag had been removed from churches, both metaphorically and physically, after Vietnam and the Watergate scandal to protest the appalling use of civil religion made by government leaders. But after September 11 it thought the time had come for the churches "to recommit themselves to our nation and to its highest purpose." This meant, the publication added, that the American churches "should not hesitate to celebrate our fundamental political values. We should prepare the occasional sermon and Sunday-school class that shows the connection between theological and political liberty. We should sing the occasional hymn asking God's blessing on our nation. We should honor members of the armed services, and recognize members who work in the judicial system, politics, or law enforcement—callings that attempt to pursue real justice in the real world," suggesting "that the era of cynicism and despair regarding the American experiment is over. We should once again plant 'the flag'—the national pursuit of liberty and justice for all—in the midst of our churches' life and mission."[61] When commenting on Bush's speech to the nation on September 20, 2001, the publication stated that civil religion was not a threat to the highest levels of national existence, because the president had not used religious expressions to present his topics. However, several readers contested the statement that civil religion was not dangerous, objecting that the description of the war on terror as a war on evil had been expressed by the president "through themes and symbols common to most religions," so as to legitimize the government's actions.[62]

Actually the reawakening of civil religion after September 11 posed serious theological and moral problems, as well as political ones, particularly in the new version proposed in President Bush's war theology. The religious consciences of Christian Americans deplored the continuous reference by Bush, and by many members of his administration, to their devoutness in order to legitimize their policies, accusing them of transforming, in this way, a universal religion based on love and peace into a national religion to justify an act of war. Thus they demonstrated a precise aversion to civil religion, judging it incompatible with Christianity. This last attitude was not brought on only by the president's policies. In fact, diffidence and hostility towards civil religion had been apparent from the beginning when the term was coined to describe the peculiar American phenomenon whereby religion and politics are entwined. And this led, in the course of history, to the tendency to confer an air of sacredness on the American nation, its institutions, its symbols, and its politics, by means of the myth of the chosen people, blessed by God.

In 1966 the Democratic Senator J. William Fulbright, chairman of the Senate Committee on Foreign Relations and decidedly against the war in Vietnam, published a book *The Arrogance of Power,*[63] in which he warned the American nation not to be seduced by the myth of mission and the sense of almightiness; not to believe that "its power is a sign of God's favor" or proof that God has assigned the United States the special task of making other nations richer, happier, and wiser, that is, remaking them according to its own shining image: "Power confuses itself with virtue and tends also to take itself for omnipotence." Infatuated by an exaggerated sense of power and an imaginary sense of mission, Fulbright added, a nation could easily be convinced that it has the means and duty to perform God's work. However, it is precisely this type of infatuation which generates an arrogant and disastrous imperialist policy, observed the senator, recalling examples from past empires, starting from ancient times to Hitler.[64]

Warnings against the sacralization of America became more insistent during the debate over civil religion, particularly when Nixon was president in the early 1970s. As we have seen, Nixon strongly encouraged the celebration of American religion, which many of his adversaries considered nothing other than a political expedient or some form of nationalist worship. Even Bellah had to defend himself from being accused of promoting an idolatrous cult of the nation. In 1970 he confirmed his idea that civil religion should not be taken as a way for the nation to praise itself, but rather as the subordination of the nation to the ethical principles that transcend it and upon which it shall be judged.[65] The sociologist maintained that since civil religion was an inevitable fact, because every nation and every population reaches some form of religious self-representation, it was just as well to accept the fact that it exists, and to try to understand the criticism moved by civil religion so as to prevent the nation from being turned into an idol. In 1974 the Catholic theologian Michael Novak wrote that civil religion does not prescribe worship of the American nation and clearly states that America has not taken the place of God, but the tendency to worship the nation persists naturally, despite this prohibition.[66] The Protestant theologian Martin Marty observed that civil religion may have positive or negative effects depending on whether it has a "prophetic" function, in other words, if it criticizes the nation's morality when it deviates from its ethical principles and duties, urging it to correct itself and behave properly, or a "priestly" role, exalting the nation, glorifying it as a model of innocence, virtue, and rectitude for humanity.[67] Other experts have considered civil religion a way to legitimize American democracy, which assumes different aspects depending on political trends. Sociologist Robert Wuthnow made a distinction between "liberal" civil religion and "conservative" civil religion.[68]

Others have considered it a double-edged sword which can be favorable or damaging depending on the causes it supports. In fact, in the history of the United States, civil religion has been interpreted in different ways to support contrasting causes: to defend slavery or call for its abolition; to promote civil rights or deny them; to legitimize war or condemn it; to support the separation of church and state or encourage their cooperation; to glorify America or admonish it; to be tolerant and ecumenical or intolerant and selective. The most tragic collective occurrence experienced by America was the Civil War. It was fought by United States citizens who read the same Bible but interpreted it differently, and who also conceived of and practiced civil religion differently.[69]

In February 2002 the Pew Forum on Religion and Public Life organized a meeting on the reawakening of civil religion. At the meeting the Christian participants put forward their different points of view on the topic, arguments that had already been debated in previous situations. However, the non-Christian participants voiced opinions that constituted a real novelty.[70] For them, civil religion was a disturbing problem, both because of its Christian matrix and, as one Islamic participant said, because it tended to encourage a religious ecumenism which diluted one's specific religious beliefs, turning them into generic patriotic devoutness. This same devoutness was evident in the numerous interreligious ceremonies held after September 11 where participants, waving "Old Glory," sang patriotic anthems and "God Bless America." Moreover, said a Sikh participant, this civil religion is founded mainly on a tradition created by white, Christian Americans. Christian African-Americans or Americans who believe in other religions could refuse it and yet feel they are equally good, loyal, patriotic citizens, but they run the risk of being considered *un-American*. This epithet was used in the past by white Americans and Protestant "nativists" who organized xenophobic crusades against Catholic and Jewish immigrants.[71]

In the wake of a distinction between two types of civil religion, the theologian Robert Jewett and the philosopher John Schelton Lawrence suggested differentiating the two traditions: the first, where they place President Bush, they called "zealous nationalism," which claims it shall redeem the world by destroying its enemies; it expresses itself through the myth of a conspiracy of wicked spirits, the demonization of the enemy, mystical violence, obsession with victory, and the cult of national symbols. The second tradition, called "prophetic realism," avoids taking an outright innocent and unselfish stand, and it tries to redeem the world through coexistence and an impartial justice which does not claim a privileged role for any single nation, as has been made evident throughout the history of America by the movements that have criticized the prevailing opinions.[72] Following the terrorist attacks the two different, conflicting interpretations of civil religion were once again under debate. This occurred, as professor of religion Diana Butler Bass commented in 2004, after a long period during which many observers and experts thought the "idea of a civic faith—the belief in some transcendent dimension of American identity and its destiny" was "untenable in the secular and pluralistic United States."[73] Instead, from September 11 on, "civil religion reemerged as part of the nation's social fabric," with its original ambiguity: "Will America's emerging civil religion be priestly or prophetic? Militant or realistic? Exclusive or ecumenical? These are the choices America's faith communities must make—and they are profoundly important because these choices will determine how we understand justice, peace-making, reconciliation, community, and America's sense of global vocation."[74]

Among those who considered civil religion favorably, yet without hiding its ambiguities, was historian Barry Hankins,[75] who wrote in 2004 that, over the course of time, American religion had become more and more tolerant and inclusive while the nation became more pluralistic, to the extent that it was a generic religion which spoke of God and providence in such vague terms that everyone except atheists could be included. Also Robert Benne gave a positive assessment of civil religion, however considering it a double-edged weapon. An article of his published in April 2005 in the *Journal of Lutheran Ethics* sparked a debate between contrasting opinions which, nevertheless, confirmed the importance that civil religion continues to have for those who consider it a feature of American society, one to be preserved in its best manifestation, that is, in rallying the American nation around its fundamental values.[76] Other experts, for instance, Michael E. Bailey and Kristen Lindholm, were more skeptical. They examined the presidential rhetoric in his inaugural speeches and published their conclusions in an essay in 2003. They found that the United States' growing economic, political, and military might had caused American civil religion to gradually abandon its modest, prudent, realistic position and sense of perspective—which had characterized civil religion when the American democracy was considered a temporary experiment, subject to failure, and for this reason continually subject to God's judgment—to assume one of proud satisfaction and self-glorification as God's democracy, constantly protected and blessed by Providence. A new civil religion emerged from this transformation. It deifies America and is absolute in predicting that an inevitably glorious future is awaiting. It has blind faith in its own unlimited power over the world, but has lost the sense of reality and limitation which had animated civil religion initially. According to these two experts, therefore, the new civil religion is dangerous for a good political situation because it exalts and sacralizes an abstract, homogeneous American identity, whereas the real Americans have a multi-faceted variety of identities. It threatens to foster an undifferentiated view of life which discourages differences of opinion, social pluralism, and the recognition of specific responsibilities which lie with different roles.[77] The British political expert George Monbiot reached this same conclusion after the fall of the regime in Iraq:

> The United States is no longer just a nation. It is now a religion. Its soldiers have entered Iraq to liberate its people not only from their dictator, their oil and their sovereignty, but also from their darkness.... So American soldiers are no longer merely terrestrial combatants; they have become missionaries. They are no longer simply killing enemies; they are casting out demons.

Consequently, Monbiot added, the notion of the "chosen nation" gradually "has been conflated with another, still more dangerous idea. It is not just that the Americans are God's chosen people, America itself is now perceived as a divine project.... The United States of America no longer needs to call upon God; it is God, and those who go abroad to spread the light do so in the name of a celestial domain. The flag has become as sacred as the Bible, the name of the nation as holy as the name of God. The presidency is turning into a priest-hood. So those who question George Bush's foreign policy are no longer merely critics; they are blasphemers, or 'anti-American.'"[78]

For these reasons there are Christian Americans who believe that civil religion, however it is understood, is incompatible with Christianity. On many occasions they have openly condemned it as being a false religion which places Christianity at the service of politics, mixing Christian principles and patriotism in the symbols, the rhetoric, and the nation's public ceremonies.

Is This Perhaps Idolatry?

A public protest against civil religion was made in 1973 by Senator Mark Hatfield at the National Prayer Breakfast. Similar ceremonies, said the senator, represent the "real danger of misplaced allegiance, if not downright idolatry, to the extent that they fail to distinguish between the god of an American civil religion and the God who reveals Himself in the Holy Scriptures and in Jesus Christ."[79] In that same year various experts studying Christianity spoke out against civil religion and the confusion created between Christianity and patriotism by the nation's representatives. There is an almost inevitable tendency on the part of some government exponents to foster a kind of civil religion, commented Walfred Peterson, professor of political science, with regards to Senator Hatfield's statements:

> Why are political leaders so tempted? Some are seeking any means to gain support and national unity. They are willing to prostitute religion to political ends. But many leaders are not so crassly motivated. Often, state officials upon coming to high office are much impressed with the gravity of their new responsibilities. They feel inadequate. Therefore, they feel an urge to reach out beyond themselves—to religion—for a source of power and authority that will aid them.... All political leaders want to be sure that God is on their side. The best way to ensure that is to create, even though it is done unconsciously, a god that is defined in terms of national life, a god who unites the citizens, a god who urges those civil virtues needed by the state. This is very different from the God of the Bible, who calls out His people to a separated life. This is why the Christian in America must be on guard lest the state begin tampering with religion. Its tampering will end in false religion.[80]

In commenting on this judgment, historian W. Stanford Reid stated that the civil religion described by Peterson for America was the same against which the Christians fought when they refused to burn incense before the emperor's statue and against which German evangelicals resisted when Hitler formed his state-controlled German Church. "If we accept the present civil religion in North America," Reid added, "without protest we may soon find ourselves faced with the necessity of resisting, even to death, similar demands."[81] Such a dreadful outlook for resistance against civil religion was surely an exaggeration, but it expressed the state of mind of many American Christians alarmed by the pervasive influence of civil religion which, in the end, also spread to the churches, involving them in the rites, symbols, and myths that sacralized the American nation. In 1976, following the bicentennial celebration of the American revolution, a gaudy exhibition of American civil religion, Donald B. Kraybill published a harsh though well-documented criticism of the myths, symbols, and rites of American civil religion, which he defined as *a maverick religion* "which has blossomed into a marriage between politics and piety."[82] It was a combination of elements of American patriotism mixed with ingredients from the Judaic-Christian tradition "to form a national religion of patriotism,"[83] addressed to ordinary people and useful for both Republicans and Democrats. But civil religion, Kraybill added, "quickly becomes idolatrous nationalism with many public displays of piety. The nation itself emerges as the 'Golden Calf' and lures many away from the true object of worship," offering them a "watered-down, Americanized gospel with much form and little content."[84] According to Kraybill, American religion glorified the nation as made up of a chosen people, sanctified its institutions as if they were the realization of the kingdom of God, legitimized its conduct in the name of God even when said conduct was not at all religious or was clearly in contrast with Christian principles, and considered its successes and its might confirmation that, indeed, the nation did enjoy special divine protection in its fight to free the world of evil. "The Fourth of July celebrations in '76 proclaim to other nations that God and United States have enjoyed a triumphant victory over the forces of evil for 200 years."[85]

Twenty-five years later, in the face of a reawakening of civil religion, Kraybill renewed his condemnation, advising Christian Americans that they "must distinguish between the god of American civil religion and the God revealed in Jesus of Nazareth," and not to turn the invocation "God Bless America" into an idolatrous formula which justifies everything that the nation does, including war, because in this way "wars turn into 'holy' wars with tribal gods applauding on both sides of the trenches."[86]

The rebirth of civil religion, its renewed cult of the flag and of the invocation "God Bless America," were considered dangerous by Christian pacifists for those who really believed in Christ, because it "may elevate America above Christ."[87] Christian Americans were citizens of two worlds, the United States and the kingdom of God, and they were not to mix the two by identifying the United States with the kingdom of God—thus transforming America into an idol, "Old Glory" into a totem, and preventive war into a holy war against evil. For this reason some Christians in America refused to display "Old Glory" after September 11 when patriotism and devoutness were at their peak, even risking to seem unpatriotic. They hoped to discourage the reawakening of civil religion, viewed as idolatrous of the nation, and saw the flag as a symbol of militarism, nationalism, and imperialism, all incompatible with the fundamental pacifism of Christianity. "I believe it is never appropriate to have a U.S. flag at a worship service. The church is the body of Christ. The 'God-with-us' whom we know in Jesus Christ is a universal God," Reverend Ralph Detrick complained.[88] Theologians and ministers of different Christian faiths declared they were against displaying the national flag in places of worship, fearing that this could eclipse a much more important symbol, the cross, and transform the flag into an idolatrous object, considered a sin by the Christian Church.[89] "As North American Christians," stated author Valerie Weaver-Zercher, "we must disentangle ourselves from civil religion, the fusion of Christianity and patriotism, invoking God's name to bless our nation and all its actions"—"Civil religion helps politicians because it turns critique of government actions into sin, or sign of disrespect for God. We must always be cautious when Caesar quotes the Scriptures.... If God is on our side, we can justify just about anything."[90] Paul Keim, professor of biblical studies, judged the nation's political and religious leaders' incessant invocation to God for his blessing, a sacrilege.[91]

The main target of the controversy over civil religion was President Bush's use of religion in politics and his war theology. David Domke, communications sociologist, studied the communicative strategy of Bush and his administration. He defined Bush's civil religion as a form of "political fundamentalism," which had exploited the emotional situation caused by the September 11 attacks to monopolize the political situation, imprinting it with religious conservatism and with a Manichaean view of reality. The aim was to obtain widespread approval of the Republican administration's internal and foreign policies as the only ones capable of defending the American nation's fundamental principles and interests. Any difference of opinion or dissent from Bush's decisions was considered unpatriotic, bowing to terrorism, and treacherous for the common good and moral health of America. According to Domke, "political fundamentalism" constituted a threat for American democracy because it was, by nature, intolerant and exclusive, claiming to identify the cause of a party and a religious group with the cause of God and America.[92]

Another pretext or target of the Christian argument against civil religion was Bush's imperialist theology, that Wallis considered more dangerous than the fundamentalism of Jerry Falwell and Pat Robertson. According to Wallis, "the real theological problem in America today is no longer the Religious Right but the nationalist religion of the Bush administration—one that confuses the identity of the nation with the Church, and God's purpose with the mission of the American empire," while it is considered a Christian's duty to continuously challenge any imperial power which threatens to border on paganism and substitute secular designs for those of God. Bush's imperial theology, Wallis also stated, "is more American civil religion than Christian faith...To confuse the role of God with that of the American nation, as George Bush seems to do, is a serious theological error that some might say borders on idolatry or blasphemy."[93] Much more drastic is the opinion of a Swiss theologian who says, "Bush's God is an idol and his theology, founded on the Holy Trinity, Nation, Family and God, is a totalitarian-type civil religion," because it claims it is the only true interpretation of politics inspired by religion, but it sacralizes the powerful American nation.[94]

Describing Bush's civil religion as being totalitarian is an exaggeration, and those who exclude any risk of totalitarianism in the United States are right.[95] However, the reference to totalitarianism—if it refers to one of its essential aspects, that is, the feature of an exclusive and intolerant political religion— could be useful in making some observations and drawing some conclusions as to the actual changes in American civil religion resulting from September 11, from Bush's war theology, and from the symbiosis between the Religious Right and the Republican Party. The tragically new and extraordinary situation the Americans found themselves in after September 11 induced the Republican Party, under the leadership of Bush and with strong backing from the Religious Right, to carry out an experiment by transforming American civil religion into American-style political religion. The aim was to become the one and only party, made up of "good, religious, patriotic Americans," which would guarantee the Republican Party the exclusive privilege of being God's party.

The study of God's democracy in an age of empire and terror draws to an end taking into consideration this last aspect. In the last chapter we postulate an over-all interpretation of the events we have described. Meanwhile, the phenomenon that originated this study, the reawakening of American civil religion after September 11, persists and will probably continue to last, in ways and forms that are hard for historians to foresee.

——— 9 ———

A Political Religion, American Style?

As we have seen in the previous chapters, many of Bush's supporters, as well as his critics, considered his religious rhetoric an expression of American civil religion, particularly after the attack on Iraq, but they have voiced different opinions as to how much the Religious Right has influenced the new version of American religion formulated by the president. For example, Carl Cannon defended Bush, accused of favoring the conservative evangelicals or fundamentalists, by drawing attention to the fact that his references to religion were generic because when he mentioned God, he did so in a general sense using neutral paraphrases that lie within the realm of American civil religion.[1] Welton Gaddy, however, was of a different opinion. He maintained that there was a difference between American civil religion and Bush's use of religious expressions derived from a specific Christian evangelical concept.[2]

Even after the fall of Saddam Hussein's regime and up to the reelection of Bush, the president's devoutness and, in general, religion, politics, and civil religion continued to be topics for discussion. During that period, interest in civil religion was augmented not only by the debate over the role of religion in politics, but also by the identity crisis that permeated American society, owing to the divisions created by the president's internal and foreign policies.

Following the fall of the regime in Iraq, the nationwide patriotism sparked by September 11 faded, and during the subsequent two years America appeared to be torn by internal divisions, split into two. Meanwhile, after the illusion of a quick victory, the consequences of the war in Iraq began to affect the president's popularity, which fell drastically—causing, at the same time, a growing hostility towards the United States not only in Muslim countries but also in the Western world. Consensus fell in America to its lowest since September 11, dropping from 71 percent in April 2003, when the toppling of Saddam Hussein was still considered a brilliant victory, to 52 percent the following September and 33 percent in

March 2006.[3] The day after the September 11 attacks, the French newspaper *Le Monde* headlined the front page "We Are All Americans," expressing the world's true feelings of collective solidarity with the American people. Even such hostile regimes as Iran announced as much. Two years later this global solidarity had disappeared and all because of the preventive war against the regime of Saddam Hussein:

> In the two years since Sept. 11, 2001, the view of the United States as a victim of terrorism that deserved the world's sympathy and support has given way to a widespread vision of America as an imperial power that has defied world opinion through unjustified and unilateral use of military force.[4]

The European weekly the *Economist,* known to be friendly towards the Bush administration, when commenting on the second anniversary of September 11 wrote that it makes no sense to talk, as some Americans do, of "pressuring other Muslim countries to adopt democracy. September 11 was not a license to try to impose American choices on everyone else. To do that would risk intensifying the very conflict that the terrorists presumably hoped to provoke on the murderous day two long years ago."[5]

Two years after the terrorist attack on America, anti-Americanism was growing everywhere in the world. According to a survey by the Pew Research Center at the end of 2003, 53 percent of the Europeans placed the United States with Iran and North Korea as countries that threatened world peace, while 59 percent indicated Israel and 21 percent Russia.[6] The number of Europeans who viewed America positively was clearly declining, not only in the countries that had opposed the war in Iraq, that is, France and Germany, but also in the countries whose governments had supported it: England, Spain, and Italy. The Europeans detected a growing moral, cultural, and political divide between the United States and Europe. One of the main causes was the increasingly evident difference between a secular Europe and a religious America.[7] During a meeting organized by the Pew Center on July 10, 2003 to discuss relations between Europe and the United States, the moderator, syndicated columnist E. J. Dionne Jr., opened the discussion reading a quotation from François Heisbourg, director of the Foundation for Strategic Research, a Paris think tank, which efficaciously summarized the situation:

> The biblical references in politics, the division of the world between good and evil, these are things that we simply don't get. In a number of areas, it seems to me that we are no longer part of the same civilization. You have a fairly religious society on one hand and generally secular societies on the other, operating with different references. What would unite us does not seem to be in the forefront.[8]

Less than a year later, on April 7, 2004 the *International Herald Tribune* published an article by the German writer Peter Schneider, titled: "Separated by Civilization: Trans-Atlantic Impasse."[9]

However, surveys conducted through 2004 showed that the Europeans who were hostile towards the United States made a distinction between a predominant aversion to President Bush and their liking of the American people. This distinction virtually disappeared when Bush was reelected because, as Dominique Moisi, French professor of international studies, said on January 21, 2005, it was no longer possible for the Europeans to consider the Americans alien to their president's policy-making.[10]

While many lay Europeans feared a clash between the two Western civilizations, a religious America and a secular Europe, in the United States there were those who feared a "clash of civilization" within American society—where the Bush administration, instead of working as promised to mend the divisions and reunite the nation, had deliberately intensified the "culture war" against secular America to supposedly restore the traditional values supported by the Religious Right. In 2004, Samuel P. Huntington, author of a book on the clash of civilizations, published *Who Are We?*—a book full of pessimistic forecasts regarding America's national identity crisis. The book is centered on the problem of religion and the plight of the original "American creed," which was derived from the Anglo-Protestant culture and was now facing a religious, ethnical, and cultural challenge in a more and more varied and heterogeneous society.[11] The presidency under Bush proved that religion still played a central role in American politics and that America, despite its continuously changing society, was basically a Christian nation. Meanwhile, powerful external forces augmented the relevance of religion to the American identity and the probability that the Americans would continue to consider themselves a religious, Christian population. Huntington proposed defense of an Anglo-Puritan religious tradition as the cure for the nation's identity crisis: "The alternative to cosmopolitanism and imperialism is nationalism devoted to the preservation and enhancement of those qualities that have defined America since its foundation."[12] From this point of view also American civil religion was granted a therapeutic function. Huntington defined it as "Christianity without Christ."[13]

Once again, God and religion were in the limelight during the 2004 presidential campaign, because the candidates' religious faiths were considered topics of great importance. In part this was due to the fact that John F. Kerry was a Catholic, the third major-party Catholic nominee for president in American history, but he was not supported by the Catholic hierarchy because of his pro-choice stand on abortion. Bush had an advantage in the confrontation on religion, as he had successfully and patiently built up an electoral strategy in the four years of his first term as president. Therefore, he managed to obtain the vote of millions of Christian evangelicals who had not participated in the previous election, thus favoring the identification of the Republican Party with the Religious Right and intensifying the cultural war within American society. The Republican Party's propaganda depicted the Democrats as liberal enemies of religion in public life, favorable towards abortion and matrimony between homosexuals, promoters of a hedonistic, permissive culture, and, above all, morally weak and unable to defend the nation in the era of terrorism or fight in the war against terror. When the Democrats criticized Bush's policies, they were described as not very patriotic or even anti-American, as if they had opened the gateway to America for the terrorists. Bush's claim that his was true patriotism, and that he represented America's true moral and religious values, was the most obvious sign of his attempt to monopolize American religion. The strategy adopted to obtain votes from the Religious Right was successful and led to the reelection of Bush with 51 percent, compared to 48 percent for the Democratic candidate. The decisive factors were over three million new Republican voters, mostly traditionalist Christians, and the convergence on the Republican candidate of the majority of conservative white evangelicals and Catholics, in addition to the Hispanic Catholics.

What emerged from the November 2, 2004 election was a nation divided down the middle between Republicans and Democrats and one that was much more focused on ideology and religion. "Two nations under God," commented *New York Times* columnist Thomas L. Friedman, the day after the election. However, as Michael Sandel, a political theorist, stated, there was an important difference, and that was that the Democrats had ceded their domination over the moral and spiritual sources of American politics to the Republicans.[14] Among the reasons for choosing a candidate, the voters had given top priority to "moral values." Bush's reelection was hailed by his supporters as the victory of a religious and traditionalist America over a secular and liberal nation in the "culture war." This war was fought by the Religious Right and the Republican Party to assert their own principles and values in society and politics as those of the religious and patriotic "true American," who was fighting evil which, internally and externally, aimed at destroying God's democracy. This Manichaean simplification, typical of the fundamentalist mentality, was another evident sign that Bush and the Religious Right wanted to arrogate to themselves morality and patriotism, claiming to be the only ones embodying authentic American values. Such a claim was only an intensification of the origins of the Religious Right, which had developed and consolidated itself, albeit with ups and downs, during the last two decades.[15]

In 1992, Yale professor Harold Bloom wrote that American religion was becoming "post-Protestant," moving "towards the twenty-first century with unrestrained triumphalism, easily convertible into our political vagaries."[16] After examining the increasingly influential role of the conservative Protestant churches in the Republican Party, the political mobilization of the Religious Right, and American religion's triumphalism during the first Gulf War, Bloom concluded: "We are on the verge of being governed by a nationally established religion, an ultimate parody of the American religion" based on a "multiform alliance" between the conservative and traditionalist churches, "that will transform our nation by the year 2000, under the leadership of a Republican Party that since 1979 has become the barely secular version of the American Religion."[17]

With the arrival of George W. Bush in the White House in the year 2000 and his reelection in 2004, the above-mentioned forecast seemed about to take effect. This was also due to the awakening of civil religion and a revitalized sacralization of politics after September 11, which the Republican administration was clever enough to use in order to gain a predominant position over American religion so as to identify it with its own ideology and religious beliefs. In this way the Republican Party, with the help of neoconservatives and leaders of the Religious Right, was able to start transforming American civil religion so that it could considerably modify its ecumenical, tolerant, and inclusive nature to become a partisan, exclusive, and intolerant religion. In fact, Mark Silk observed, the rhetoric of civil religion "at least since the Civil War, mostly served to unify the country. While there have always been those prepared to turn it to partisan purposes, the American civil religion has meant to be inclusive, to unfurl a sacred banner above the political fray"; instead, during the last 25 years, American civil religion has been transformed into "an instrument for domestic political combat."[18] Evident in this change is the Republican Party's tendency to transform *civil religion,* intended as a sort of sacralization of politics that does not coincide with the ideology of any one party or movement, into a *political religion,* intended as the sacralization of politics by one party or movement, which arrogates the sole right to define good and evil according to its own ideology.[19] The original characteristics of this transformation are of great interest for those studying political religions, because American religion has its own peculiarities, as it is a civil religion deriving from a traditional one—that is, Protestant Christianity— but adapted to a growing religious pluralism. Therefore, it is entirely different from many European civil religions, which originated from secular political movements that were often anti-Christian. Furthermore, this transformation, if it ever occurs, would be a new experience in political religion, because previous political religions have been mainly the expression of totalitarian movements which have asserted themselves in single-party regimes, although in the past there have been some attempts in democratic regimes—for example, in France and the United States in the nineteenth century.[20] The institution of a political religion that controls a society where religious pluralism and individualism are fundamental pillars of its existence would be an unprecedented phenomenon that could not be analyzed using models of the past.

It is thought, however, that individualism and religious pluralism, together with a deeply-rooted tradition in liberal democracy, provide barriers capable of preventing domination over American religion by a single party or a religious movement that claims it possesses exclusive knowledge about good and evil. According to Alan Wolfe, an individualistic and pluralist religion is propitious for American democracy.[21] On the other hand, the vicissitudes marking President Bush's second term do not seem to favor the Republican Party's attempt to transform American civil religion into an "American-style" political religion, nor the Religious Right's ambitions to impose its principles and values in the name of a traditionalist, fundamentalist, bellicose Christianity that appears to be opposed to putting into practice the Beatitudes of the Sermon on the Mount.

President Bush's troubled second term seriously undermined the likelihood that an "American-style" political religion could actually come about. In 2005, the commemoration of the fourth anniversary of September 11 was overshadowed by the administration's disastrous show of incompetence in the wake of the devastation of New Orleans by Hurricane Katrina. During this natural disaster many Americans wondered where the president was and not where God was. In the spring of 2006, the president's popularity was at a historical low, declining even among the Republicans. In the meantime, the number of American soldiers who were dying in Iraq had almost reached the number of victims of September 11, and the repatriation of their bodies took place without any public ceremony, in an unreal silence. And the image of God's democracy was badly damaged by the pictures of the tortures practiced at Abu Ghraib, the massacre of civilians by the Marines at Haditha, and the conditions of the prisoners at Guantánamo. These events did not help raise the moral prestige of God's democracy, nor did they aid the president's aspirations to remodel America according to the principles and values of the Religious Right.

The defeat of the Republican Party in the November 2006 midterm election, establishing a Democratic majority in Congress, confirmed the declining popularity of George W. Bush. The 2006 election also decisively thwarted the Republican Party's attempt to monopolize American civil religion by transforming it into an American-style political religion. That is what happened during the 2004 presidential campaign, when the polarization around politics and religion resulted in the so-called "God gap" between truly religious Republicans, therefore, "true" Americans, and the less religious, therefore, "un-American" Democrats. President Bush's victory confirmed the decisive role played by the Religious Right in the reelection of a president who had made religion his banner.[22] The Democratic Party's success in the 2006 congressional election halted the Religious Right's march forward. In fact, although the Democrats still have difficulty making a breach among the most-religious Americans, the number of less-religious Americans among the voters for Republican candidates is not increasing. As both Mark Silk and John Green noted, "the growth in the votes of religiously unaffiliated voters for Democratic congressional candidates rose from 61 percent in 2002 to 70.9 percent in 2004 to 75.3 percent last year. Overall, the political bottom line for 2006 was that the Republicans had a bigger problem with less religious voters than the Democrats had with more religious ones—a sharp reversal of fortunes from 2004."[23]

For most Americans such important "issues" as abortion and same-sex marriages, while still determining the political choices of religious conservatives, have dropped to second place against problems such as the war in Iraq and the economic recession. For this reason the 2006 elections are considered by some observers a turning point, because they marked the beginning of the decline of the Religious Right's political supremacy. After 2006 there was no need to fear what Reverend Barry W. Lynn called an "assault on religious freedom" by the Religious Right.[24] At the same time, the threat of a new move forward by the fundamentalist hardliners of "Christian nationalism," as Michelle Goldberg defined them, seemed to have been averted.[25] Meanwhile, some of Bush's assistants who arrived in Washington to work out and implement a policy inspired by religion, in particular David Kuo, revealed that they were disappointed when they realized that religion was manipulated in the White House for political purposes that contradicted the teachings of Jesus.[26]

This does not mean that the importance of the religious factor in the American presidential campaign has decreased. Most Americans continue to declare that they prefer a president with strong religious convictions. They do not find it inappropriate for the candidates to manifest their religious faiths but deplore excessive religious rhetoric on the part of the candidates and declare they are against outright support of a candidate by the church. The religious factor has been widely treated by both parties during the primaries for the 2008 election.[27] All the candidates, both Republican and Democrat, up for nomination have manifested extensively their religious faiths. The Democratic candidates learned their lesson in the 2004 election, and in the 2008 primaries they have frequently mentioned their religious faiths so as to reach the evangelical voters. It is not possible in March 2008 to predict what role religion will play in the Americans' final decisions when choosing their new president. However, on the eve of the end of the Bush era, it is possible to make some considerations regarding American civil religion.

The success of the Democrats in 2006 demonstrated that many Americans were tired of the culture wars and polarization around politics and religion fomented by the Bush presidency. During a debate at the Pew Forum Faith Angle Conference in Key West, Florida (December 4, 2007), on the role to be played by the religious factor in the 2008 election, Michael Barone stated that, "Between 2004 and 2006 we moved from one period in politics to another, from a period of trench-warfare politics, in which we had two armies lined up in a culture war in the trenches, nobody deserting to the other line; the only question was how many people you could muster to go over the lines and capture that very narrow margin of contested territory that meant the difference between victory and defeat. That's the wonderful ambivalence that people have. They want to have candidates that are highly religious, and they want to hear about it somewhat but not too much." And E. J. Dionne added that the 2006 election "did close an era in American politics. Americans seemed tired of culture wars, tired of polarization around cultural issues, tired of the use of these issues as electoral cudgels. I think the culture wars and the religious wars exploit our discontents; the task of politics is to heal them. And I think right now there's a great hunger across religious denominations and across levels of political commitment for a politics of remedy to replace a politics of polarization."[28]

After decades of harsh divisions in American society, opposition to political and religious polarization has contributed to a redirection of American civil religion toward its traditional function of unification. "A soft civil religion is something our country desperately needs at a time of deep partisanship," declared Alan Wolfe.[29] The election in 2006 of the first Muslim American in Congress, the Democrat Keith Elisson, who was sworn in on the Koran, was perhaps a symbolically important sign that American religion was redirecting itself toward an inclusive pluralism, toward a "soft civil religion." The charisma of Barack Obama, who has called for the nation to unite in the common belief in the "American dream" attested to by his life as an African-American, has been considered a sign that there is an awakening of a "soft civil religion." "Mr. Obama is simply understandably making an emotional appeal to those yearnings. Politics is about policy, but it's also about giving people some kind of sense of participating in a common venture with their fellow citizens."[30] Mr. Obama is presenting himself as the heir of the civil rights movement with his appeal for unity to overcome religious divisions and political polarizations. According to Mark Silk, Obama "is running on America's civil religion and he needs to bring people together."[31]

At the end of the Bush era, an awakening of civil religion is desired by those who consider religion "a force for unity, not division, in the nation and the world," as Jon Meacham wrote.[32] But this can only occur, warns Gary Scott Smith, historian of the religions of the presidents, if differences and plurality are respected and the principle of the separation of church and state is preserved: "To participate effectively in contemporary politics, faith communities must . . . accept basic rules for the political game, such as not resorting to appeals to divine revelation to justify their position."[33]

It seems that the need to redirect civil religion toward its inclusive function is spurred by the changes taking place in the American religious landscape. Almost half (44 percent) of the Americans change their religious affiliations, 16 percent are religiously "unaffiliated," and there is a growing number of non-Christian Americans.[34] This situation might also influence the future of civil religion, according to Alan Wolfe, who, commenting on these data said:

> Americans have long viewed themselves as belonging to God's chosen country, charged by the Creator to fulfill his special providence.
>
> As the United States begins to resemble the rest of the world in the astonishing variety and volatility of its religious traditions, it will become increasingly difficult for leaders to rally around the flag by rallying around the faith. That may make some Americans, especially those who believe we once were, and should always be, a Christian country, unhappy. But it ought to make those who take pride in its diversity and tradition of religious freedom proud.[35]

The attempt to transform American civil religion into an "American-style" political religion, implemented by President Bush, was initially favored by the situation that followed the terrorist attack of September 11, 2001. In the era of empire and terror after September 11, the awakening of civil religion had enabled Bush to gain the consensus of most Americans, allowing him to appear as the charismatic chief capable of guiding the United States in the "war against terror." In the last years of his presidency the charisma has faded away, thwarting the idea of imposing a conservative Republican monopoly on American civil religion.

It is doubtful whether the attempt to transform American civil religion into an "American-style" political religion could ever be successful. But the very fact that an attempt has been made with such deliberate ostentation in the world's currently most-powerful democracy is a serious occurrence, one which leaves its mark and could be a seductive example for others to follow if the aim is to monopolize politics and religion in a democratic society.

It is not up to the historian to make prophesies. However, the study of American civil religion in the Bush era can be useful in making considerations about current or future occurrences of the sacralization of politics, attempted through the unprecedented practice of turning religion into politics or turning politics into religion. Religion does not consist only of values and transcendence, but, like politics, it is made of power and the desire for power. When religion and politics unite their forces in the exercise of power, sacralizing politics or politicizing religion, it is possible to foresee an era of uncertainty and insecurity for liberty and human dignity, both in the field of politics and in the field of religion.

Notes

Chapter 1

1. "America's World," *Economist,* October 23, 1999.

2. Cit. in J.S. Nye Jr., *Il paradosso del potere americano: Perché l'unica superpotenza non può più agire da sola,* transl. and ed. (Turin: Einaudi, 2002), 3.

3. See M. Hertsgaard, *The Eagle's Shadow: Why America Fascinates and Infuriates the World* (New York: Farrar, Strauss and Giroux, 2002).

4. See M.H. Hunt, *Ideology and U.S. Foreign Policy* (New Haven: Yale University Press, 1987); W.A. McDougall, *Promised Land, Crusader State: The American Encounter with the World Since 1776* (Boston: Houghton Mifflin, 1997); W.R. Mead, *Special Providence: American Foreign Policy and How It Changed the World* (New York: Knopf, 2001).

5. E.L. Tuveson, *Redeemer Nation: The Idea of America's Millennial Role* (Chicago: University of Chicago Press, 1968).

6. E.M. Burns, *The American Idea of Mission: Concepts of National Purpose and Destiny* (New Brunswick, NJ: Rutgers University Press, 1957).

7. A.K. Weinberg, *Manifest Destiny: A Study of Nationalist Expansionism in American History* (Baltimore: Johns Hopkins University Press, 1935).

8. C. Cherry, ed., *God's New Israel: Religious Interpretations of American Destiny* (Chapel Hill: University of North Carolina Press, 1998).

9. L.P. Ribuffo, "Religion and American Foreign Policy: History of a Complex Relationship," *The National Interest* 52 (1998): 36–51.

10. W. Martin, "With God on Their Side: Religion and U.S. Foreign Policy," in *Religion Returns to the Public Square: Faith and Policy in America,* eds. H. Heclo and W.M. McClay (Washington, DC: Woodrow Wilson Center Press, 2003), 327–59.

11. G. Prezzolini, *America in pantofole: Un impero senza imperialisti* (Florence: Vallecchi, 1950).

12. A.M. Schlesinger Jr., *I cicli della storia americana,* transl. and ed. (Pordenone: Tesi, 1991), 202.

13. F. Fukuyama, *La fine della storia e l'ultimo uomo,* transl. and ed. (Milan: Rizzoli, 1996).

14. S.P. Huntington, *Lo scontro delle civiltà e il nuovo ordine mondiale,* transl. and ed. (Milan: Garzanti, 2000).

15. T. Smith, *America's Mission: The United States and the Worldwide Struggle for Democracy in the Twentieth Century* (Princeton, NJ: Princeton University Press, 1994), 311ff.

16. *The 9/11 Report: The National Commission on Terrorist Attacks Upon the United States* (New York: St. Martin's Press, 2004), 486.

17. A. Frachon and D. Vernet, *L'Amérique messianique: Les guerres des néoconservateurs* (Paris: Seuil, 2004).

18. P. Boyer, *When Time Shall Be No More: Prophecy Belief in Modern American Culture* (Cambridge, MA: Harvard University Press, 1992), 338–39.

19. W.W. Dixon, *Visions of the Apocalypse: Spectacles of Destruction in American Cinema* (London: Wallflower Press, 2003).

20. See D. Wojcik, *The End of the World as We Know It: Faith, Fatalism, and Apocalypse in America* (New York: New York University Press, 1997), 8.

21. Boyer, *When Time Shall Be No More,* 339.

22. G. Wills, *Under God: Religion and American Politics* (New York: Simon and Schuster, 1990), 24.

23. Wojcik, *The End of the World as We Know It,* 212.

24. D. Fishburn, ed., "Introduction," in *The World in 2001,* (London: The Economist, 2000), 9.

25. M. Kondracke, "What Augurs after the Inauguration?" ibid., 57.

26. *The 9/11 Report,* 71–72.

27. See F.I. Greenstein, ed., *The George W. Bush Presidency: An Early Assessment* (Baltimore: Johns Hopkins University Press, 2003), 106.

28. See *The 9/11 Report,* 487.

29. "The Politics of Panic," *New York Times,* September 11, 2001.

30. See D.M. Rankin, "The Press, the Public, and the Two Presidencies of George W. Bush," in *Transformed by Crisis: The Presidency of George W. Bush and American Politics,* ed. J. Kraus, K.J. McMahon, and D.M. Rankin (New York: Palgrave, 2004), 52–71.

31. S.G. Stolberg, "Scientists Urge Bigger Supply of Stem Cells," *New York Times,* September 11, 2001.

32. T.M. Freiling, ed., *George W. Bush on God and Country* (Washington, DC: Allegiance Press, 2004), 17–24.

33. K. Zernike, "School Dress Codes vs. a Sea of Bare Flesh," *New York Times,* September 11, 2001.

34. J. Perlez, "Biden Opens Wide Critique of Bush Plan for a Shield," ibid.

35. I.H. Daalder and J.M. Lindsay, "Bush's Foreign Policy Revolution," in *The George W. Bush Presidency,* ed. Greenstein, 102.

36. Ibid., 105.

37. Ibid., 109.

38. J. Risen, "Reports Disagree on Fate of Anti-Taliban Rebel Chief," *New York Times,* September 11, 2001.

39. See *The 9/11 Report,* 251ff.

40. Ibid., 250–51.

41. "Tearing a Hole in the Skyline," *Newsweek,* September 24, 2001.

42. The picture of the "third tower" is by N. Gibbs, "Life on the Home Front," *Time,* October 1, 2001.

43. "Remains of a Day," ibid., September 9, 2002.

44. T. Pzszczynski, S. Solomon, and J. Greenberg, eds., *Terror in America: The Day Our World Changed* (Washington, DC: American Psychological Association, 2003), 4.

45. J. Kornbluth and J. Papin, eds., *Because We Are Americans: What We Discovered on September 11, 2001* (New York: Warner Books, 2001), 1–2.

46. J. Adler, "Ground Zero," *Newsweek,* September 24, 2001.

47. Gibbs, "Life on the Home Front."

48. C. McGuigan, "Requiem for an American Icon," *Newsweek,* September 24, 2001.

49. A. Calandro, "To Mourn, Reflect, and Hope," in *Beauty for Ashes: Spiritual Reflections on the Attack on America,* ed. J. Farina (New York: Crossroad Publishing Company, 2001), 251–52.

50. P. Ochs, "September 11 and the Children of Abraham," *The South Atlantic Quarterly,* no. 2 (2002): 391.

51. J.B. Freeman, "The American Republic, Past and Present," *The Chronicle of Higher Education,* September 28, 2001.

52. *The 9/11 Report,* lxxxi.

53. F. Zakaria, "The End of the End of History," *Newsweek,* September 24, 2001.

54. E.T. Linenthal, "Toward the 'New Normal,'" *The Chronicle of Higher Education,* September 28, 2001.

55. Cit. in J. Stein, "Nation on the Couch," *Time,* October 1, 2001.

56. K. Kelly, "After the Fall: Struggling for Emotional Balance after September 11," *U.S. News & World Report,* November 12, 2001.

57. G.Y. DeNelsky, "The Day the Psychology of America Changed Forever," *The National Psychologist,* November–December 2001, http://nationalpsychologist.com/archives.

58. G. Cowley, "After the Trauma," *Newsweek,* October 1, 2001.

59. See S. Body-Gendrot, *La société américaine après le 11 septembre* (Paris: Presses de Science Po, 2002), 18.

60. Cit. in R. Jewett, J.S. Lawrence, *Captain America and the Crusade against Evil: The Dilemma of Zealous Nationalism* (Grand Rapids, MI: William B. Eerdmans, 2003), 10.

61. Cit. ibid., 9.

62. W. Langewiesche, *American Ground,* transl. and ed. (Milan: Adelphi, 2003), 97.

63. G.W. Bush, Remarks by the President After Two Planes Crash into World Trade Center, September 11, 2001.

64. Id., Remarks by the President upon Arrival at Barksdale Air Force Base, September 11, 2001.

65. Id., Statement by the President in His Address to the Nation, September 11, 2001.

66. I shall mention only a few of the comments about, and the interpretations of, the events of September 11 and the "war on terror" and its effects—representative studies with different points of view: J.F. Hoge Jr. and G. Rose, eds., *How Did This Happen? Terrorism and the New War* (New York: Public Affairs, 2001); S. Talbott and N. Chanda, eds., *The Age of Terror: America and the World After September 11* (New York: Basic Books, 2001); R. Bernstein, *Out of the Blue: The Story of September 11, 2001 from Jihad to Ground Zero* (New York: Holt, 2002); R. Burbach and B. Clarke, eds., *September 11 and the U.S. War* (San Francisco: City Lights Books and Freedom Voices Press, 2002); C. Calhoun, P. Price, and A. Timmer, eds.,*Understanding September 11* (New York: The New Press, 2002); S. Hauerwas and F. Lentricchia, eds., *Dissent from the Homeland: Essays after September 11* (Durham, NC: Duke University Press, 2002; special issue of *The South*

Atlantic Quarterly, no. 2, 2002); E. Hershberg and K. W. Moore, eds., *Critical Views of September 11: Analysis from Around the World* (New York: The New Press, 2002); S. Brill, *After: How America Confronted the September 12 Era* (New York: Simon and Schuster, 2003); R. Falk, *The Great Terror War* (New York: Olive Branch Press, 2003); J. Meyerowitz, ed., *History and September 11th* (Philadelphia: Temple University Press, 2003).

Chapter 2

1. Cit. in Voltaire, J.-J. Rousseau, and I. Kant, *Sulla catastrofe: L'illuminismo e la filosofia del disastro,* introduction and ed. A. Tagliapietra (Milan: Bruno Mondadori, 2004), x.

2. Ibid., 3.

3. Ibid., 7.

4. C. Zaleski, "Faith and Doubt at Ground Zero," *The Christian Century,* December 18, 2002.

5. E. Hankiss, "Symbols of Destruction," *Social Science Research Council, After Sept. 11,* http://www.ssrc.org/sept11/essays/hankiss.htm.

6. E. Becker, *The Denial of Death* (New York: Free Press, 1973).

7. M. Marshall Clark, "The September 11, 2001, Oral History Narrative and Memory Project: A First Report," in *History and September 11th,* ed. J. Meyerowitz (Philadelphia: Temple University Press, 2003), 128.

8. K. Armstrong, "Seeing Things as They Really Are," in *Walking with God in a Fragile World,* eds. J. Langford and L. S. Rouner (Lanham, MD: Rowman and Littlefield, 2003), 107.

9. S. Neiman, *Evil in Modern Thought: An Alternative History of Philosophy* (Princeton, NJ: Princeton University Press, 2004), 282.

10. Ibid., 281.

11. Ibid., xii.

12. Ibid., xi.

13. A. Delbanco, *The Death of Satan: How Americans Have Lost the Sense of Evil* (New York: Farrar, Strauss and Giroux, 1996), 3.

14. Ibid., 9.

15. Ibid., 4.

16. Delbanco, *The Death of Satan,* 6.

17. U. Siemon-Netto, "Poll Shows Protestant Collapse," *United Press International,* June 28, 2001, http://www.vny.com/cf/News/upidetail.cfm?QID=198421 (accessed June 26, 2008).

18. PBS, "America Responds," Broadcast on September 12, 2001, http://www.pbs.org/americaresponds/moyers912.html.

19. M. Simmons and F. A. Thomas, eds., *9.11.01: African American Leaders Respond to an American Tragedy* (Valley Forge, PA: Judson Press, 2001), ix.

20. C. Cherry, ed., *God's New Israel: Religious Interpretations of American Destiny* (Chapel Hill: University of North Carolina Press, 1998).

21. T. Peterson, "Searching for God in September 11," *BusinessWeek Online,* September 10, 2002.

22. W. D. Watley, "Seeking God's Face," in *9.11.01,* eds. Simmons and Thomas, 133–34.

23. F. Mathewes-Green, "How Can God Permit Suffering?" in *Where Was God on Sept. 11? Seeds of Faith and Hope,* eds. D. B. Kraybill and L. G. Peachey (Scottdale, PA: Herald Press, 2002), 27.

24. In *Beauty for Ashes: Spiritual Reflections on the Attack on America,* ed. J. Farina (New York: Crossroad Publishing Company, 2001), 15.

25. L.S. Rouner, "Terror and the Christian Faith," in *Walking with God,* eds. Langford and Rouner, 74.

26. F. Buechner, "Walking in the World with a Fragile God," ibid., 8.

27. In Kraybill and Peachey, eds., *Where Was God on Sept. 11?,* 29.

28. Farina, ed., *Beauty for Ashes,* 31–34.

29. In *Where Was God on Sept. 11?,* eds. Kraybill and Peachey, 30–31.

30. E.T. Linenthal, "Toward the 'New Normal,'" *The Chronicle of Higher Education,* September 28, 2001.

31. P. Steinfels, "Where Was God? It Is a Question That Might Be Asked Every Day—Or Perhaps Not At All," *New York Times,* August 31, 2002.

32. Beliefnet, ed., *From the Ashes: A Spiritual Response to the Attack on America* (n.p.: Rodale, 2001), 54–60.

33. H. Jonas, *Il concetto di Dio dopo Auschwitz: Una voce ebraica,* transl. and ed. (Genoa: Il Melangolo, 1990).

34. The text of the interview is published in B. Lincoln, *Holy Terrors: Thinking about Religion after September 11* (Chicago: University of Chicago Press, 2003), 104–107.

35. In *Beauty for Ashes,* ed. Farina, 126–27.

36. Ibid.

37. Cit. in Lincoln, *Holy Terrors,* 104.

38. In *Beauty for Ashes,* ed. Farina, 122–26.

39. P. Eaton, "United in a New Kind of Grief," in *Where Was God on Sept. 11?,* eds. Kraybill and Peachey, 22.

40. J. Moltmann, "Watching for God," in *Walking with God,* eds. Langford and Rouner, 69.

41. A.M. Greeley, "Where Was God?" in *From the Ashes,* ed. Beliefnet, 42–43.

42. In *Walking with God,* eds. Langford and Rouner, 3.

43. See Z. Sardar and M.W. Davies, *Why Do People Hate America?* (New York: Disinformation, 2002).

44. In *Walking with God,* eds. Langford and Rouner, 65.

45. Ibid., 41.

46. In *Where Was God on Sept. 11?,* eds. Kraybill and Peachey, 109.

47. M. Simmons, "In Times Like These," in *9.11.01,* eds. Simmons and Thomas, x.

48. C.A. Knight, "Preaching While the World Is at War," ibid., 119.

49. C.G. Adams, "Meeting God Again, the First Time," ibid., 146.

50. R.M. Franklin, "Piety and the Public Square," ibid., 80.

51. W.D. Watley, "Seeking God's Face," ibid., 135–36.

52. V.M. McKenzie, "It Is Time to Move Forward!" ibid., 121–22.

53. C.E. Booth, "What's Going On," ibid., 51.

54. Ibid., 53_54.

55. C.H. Felder, "An African American Pastoral on Recent Acts of Terrorism in America," ibid., 14–15.

56. Cit. in Zaleski, "Faith and Doubt."

57. J. Lampman, "Americans See Religion as Gaining Clout in Public Life," *The Christian Science Monitor,* December 7, 2001.

58. P. Noonan, "God Is Back," *Wall Street Journal,* September 28, 2001.

59. P.J. Gomes, "Outer Turmoil, Inner Strength," in *9.11.01,* eds. Simmons and Thomas, 155.

60. Pew Forum on Religion & Public Life, *Lift Every Voice: A Report on Religion in American Public Life 2002,* http://pewforum.org.

61. T. Pzszczynski, S. Solomon, and J. Greenberg, *In the Wake of 9/11: The Psychology of Terror* (Washington, DC: American Psychological Association, 2003), 100–101.

62. Pew Forum on Religion & Public Life, *Post 9-11 Attitudes: Religion More Prominent, Muslim-Americans More Accepted,* December 6, 2001, http://pewforum.org.

63. J. Gomez, "How Do We Keep Our Faith When God Seems to Be Silent?" in *Beauty for Ashes,* ed. Farina, 112.

64. Ibid., 18.

65. Ibid., 19–20.

Chapter 3

1. Pew Forum on Religion & Public Life, *Post 9-11 Attitudes: Religion More Prominent, Muslim-Americans More Accepted,* December 6, 2001, http://pewforum.org.

2. Explanations of Bush's religion can be found in S. Mansfield, *The Faith of George W. Bush* (New York: Tarcher-Penguin, 2003), and P. Kengor, *God and George W. Bush: A Spiritual Life* (New York: ReganBooks, 2004).

3. See M. Molinari, *George W. Bush e la missione americana* (Rome-Bari: Laterza, 2004); K.P. Phillips, *Una dinastia americana,* transl. and ed. (Milan: Garzanti, 2004).

4. G.W. Bush and M. Herskowitz, *A Charge to Keep: My Journey to the White House* (New York: ReganBooks-HarperCollins, 2001), 136.

5. Cit. in D. Frum, *The Right Man: An Inside Account of the Bush White House,* (New York: Random House, 2003), 283.

6. For a critical appraisal of the role of religion in Bush's politics, from different points of view, see S. Fath, *Dieu bénisse l'Amérique: La religion de la Maison-Blanche* (Paris: Seuil, 2004); P. Singer, *The President of Good and Evil: Taking George W. Bush Seriously* (London: Granta Books, 2004); D. Domke, *God Willing? Political Fundamentalism in the White House, the "War on Terror," and the Echoing Press* (London: Pluto Press, 2004); J. Wallis, *God's Politics: Why the Right Gets It Wrong and the Left Doesn't Get It* (New York: HarperCollins, 2005).

7. Kengor, *God and George W. Bush,* 31–32.

8. Texas State Archives, State of Texas, Office of the Governor, Memorandum, April 3, 1995.

9. Texas State Archives, State of Texas, Office of the Governor, Official Memorandum, The "Jesus Day" Proclamation, March 17, 2000.

10. Cit. in www.presidencyusbc.edu/ws/index.php?pid=76120; see H. Fineman, "Words from the Heart," *Newsweek,* January 1, 2000.

11. M. Dowd, "Playing the Jesus Card," *New York Times,* December 15, 1999.

12. "George W. Bush: Running on His Faith," *U.S. News & World Report,* December 6, 1999.

13. J. Lee Grady, "God and the Governor," *Charisma,* August 29, 2000, http://www.charismamag.com/display.php?id=643.

14. K. Ettenborough, "Christianity on Campaign Trail," *The Milwaukee Journal Sentinel,* September 3, 2000.

15. The Pew Center for the People and the Press, *Religion and Politics: The Ambivalent Majority,* September 20, 2000, http://pewforum.org.

16. Steve Farkas et al., *For Goodness' Sake: Why So Many Want Religion to Play a Greater Role in American Life,* New York: Public Agenda, 2001.

17. S.L. Byrd, "Religious Expression in the 2000 Presidential Campaign: Civil Religion or Private Belief?" (paper), http://www.geocities.com/Athens/-Olympus/5357/crbyrd.html (accessed May 23, 2003).

18. Fineman, "Words from the Heart."

19. N. Walter, "It's Policies, not Prayers, That We Want," *The Independent,* September 4, 2000.

20. S.E. Ahlstrom, *A Religious History of the American People* (New Haven: Yale University Press, 1972), 878–79.

21. B.F. Donahue, "The Political Use of Religious Symbols: A Case Study of the 1972 Presidential Campaign," *The Review of Politics,* January 1975, 48–65. About Nixon's religion, see C.P. Henderson, *The Nixon Theology* (New York: Harper and Row, 1972).

22. Donahue, "The Political Use of Religious," 52–54.

23. "The 1976 Elections," *Journal of Church and State,* December 1976.

24. L.P. Ribuffo, "God and Jimmy Carter," in *Transforming Faith: The Sacred and the Secular in Modern American History,* eds. M.L. Bradbury and J.B. Gilbert (New York: Greenwood Press, 1989), 141.

25. B.A. Kosmin and S.P. Lachman, *One Nation under God: Religion in Contemporary American Society* (New York: Crown Publisher, 1993), 158.

26. Ibid., 160–61.

27. W. Safire, "God Bless Up," *New York Times,* August 27, 1992.

28. "Faith Is a Factor in Presidential Campaign," *Star Tribune,* October 25, 1992.

29. Kosmin and Lachman, *One Nation under God,* 160.

30. Ibid.

31. Ibid., 161.

32. Ibid., 162.

33. See R.D. Linder, "Universal Pastor: President Bill Clinton's Civil Religion," *Journal of Church and State,* no. 38 (1996): 733–49.

34. Ibid.

35. Ibid.

36. J. Tapper, *God Is Their Co-Pilot,* http://archive.salon.com/politics/feature/2000/07/07/born_again.

37. Cit. in Mansfield, *The Faith of George W. Bush,* 106.

38. See M.C. Segers, ed., *Piety, Politics, and Pluralism: Religion, the Courts, and the 2000 Election* (Lanham, MD: Rowman and Littlefield, 2002), 127.

39. K.L. Woodward, "God's Place in Politics," *Newsweek,* September 11, 2000.

40. G. Baker, "Gore Trusts God to Deliver a Moral Majority," *The Financial Times,* August 10, 2000.

41. Segers, ed., *Piety, Politics, and Pluralism,* 137–40.

42. J. Lieberman and M. D'Orso, *In Praise of Public Life* (New York: Simon and Schuster, 2000).

43. Segers, ed., *Piety, Politics, and Pluralism,* 137.

44. Ibid.

45. Barna Group, *Annual Study Reveals America Is Spiritually Stagnant,* March 5, 2001, http://www.barna.org.

46. U. Siemon-Netto, "Poll Shows Protestant Collapse," *United Press International,* June 28, 2001, http://www.vny.com/cf/News/upidetail.cfm?QID=198421 (accessed June 26, 2008).

47. Barna Group, *One-Quarter of Self-Described Born Again Adults Rely on Means Other than Grace to Get to Heaven,* November 29, 2005, http://www.barna.org.

48. A. Kohut, J.C. Green, S. Keeter, and R.C. Toth, *The Diminishing Divide: Religion's Changing Role in American Politics* (Washington, DC: Brookings Institution Press, 2000), 4.

49. See W. Martin, *With God on Our Side: The Rise of the Religious Right in America* (New York: Broadway Books, 1996).

50. See F. Colombo, *Il Dio d'America: Religione, ribellione e Nuova destra* (Milan: Mondadori, 1983); J. Micklethwait and A. Wooldridge, *The Right Nation: Conservative Power in America* (New York: Penguin, 2004).

51. P. Boyer, *When U.S. Foreign Policy Meets Biblical Prophecy,* February 20, 2003, http://www.alternet.org.

52. J.C. Green, M.J. Rozell, and C. Wilcox, eds., *The Christian Right in American Politics: Marching to the Millennium* (Washington, DC: Georgetown University Press, 2003).

53. See M.J. Rozell, "The Christian Right in the 2000 GOP Presidential Campaign," in *Piety, Politics, and Pluralism,* ed. Segers, 57–58.

54. See A.J. Reichley, *Faith in Politics* (Washington, DC: Brookings Institution Press, 2002), 332.

55. C. Wilcox, "Laying Up Treasures in Washington and in Heaven: The Christian Right and Evangelical Politics in the Twentieth Century and Beyond," *Magazine of History,* January 2003, 28–29.

56. C. Thomas and E. Dobson, "Blinded by Might: The Problem with Heaven on Earth," cit. in *What's God Got to Do with the American Experiment?,* eds. E.J. Dionne Jr. and J.J. DiIulio Jr.(Washington, DC: Brookings Institution Press, 2000), 52.

57. Frum, *The Right Man,* 9.

58. Cit. in Kengor, *God and George W. Bush,* 79.

59. Green, Rozell, and Wilcox, eds., *The Christian Right,* 1.

60. G.W. Bush, National Day of Prayer and Thanksgiving, January 21, 2001.

61. "Avec Bush, la religion à la Maison Blanche," *Le Monde,* February 3, 2001.

62. For references to the chief members of the Bush administration, see B. Woodward, *La guerra di Bush,* transl. and ed. (Milan: Sperling & Kupfer, 2003); E. Kaplan, *With God on Their Side: How Christian Fundamentalists Trampled Science, Policy, and Democracy in George W. Bush's White House* (New York: New Press, 2004); R. Kessler, *A Matter of Character: Inside the White House of George W. Bush* (New York: Sentinel, 2004); F. Rampini, *Tutti gli uomini del presidente: George W. Bush e la nuova destra americana* (Rome: Carocci, 2004); R. Suskind, *I segreti della Casa Bianca,* transl. and ed. (Milan: Il Saggiatore, 2004).

63. Cit. in Mansfield, *The Faith of George W. Bush,* 154.

64. H. Fineman, "Bush and God," *Newsweek,* March 10, 2003.

65. Frum, *The Right Man,* 3–4.

66. G. Wills, "With God on His Side," *New York Times,* April 13, 2003.

67. R.G. Hutcheson Jr., *God in the White House: How Religion Has Changed the Modern Presidency* (New York: Macmillan, 1988).

68. Cit. in R.V. Pierard and R.D. Linder, *Civil Religion and the Presidency* (Grand Rapids, MI: Zondervan, 1988), 185.

69. W.L. Miller, *Piety Along the Potomac: Notes on Politics and Morals in the Fifties* (Boston: Houghton Mifflin, 1964), 40.

70. Pierard and Linder, *Civil Religion and the Presidency,* 201.

71. M. Gustafson, "The Religious Role of the President," *Midwest Journal of Political Science,* November 1970, 708–22.

72. See J. Snow Wolfe, *The Kennedy Myth: American Civil Religion in the Sixties,* PhD dissertation presented to the Faculty of the Graduate Theological Union, Berkeley, CA, May 1975 (Ann Arbor, MI: UMI Dissertation Services, 1993).

73. R.S. Alley, *So Help Me God: Religion and the Presidency, Wilson to Nixon* (Richmond, VA: John Knox Press, 1973), 96.

74. Cit. in R.N. Bellah, *Beyond Belief: Essays on Religion in a Post-Traditional World* (New York: Harper and Row, 1970), 181.

75. Hutcheson, *God in the White House,* 81.

76. Pierard and Linder, *Civil Religion and the Presidency,* 216.

77. Ibid., 224.

78. See A.M. Schlesinger Jr., *La presidenza imperiale,* transl. and ed. (Milan: Comunità, 1980).

79. Hutcheson, *God in the White House,* ix.

80. W. Edel, *Defenders of the Faith: Religion and Politics from the Pilgrim Fathers to Ronald Reagan* (New York: Barger, 1987), 149.

81. P. Kengor, *God and Ronald Reagan: A Spiritual Life* (New York: ReganBooks-HarperCollins, 2004), 164.

82. Linder, *Universal Pastor,* 741.

83. Kengor, *God and George W. Bush,* 182–84.

Chapter 4

1. George W. Bush, interviewed by the Baptist Press, the national information service of the Southern Baptist Convention, August 31, 2000, http://www.beliefnet.com/story/33/story_3345_1.html.

2. G.W. Bush and M. Herskowitz, *A Charge to Keep: My Journey to the White House* (New York: HarperCollins, 2001), 1–13.

3. P. Kengor, *God and George W. Bush: A Spiritual Life* (New York: ReganBooks-HarperCollins, 2004), 61.

4. Cit. in S. Mansfield, *The Faith of George W. Bush* (New York: Tarcher-Penguin, 2003), 109.

5. Kengor, *God and George W. Bush,* 85.

6. Ibid., 118.

7. Cit. in T.M. Freiling, ed., *George W. Bush on God and Country* (Washington, DC: Allegiance Press, 2004), 253–55.

8. J. Tapper, *God Is Their Co-Pilot,* http://archive.salon.com/politics/feature/2000/07/07/born_again/.

9. Cit. in Mansfield, *The Faith of George W. Bush,* 95.

10. J. Lee Grady, "God and the Governor," *Charisma,* August 29, 2000, http://www.charismamag.com/display.php?id=643.

11. G.W. Bush, interviewed by S. Waldman, October 2000, http://www.beliefnet.com/story/33/story_3345_1.html.

12. G.W. Bush, Inaugural Address, January 20, 2001.

13. Kengor, *God and George W. Bush,* 84.

14. Cit. in ibid., 87.

15. M. Novak, *Choosing Presidents: Symbols of Political Leadership* (New Brunswick, NJ: Transaction Publishers, 1992), xxviii.

16. A.M. Schlesinger Jr., "Introduction," in *The Chief Executive: Inaugural Addresses of the Presidents of the United States from George Washington to Lyndon B. Johnson* (New York: Crown Publishers, 1965), iv.

17. C.V. La Fontaine, "God and Nation in Selected U.S. Presidential Inaugural Addresses, 1789–1945: Part One," *Journal of Church and State,* no. 1 (1976): 39–40.

18. See L. Baritz, *City on a Hill: A History of Ideas and Myths in America* (New York: Wiley, 1964).

19. J.G. Hunt, ed., *The Inaugural Addresses of the Presidents* (New York: Gramercy Books, 1997), 3–7.

20. Ibid., 13–20.

21. Ibid., 23–35.

22. D. Milbank, "Religious Right Finds Its Center in Oval Office," *Washington Post,* December 24, 2001.

23. See F.I. Greenstein, "The Leadership Style of George W. Bush," in *The George W. Bush Presidency: An Early Assessment,* ed. F.I. Greenstein (Baltimore: Johns Hopkins University Press, 2003), 7–8.

24. J. Kraus, "September 11th and Bush's Presidency," in *Transformed by Crisis: The Presidency of George W. Bush and American Politics,* eds. J. Kraus, K.J. McMahon, D.M. Rankin (New York: Palgrave, 2004), 1.

Chapter 5

1. On Bush's political and religious rhetoric, see S. Silberstein, *War of Words: Language, Politics and 9/11* (London: Routledge, 2002).

2. G.W. Bush, National Day of Prayer and Remembrance for the Victims of the Terrorist Attacks on September 11, 2001, September 13, 2001.

3. Id., President's Radio Address, July 6, 2002.

4. B. Broadway, "September 11, 2001: War Cry from the Pulpit," *Washington Post,* September 22, 2001; G.W. Bush, Remarks at the National Day of Prayer and Remembrance Service, September 14, 2001.

5. G.W. Bush, Remarks at the National Day of Prayer and Remembrance Service, September 15, 2001.

6. Cit. in R.V. Pierard and R.D. Linder, *Civil Religion and the Presidency* (Grand Rapids, MI: Zondervan, 1988), 78.

7. See E. Gentile, *Politics as Religion,* transl. by G. Staunton (Princeton, NJ: Princeton University Press, 2006), 16ff.

8. J.F. Meyer, *Myths in Stone: Religious Dimension of Washington D.C.* (Berkeley: University of California Press, 2001), 76–81.

9. For information about the cathedral, http://www.cathedral.org/cathedral/discover/history.shtml.

10. Cit. in S. Silberstein, *War of Words: Language, Politics and 9/11* (London: Routledge, 2002), 41.

11. E.L. Tuveson, *Redeemer Nation: The Idea of America's Millennial Role* (Chicago: University of Chicago Press, 1968), 197–98.

12. Broadway, "September 11, 2001."

13. See P. Kengor, *God and George W. Bush: A Spiritual Life* (New York: ReganBooks-HarperCollins, 2004), 134.

14. H.R. Kreider, "Jesus at the National Cathedral," in *Where Was God on Sept. 11? Seeds of Faith and Hope,* eds. D.B. Kraybill and L.G. Peachey (Scottdale, PA: Herald Press, 2002), 61.

15. M. Silk, "The Civil Religion Goes to War," *Religion in the News,* no. 3, 2001.

16. Kengor, *God and George W. Bush,* 126.

17. G.W. Bush, Address to a Joint Session of Congress and the American People, September 20, 2001.

18. Ibid.

19. See D. Domke, *God Willing? Political Fundamentalism in the White House, the "War on Terror," and the Echoing Press* (London: Pluto Press, 2004), 36.

20. J. Kraus, K.J. McMahon, and D.M. Rankin, eds., *Transformed by Crisis: The Presidency of George W. Bush and American Politics* (New York: Palgrave, 2004), 41.

21. See R. Harvey and H. Volat, *USA Patriot Act: De l'exception à la règle* (Paris: Lignes, 2006).

22. G.W. Bush, Address to the Nation, October 7, 2001.

23. See D.L. Green, "Bush Turns Increasingly to Language of Religion," *Baltimore Sun,* February 10, 2003.

24. Kengor, *God and George W. Bush,* 135.

25. Cit. in Kengor, *God and George W. Bush,* 138.

26. G.W. Bush, "Islam Is Peace" Says President: Remarks by the President at Islamic Center of Washington DC, September 17, 2001.

27. Id., President Meets with Muslim Leaders, September 26, 2001.

28. Pew Forum on Religion & Public Life, *Post 9-11 Attitudes: Religion More Prominent, Muslim-Americans More Accepted,* December 6, 2001, http://pewforum.org.

29. The Pew Research Center for the People and the Press, *American Struggle with Religion's Role at Home and Abroad,* Washington, DC, 2002.

30. Cit. in Kengor, *God and George W. Bush,* 139.

31. Cit. in Kengor, *God and George W. Bush,* 135–36.

32. See E. Kaplan, *With God on Their Side: How Christian Fundamentalists Trampled Science, Policy, and Democracy in George W. Bush's White House* (New York: New Press, 2004), 12–18.

33. Ibid., 139.

34. Ibid., 137.

35. H. Fineman, "Bush and God," *Newsweek,* March 10, 2003.

36. N.D. Kristof, "Giving God a Break," *New York Times,* June 10, 2003.

37. Cit. in *Beauty for Ashes: Spiritual Reflections on the Attack on America,* ed. J. Farina (New York: Crossroad Publishing Company, 2001), 41–45.

38. Kengor, *God and George W. Bush,* 169.

39. Cit. in D. Caldwell, "George Bush's Theology: Does the President Believe He Has a Divine Mandate?" *National Catholic Reporter,* February 21, 2003.

40. Cit. in G. Wills, "Fringe Government," *The New York Review of Books,* October 6, 2005.

41. D. Frum, *The Right Man: An Inside Account of the Bush White House* (New York: Random House, 2003), 148.

42. T. Carnes, "Bush's Defining Moment," *Christianity Today,* November 12, 2001.

43. See S. Mansfield, *The Faith of George W. Bush* (New York: Tarcher-Penguin 2003), 174.

Chapter 6

1. D. Frum, *The Right Man: An Inside Account of the Bush White House* (New York: Random House, 2003), 244ff.

2. G.W. Bush, Remarks by the President upon Arrival at Barksdale Air Force Base, September 11, 2001.

3. Id., Honoring the Victims of the Incidents on Tuesday, September 11, 2001, September 12, 2001.

4. Ibid.

5. Id., National Day of Prayer and Remembrance for the Victims of the Terrorist Attacks on September 11, 2001, September 13, 2001.

6. Id., President Pays Tribute at Pentagon Memorial: Remarks by the President at the Department of Defense Service of Remembrance, October 11, 2001.

7. Id., The President's State of the Union Address, January 29, 2002.

8. R. Fuller, *Naming the Antichrist: The History of an American Obsession* (New York-Oxford: Oxford University Press, 1995).

9. Ibid., 45–50.

10. See C.L. Albanese, *Sons of the Fathers: The Civil Religion of the American Revolution* (Philadelphia: Temple University Press, 1976).

11. Fuller, *Naming the Antichrist,* 138–48.

12. E.L. Tuveson, *Redeemer Nation: The Idea of America's Millennial Role* (Chicago: University of Chicago Press, 1968), 187–214.

13. See R.H. Abrams, *Preachers Present Arms: The Role of the American Churches and Clergy in World Wars I and II, with Some Observations on the War in Vietnam* (Scottdale, PA: Herald Press, 1969).

14. Cit. in R.V. Pierard and R.D. Linder, *Civil Religion and the Presidency* (Grand Rapids, MI: Zondervan, 1988), 158.

15. Ibid., 161.

16. P. Kengor, *God and Ronald Reagan: A Spiritual Life* (New York: ReganBooks-HarperCollins, 2004), 234–41.

17. See R.L. Coles, "Manifest Destiny Adapted for 1990s' War Discourse: Mission and Destiny Intertwined," *Sociology of Religion* 63, 4 (2002): 403–26.

18. G.W. Bush, Remarks Following a Meeting with the National Security Team, September 12, 2001.

19. Id., President Discusses War on Terrorism in Address to the Nation World Congress Center, Atlanta, GA, November 8, 2001.

20. Id., "Securing Freedom's Triumph," *New York Times,* September 11, 2002.

21. Ibid., September 12, 2002.

22. A.M. Schlesinger Jr., *Crisi di fiducia: Idee, potere e violenza in America,* transl. and ed. (Milan: Rizzoli, 1971), 7.

23. R.N. Bellah, *The Broken Covenant: American Civil Religion in Time of Trial* (New York: Seabury Press, 1975).

24. J.O. Robertson, *American Myth, American Reality* (New York: Hill and Wang, 1980).

25. Cit. in R.A. Sherrill, ed., *Religion and the Life of the Nation: American Recoveries* (Urbana: University of Illinois Press, 1990), 3.

26. R. Wuthnow, *The Struggle for America's Soul: Evangelicals, Liberals, and Secularism* (Grand Rapids, MI: William B. Eerdmans, 1989), xii.

27. Ibid., 21–26.

28. J.D. Hunter, *Culture Wars: The Struggle to Define America* (New York: Basic Books, 1991).

29. Cit. in J.A. Morone, *Hellfire Nation: The Politics of Sin in American History* (New Haven: Yale University Press, 2003), 453.

30. Ibid.

31. J.J. Kirkpatrick, *The Reagan Phenomenon, and Other Speeches on Foreign Policy* (Washington, DC: American Enterprise Institute for Public Policy Research, 1983), 12.

32. Arthur S. DeMoss Foundation, *The Rebirth of America* (Philadelphia, 1986).

33. Ibid., 78.

34. R.N. Bellah, R. Madsen, W.M. Sullivan, A. Swidler, and S.M. Tipton, *Habits of the Hearts* (New York: Harper and Row, 1985).

35. A.M. Schlesinger Jr., *The Disuniting of America* (Knoxville, TN: Whittle Direct Book, 1991), 2.

36. S.L. Carter, *The Culture of Disbelief: How American Law and Politics Trivialize Religious Devotion* (New York: Basic Books, 1993).

37. Cit. in D.G. Mayer, *The American Paradox: Spiritual Hunger in an Age of Plenty* (New Haven: Yale University Press, 2000), 257.

38. Ibid., xi.

39. E.J. Eisenach, *The Next Religious Establishment: National Identity and Political Theology in Post-Protestant America* (Lanham, MD.: Rowman and Littlefield, 2000), 1–2.

40. Ibid., 258ff.

41. Ibid.

42. Cit. in J.G. Hunt, ed., *The Inaugural Addresses of the Presidents* (New York: Gramercy Books, 1997), 501.

43. F. Clarkson, *Eternal Hostility: The Struggle between Theocracy and Democracy* (Monroe, ME: Common Courage Press, 1997).

44. R. Putnam, "Bowling Alone: America's Declining Social Capital," *Journal of Democracy* 6 (1995): 65–78; Id., *Bowling Alone: The Collapse and Revival of American Community* (New York: Simon and Schuster, 2000).

45. Id., "Bowling Together," *The American Prospect,* February 11, 2002.

46. A. Etzioni, "The Silver Lining of 9/11," *The Christian Science Monitor,* September 13, 2001.

47. *America Rebounds: A National Study of Public Response to the September 11th Terrorist Attacks: Preliminary Findings,* prepared by T.W. Smith, K.A. Rasinski, and M. Toce, October 25, 2001, NORC, A National Organization for Research at the University of Chicago, http://www.norc.org/NR/rdonlyres/51AA73B5-EB68-4E2A-AC63-75D652AA7D41/0/pubresp.pdf.

48. G.W. Bush, President Bush Calls for Action on Economy, Energy, October 26, 2001.

49. See R.T. Hughes, *Myths America Lives By* (Urbana: University of Illinois Press, 2003), 152–89.

50. G.W. Bush, President Holds Prime Time News Conference, October 12, 2001.

51. F. Merk, *Manifest Destiny and Mission in American History* (New York: Vintage Books, 1966).

52. The most recent studies on the myth of the American nation as the chosen people: see: C. Longley, *Chosen People: The Big Idea That Shapes England and America* (London: Hodder and Stoughton, 2002); R. Jewett and J.S. Lawrence, *Captain America and the Crusade Against Evil: The Dilemma of Zealous Nationalism* (Grand Rapids, MI: William B. Eerdmans, 2003); N. Guétin, *États-Unis: l'imposture messianique* (Paris : L'Harmattan, 2004); A. Lieven, *America Right or Wrong: An Anatomy of American Nationalism* (Oxford: Oxford University Press, 2004; M. Northcott, *An Angel Directs the Storm: Apocalyptic Religion and American Empire* (London: I.B. Tauris, 2004); G. Besier and G. Lindemann, *In Namen der Freiheit: Die amerikanische Mission* (Gottingen: Vandenhoeck and Ruperecht, 2006).

53. National Security Council, The National Security Strategy of the United States of America, September 17, 2002, http://www.whitehouse.gov/nsc/print/nssall.html.

54. R.N. Bellah, "The New American Empire," *Commonwealth,* October 25, 2002.

55. Id., "Righteous Empire," *The Christian Century,* March 8, 2003.

56. Ibid., 25.

57. M. Northcott, *An Angel Directs the Storm: Apocalyptic Religion & American Empire* (London: I.B. Tauris, 2004), 75.

58. The Pew Research Center for the People and the Press, *U.S. Needs More International Backing,* February 20, 2003, http://www.people-press.org.

59. Id., "Different Faiths, Different Messages," March 19, 2003.

60. Id., "Religion and Politics: Contention and Consensus," July 24, 2003.

61. Id., "Among Wealthy Nations...U.S. Stands Alone in Its Embrace of Religion," December 19, 2002, http://www.people-press.org.

62. C. Marvin and D.W. Ingle, *Blood Sacrifice and the Nation: Totem Rituals and the American Flag* (Cambridge: Cambridge University Press, 1999); A. Boime, *The Unveiling of the National Icons: A Plea for Patriotic Iconoclasm in a Nationalist Era* (Cambridge: Cambridge University Press, 1998); R.J. Ellis, *To the Flag: The Unlikely History of the Pledge of Allegiance* (Lawrence: University Press of Kansas, 2005).

63. S.P. Huntington, *Who Are We? The Challenges to America's National Identity* (New York: Simon and Schuster, 2004), 3.

64. W.N. Guthrie, *The Religion of Old Glory* (New York: Doran, 1919), 10.

65. Ibid., 370.

66. M.M. Quaife, *The Flag of the United States* (New York: Grosset and Dunlop, 1942), 195.

67. K.A. Marling and J. Wetenhall, *Iwo Jima: Monuments, Memories, and the American Hero* (Cambridge, MA: Harvard University Press, 1991, 73.

68. R.J. Goldstein, *Saving "Old Glory": The History of the American Flag Desecration Controversy* (Boulder, CO: Westview Press, 1995).

69. Jewett and Lawrence, *Captain America,* 294.

70. Cit. Goldstein, *Saving "Old Glory,"* 252.

71. Ibid., 215–20.

72. G.W. Bush, A Proclamation by the President: Flag Day and National Flag Week, June 7, 2001.

73. S. Willis, "Old Glory," in *The South Atlantic Quarterly* 2 (2002): 377.

74. I. Molotosky, *The Flag, the Poet & the Song: The Story of the Star-Spangled Banner* (New York: Plume, 2001), 215–17.

75. Ibid., 219.

76. Jewett and Lawrence, *Captain America,* 296.

77. S. Silberstein, *War of Words: Language, Politics and 9/11* (London: Routledge, 2002), 114.

78. Huntington, *Who Are We?*, 4.

79. W.D. Baker and J.R. Oneal, "Patriotism or Opinion Leadership? The Nature and Origins of the 'Rally'Round the Flag' Effect," *Journal of Conflict Resolution*, October 2001, 661–87.

Chapter 7

1. G.W. Bush, Patriot Day 2002, September 4, 2002.

2. R. Dannheisser, "In New York, Washington and Across Nation, Americans Remember 9-11, September 6, 2002," September 6, 2002, http://www.usembassy.it/file2002_09/alia/a2090608.htm.

3. Cit. in J. Steinhauer, "Threats and Responses—Perspectives," *New York Times,* September 11, 2002.

4. A. Harmon, "Real Solace in a Virtual World: Memorials Take Root on the Web," ibid.

5. B. Fraenkel, *Les écrits de septembre: New York 2001* (Paris: Textuel, 2002).

6. "Art and Culture," *Gotham Gazette,* September 9, 2002, http://www.gothamgazette .com/print/52.

7. P. Nobel, *64.784 mq: La feroce battaglia per la ricostruzione di Ground Zero,* transl. (Milan: Isbn Edizioni, 2005).

8. E.D. Hudson, "New York," *Mediaweek,* September 9, 2002.

9. "Blueprint for Ground Zero Begins to Take Shape," *New York Times,* May 4, 2002. See P. Nobel, *64.748 mq: La feroce battaglia per la ricostruzione di Graund Zero,* transl. it., (Milan: Isbn Edizioni, 2005).

10. G. Laderman, "9/11 on Our Mind," *Religion in the News* 3 (2002).

11. Fraenkel, *Les écrits,* 84–85.

12. J.-P. Dupuy, *Avions-nous oublié le mal? Penser la politique après le 11 septembre* (Paris: Bayard, 2002), 58.

13. K. McManus, "Saving the Flesh," in *Walking with God in a Fragile World,* eds. J. Langford and L.S. Rouner (Lanham, MD: Rowman and Littlefield, 2003), 136.

14. C. Bohlen, "Sudden Warnings Statement Adds Drama to Anxious Day,"*New York Times,* September 11, 2001.

15. See C. Cherry, ed., *God's New Israel: Religious Interpretation of American Destiny* (Chapel Hill: University of North Carolina Press, 1998); J.F. Berens, *Providence & Patriotism in Early America, 1640–1815* (Charlottesville: University of Virginia Press, 1978).

16. On the relationship between nationalism and religion in the United States: see D. Dohen, *Nationalism and American Catholicism* (New York: Sheed and Ward, 1967); H.S. Hudson, ed., *Nationalism and Religion* (New York: Harper and Row, 1970); C. Strout, *The New Heavens and New Earth: Political Religion in America* (New York: Harper and Row, 1974); R.J. Neuhaus, ed., *Unsecular America* (Grand Rapids, MI: William B. Eedermans, 1986); *Religion, Ideology and Nationalism in Europe and America* (Jerusalem: The Historical Society of Israel and The Zalman Shazar Center for Jewish History, 1986), 185ff.; C.C. O'Brien, *God and Land: Reflections on Religion and Nationalism* (Cambridge, MA: Harvard University Press, 1988); W. Zelinski, *Nation Into State: The Shifting Symbolic Foundations of American Nationalism* (Chapel Hill: University of North Carolina Press, 1988); J.H. Hutson, ed., *Religion and the New Republic: Faith in the Founding of America*

(Lanham, MD: Rowan and Littlefield, 1989); M.A. Noll, ed., *Religion and American Politics: From the Colonial Period to the 1980s* (New York-Oxford: Oxford University Press, 1990); J. Bodnar, ed., *Bonds of Affection: Americans Define Their Patriotism* (Princeton, NJ: Princeton University Press, 1996); J.F. Wilson, *Religion and the American Nation: Historiography and History* (Athens, GA: University of Georgia Press, 2003); Y.T.S. Engeman and M.P. Zuckert, eds., *Protestantism and the American Founding* (Notre Dame, IN: University of Notre Dame Press, 2004).

17. W.L. Warner, *The Living and the Dead: A Study of the Symbolic Life of Americans* (New Haven: Yale University Press, 1959), 4.

18. G.K. Piehler, *Remembering War the American Way* (Washington, DC: Smithsonian Institution Press, 1995), xiv. See J.M. Mayo, *War Memorials as Political Landscape: The American Experience and Beyond* (New York-Westport, CT: Praeger, 1988); E.T. Linenthal, *Sacred Ground: Americans and Their Battlefields* (Urbana: University of Illinois Press, 1991).

19. K.E. Foote, *Shadowed Ground: America's Landscapes of Violence and Tragedy* (Austin: University of Texas Press, 1997), 6.

20. P. Metcalf and R. Huntington, *Celebrations of Death: The Anthropology of Mortuary Ritual* (Cambridge: Cambridge University Press, 1991), 213.

21. Laderman, "9/11 on Our Mind."

22. G. Wills, *Lincoln at Gettysburg* (New York: Simon and Schuster, 1992).

23. M. Kakutani, "Rituals, Improvised or Traditional," *New York Times,* September 12, 2002.

24. See B. Cabanes and J.-M. Pitte, *11 septembre: La Grande Guerre des Américains* (Paris : Colin, 2003), 112–17.

25. D. Barry, "A Day of Tributes, Tears and the Litany of the Lost," *New York Times,* September 12, 2002.

26. J. Abu-Lughod, "After the WTC Disaster: The Sacred, the Profane, and Social Solidarity," http://www.ssrc.org.

27. F.X. Clines, "President and Wife Draw Warm Response in Meeting With Families," *New York Times,* September 12, 2002.

28. D. Potorti, ed., *September 11th Families for a Peaceful Tomorrow: Turning Our Grief into Action for Peace* (New York: Rdv Books, 2003), 7.

29. Cit. in ibid., 22.

30. J. Tierney, "Vigilance and Memory—Honoring Those Lost and Celebrating a New Symbol of Resilience," *New York Times,* September 12, 2002.

31. Kakutani, "Rituals, Improvised or Traditional."

32. Laderman, "9/11 on Our Mind."

33. Clines, "President and Wife."

34. McManus, "Saving the Flesh," 137.

35. G.W. Bush, Patriot Day 2002, September 4, 2002.

36. The Pew Research Center for the People and the Press, *Among Wealthy Nations... U.S. Stands Alone in Its Embrace of Religion,* December 19, 2002, http://www.people-press.org.

37. Cit. in K. Mori, "9/11 and the 'American Civil Religion' Today," in *Journal of Interdisciplinary Study of Monotheistic Religion* 1 (2005): 1–17, http://www.cismor.jp/en/research/report/mori.pdf.

38. J. Lampman, "Americans See Religion as Gaining Clout in Public Life," *The Christian Science Monitor,* December 7, 2001.

39. See D.L. Eck, *A New Religious America: How a "Christian Country" Has now Become the World's Most Religiously Diverse Nation* (New York: HarperSan Francisco, 2001).

40. S. Waldman, "The Real Spiritual Impact of 9/11," September 2003, http://www.beliefnet.com/story/112/story_11238.html.

41. A.J. Reichley, *Faith in Politics* (Washington, DC: Brookings Institution Press, 2002), 349.

42. Cit. in J.J. DiIulio Jr., "The Lord's Work: The Church and Civil Society," in *Community Works: The Revival of Civil Society in America,* ed. E.J. Dionne Jr. (Washington, DC: Brookings Institution Press, 1998), 58; R.W. Fogel, *The Fourth Great Awakening & the Future of Egalitarianism* (Chicago: University of Chicago Press, 1999).

43. Waldman, "The Real Spiritual Impact of 9/11."

44. Ibid.

45. See P. Paul, "True Believers, in 'American Demographics,'" September 2002, 42 45.

46. Pew Forum on Religion & Public Life, *Lift Every Voice: A Report on Religion in American Public Life 2002,* http://pewforum.org.

47. The Pew Research Center for the People and the Press, *Religion and Politics: Contentions and Consensus,* July 24 2003, http://people-press.org.

48. Cit. in "Survey on American Attitudes Toward Religion in Public Life," http://www.witherspoonsociety.org.

49. Paul, "True Believers."

50. The bibliography on American civil religion and the debates caused by Robert N. Bellah's essay is extensive; therefore I shall mention only some of the main works describing the different positions: E.A. Smith, ed., *The Religion of the Republic* (Philadelphia: Fortress Press, 1971); R.S. Alley, *So Help Me God: Religion and the Presidency: Wilson to Nixon* (Richmond, VA: John Knox Press, 1972); R.E. Richey and D.G. Jones, eds., *American Civil Religion* (New York: Harper and Row, 1974); M. Novak, *Choosing Our King: Powerful Symbols in Presidential Politics* (New York: Macmillan, 1974); R.P. Hart, *The Political Pulpit* (West Lafayette, IN: Purdue University Press, 1977); R.D. Linder and R.V. Pierard, *Twilight of the Saints: Biblical Christianity and Civil Religion in America* (Downers Grove: InterVarsity, 1978); J.F. Wilson, *Public Religion in American Culture* (Philadelphia: Temple University Press, 1979); R.N. Bellah and P.E. Hammond, *Varieties of Civil Religion* (New York: Harper and Row, 1980); G. Gehrig, *American Civil Religion: An Assessment* (Storrs, CT: Society for the Scientific Study of Religion, 1981); L.S. Rouner, ed., *Civil Religion and Political Theology* (Notre Dame, IN: University of Notre Dame Press, 1986); S. Levison, *Constitutional Faith* Princeton, NJ: Princeton University Press, 1988); R.V. Pierard and R.D. Linder, *Civil Religion and the Presidency* (Grand Rapids, MI: Zondervan, 1988); T. Hase, *Zivilreligion: Religionwissenchaftliche Überlegungen zu einem theoretischen Konzept am Beispiel der USA* (Würzburg: Ergon Verlag, 2001). For a critical survey of the debate, see J.A. Mathisen, "Twenty Years After Bellah: Whatever Happened to American Civil Religion?" *Sociological Analysis* 50, no. 2 (1989): 129–46; P.E. Hammond, "American Civil Religion Revisited," *Religion and American Culture* 4 (1994): 1–23.

51. R.N. Bellah, *The Broken Covenant: American Civil Religion in Time of Trial* (New York: Seabury Press, 1975), 142.

52. M.S. Allen, "In God We Trust," *Star Tribune,* January 14, 1974.

53. C.W. Gaddy, "American Civil Religion: The Past and Present Role of Religion in Shaping the American National Identity," April 1, 2000, http://www.interfaithalliance.org.

54. C. Henderson, "The Best of Bush: Poetry not/Piety yes," http://www.christianity
.about.com/library/weekly/aa012201.htm.

55. Cit. in N.K. Gvosdev, "New President Continues Old Traditions of American Civil
Religion," January 24, 2001, http://www.geocities.com.

56. M. Angrosino, "Civil Religion Redux," *Anthropological Quarterly* 2 (2002):
239–67.

57. R. Slotkin, "Our Myths of Choice," *The Chronicle of Higher Education,*
September 28, 2001.

58. Pew Forum on Religion & Public Life, *God Bless America: Reflections on Civil
Religion After September 11,* February 6, 2002, http://pewforum.org.

59. W.M. McClay, "The Soul of a Nation," *The Public Interest* 155 (Spring 2004):
4–19.

60. Cit. "Rally Round the Flag," *Christianity Today,* November 12, 2001.

61. C. Colson, "Wake-up Call," ibid.

62. R. Benne, "That Old Time Religion," *Journal of Lutheran Ethics,* December 14,
2001, http://www.elca.org/jle/articles.

63. M.S. Allen, "Olympics Gives U.S. a Chance to Show Its 'Civil Religion,'" *Star
Tribune,* February 9, 2002.

64. McClay, "The Soul of a Nation."

65. T. Carnes, "Bush's Defining Moment," *Christianity Today,* November 12, 2001.

66. M. Silk, "The Civil Religion Goes to War," *Religion in the News,* no. 3, 2001.

67. "Bush's Messiah Complex," *The Progressive,* February 2003.

68. See N. Graebner, ed., *Manifest Destiny* (Indianapolis: Bobbs-Merrill 1968), xlviff.

69. See R.V. Pierard and R.D. Linder, *Civil Religion and the Presidency* (Grand
Rapids, MI: Zondervan, 1988), 124ff.

70. J. Carney, J.F. Dickerson, "Taking Aim at 2004," *Time,* May 5, 2003.

71. M. Whitaker, "The Editor's Desk," *Newsweek,* March 10, 2003.

Chapter 8

1. See G.J. Ikenberry, "America's Imperial Ambition," *Foreign Affairs,* September–
October 2002, 44–60.

2. M. Pei, "The Paradoxes of American Nationalism," *Foreign Policy,* May–June
2003, 31.

3. See Y. Arieli, *Individualism and Nationalism in American Ideology* (Cambridge,
MA: Harvard University Press, 1964); R.B. Nye, *This Almost Chosen People: Essays in
the History of American Ideas* (Toronto: Macmillan, 1966), 208–55.

4. S. Mead, *The Nation with the Soul of a Church* (New York: Harper and Row, 1975),
48.

5. W.S. Hudson, ed., *Nationalism and Religion in America* (New York: Harper and
Row, 1970).

6. R.N. Bellah, "Civil Religion in America," *Daedalus* 1 (1967): 118. On the separation of church and state see P. Hamburger, *Separation of Church and State* (Cambridge,
MA: Harvard University Press, 2002).

7. W. Herberg, *Protestant—Catholic—Jew: An Essay in American Religious Sociology* (1955), (Garden City, NY: Anchor Books, 1960), 1–2.

8. Ibid., 259.

9. Ibid., 263.

10. Ibid., 263–65.

11. G.W. Bush, Second Inaugural Address, January 20, 2005.

12. Cit. in J. Wallis, "Dangerous Religion," *Sojourners Magazine,* September–October 2003, 20.

13. A. Lieven, *America Right or Wrong: An Anatomy of American Nationalism* (Oxford: Oxford University Press, 2004), 28.

14. F. Zakaria, "The Arrogant Empire," *Newsweek,* March 10, 2003. On anti-Americanism after September 11 see M. Hertsgaard, *The Eagle's Shadow: Why America Fascinates and Infuriates the World* (New York: Farrar, Strauss and Giroux, 2002); J.-F. Revel, *L'obsession anti-américaine* (Paris: Plon, 2002); Z. Sardar and M.W. Davies, *Why Do People Hate America?* (Cambridge: Icon Books, 2002).

15. J. Chace, "Imperial America and the Common Interest," *World Policy Journal* 1, (2002): 1–9.

16. See J. Gray, "The Mirage of Empire," *The New York Review of Books,* January 12, 2006.

17. P. Boyer, "When U.S. Foreign Policy Meets Biblical Prophecy," February 2003, http://www.alternet.org/story/15221.

18. T. Carnes, "The Bush Doctrine," *Christianity Today,* April 25, 2003.

19. H. Meyerson, "The Most Dangerous President Ever," *The American Prospect,* May 2003.

20. Cit. in J.M. Parker, "The 'Almost Chosen': U.S. Patriotism, Piety Linked," *San Antonio Express-News,* April 12, 2003.

21. B. Broadway, "TV Debate Delineates Christian Divide on War," *The Washington Post,* March 15, 2003.

22. R. Land, "The Christian Criteria for Retribution," in *From the Ashes: A Spiritual Response to the Attack on America,* ed. Beliefnet (n.p.: Rodale, 2001), 165.

23. See T. Mitri, "Au nome de la Bible, au nome de l'Amérique," *Labor et Fides,* Geneva 2004, 130–38.

24. P. Kengor, *God and George W. Bush: A Spiritual Life* (New York: ReganBooks-HarperCollins, 2004, 230.

25. E. Bumiller, "Religious Leaders Ask if Antiwar Call Is Heard," *New York Times,* March 10, 2003.

26. "Una mobilitazione penitenziale per la pace," *L'Osservatore Romano,* March 8, 2003. On the Vatican's attitude towards the Bush presidency see M. Franco, *Imperi paralleli. Vaticano e Stati Uniti: due secoli di alleanza e conflitto 1788–2005,* (Milan: Mondadori, 2005), 121ff.

27. S. Fath, *Dieu bénisse l'Amérique: La religion de la Maison-Blanche* (Paris: Seuil, 2004), 143.

28. "Deny Them Their Victory: An Interfaith Response to Terror," in *Beauty for Ashes: Spiritual Reflections on the Attack on America,* ed. J. Farina, (New York: Crossroad Publishing Company, 2001), 45–48.

29. S. Hauerwas, "September 11, 2001: A Pacifist Response," in *Walking with God in a Fragile World,* ed. J. Langford and L.S. Rouner (Lanham, MD: Rowman and Littlefield, 2003), 121–30.

30. C.C. Black, "A Laugh in the Dark," *Theology Today* 60 (2003): 149–53.

31. D.B. Kraybill, "What Would Jesus Do?" in *Where Was God on Sept. 11? Seeds of Faith and Hope,* ed. D.B. Kraybill and L.G. Peachey (Scottdale, PA: Herald Press, 2002,) 37.

32. D.W. Shriver Jr., *Forgiveness? Now?*, ibid., 90–91.

33. A.M. Greeley, "Where Was God?" in *From the Ashes*, ed. Beliefnet, 43–44.

34. See J. Dart, "Bush Religious Rhetoric Riles Critics," *The Christian Century*, March 8, 2003; T. Carnes, "The Bush Doctrine," *Christianity Today*, May 2003.

35. "Bush's Messiah Complex," in *The Progressive*, February 2003, http://www .progressive.org.

36. Ibid.

37. Fath, *Dieu bénisse l'Amérique*, 122ff.

38. F. Rampini, *Tutti gli uomini del presidente: George W. Bush e la nuo va destra americana* (Rome: Carocci, 2004), 111.

39. C. Hitchens, "God and the Man in the White House," *Vanity Fair*, August 2003, 81.

40. B. Keller, "God and George W. Bush," *New York Times*, May 17, 2003.

41. J. Kleim, "The Blinding Glare of His Certainty," *Time*, February 24, 2003.

42. R. Suskind, "Without a Doubt," *New York Times Magazine*, October 17, 2004.

43. C. Mirra, "George W. Bush's Theological Diplomacy," *American Diplomacy*, October 15, 2003, http://www.americandiplomacy.org.

44. F. Ritsch, "Of God, and Man, in the Oval Office," *Washington Post*, March 2, 2003.

45. Cit. in D. Caldwell, "George Bush's Theology," *National Catholic Reporter*, February 21, 2003.

46. "Op/Ed on Bush's Use of Religious Language: President Plays the Christian Trump Card," http://www.interfaithalliance.org/About/About.cfm?ID=4665&c=6.

47. B.W. Lynn, "Uncivil Religion: Bush and the Bully Pulpit," *Journal of Church and State* 56, no. 3 (2003): 23.

48. R. Balmer, "Bush and God," *The Nation*, April 14, 2003.

49. M.E. Marty, "The Sin of Pride," *Newsweek*, March 10, 2003.

50. K.L. Woodward, "The White House: Gospel on the Potomac," ibid.

51. G. McGovern, "The Reason Why," *The Nation*, April 21, 2003.

52. P. Singer, *The President of Good and Evil: Taking George W. Bush Seriously* (London: Granta Books, 2004), 1.

53. Ibid., 90–111.

54. Ibid., 225.

55. J. Wallis, *God's Politics: Why the Right Gets It Wrong and the Left Doesn't Get It* (New York: HarperCollins, 2005).

56. Ibid., 145–49.

57. See M.A. Noll, *America's God: From Jonathan Edwards to Abraham Lincoln* (Oxford: Oxford University Press, 2002.

58. H.R. Niebuhr, *The Kingdom of God in America* (New York: Harper and Row, 1937).

59. See D.C. Swift, *Religion and the American Experience* (Armonk, NY: M.E. Sharpe, 1998); C.L. Albanese, *American Religions and Religion* (Belmont, CA: Wadsworth, 1999), chapt. 13; P.E. Hammond, "Civil Religion," in *Contemporary American Religion,*ed. W.C. Roof (New York: Macmillan, 2000), vol. I, 133–34.

60. On the relationship between religion and politics in the United States from the second half of the eighteenth century to September 11, see G.A. Kelly, *Politics and Religious Consciousness in America* (New Brunswick: Transaction Books, 1984); R.P. McBrien, *Caesar's Coin: Religion and Politics in America* (New York: Macmillan, 1987);

D. Chidester, *Patterns of Power: Religion & Politics in American Culture* (Englewood Cliffs, NJ: Prentice Hall, 1988); M. Silk, *Spiritual Politics: Religion and America Since World War II* (New York: Simon and Schuster, 1988); C.W. Dunn, ed., *Religion in American Politics* (Washington, DC: CQPress, 1989); K.D. Wald, *Religion and Politics in the United States* (Washington, DC: CQPress, 1992); E.J. Dionne Jr. and J.J. Di Iulio Jr., eds.,*What's God Got to Do with the American Experiment* (Washington, DC: Brookings Institution Press, 2000); A.J. Reichley, *Faith in Politics* (Washington, DC: Brookings Institution Press, 2002); H. Heclo and W.M. McClay, eds., *Religion Returns to the Public Square: Faith and Policy in America* (Washington, DC: Woodrow Wilson Center Press, 2003); R. Prätorius, *In God We Trust: Religion und Politik in den U.S.A.* (Munich: Verlag C.H. Beck, 2003); Mitri, *Au nom de la Bible, au nome de l'Amérique*; J.-F. Colosimo, *Dieu est américain: De la théodémocratie aux Etats-Unis* (Paris : Fayard, 2006).

61. "Rally Round the Flag," *Christianity Today,* November 12, 2001.

62. "Civil Religious War," ibid., January 7, 2002, 9.

63. J.W. Fulbright, *The Arrogance of Power* (New York: Random House, 1966).

64. Ibid., 3.

65. R.N. Bellah, *Beyond Belief: Essays on Religion in a Post-Traditional World* (New York: Harper and Row, 1970), 168.

66. M. Novak, *Choosing Our King: Powerful Symbols in Presidential Politics* (New York: Macmillan, 1974), 128. See *Religion and the Public Good* (Macon, GA: Mercer University Press, 1988).

67. M.E. Marty, "Two Kinds of Civil Religion," in *American Civil Religion,* eds. R.E. Richey and D.G. Jones (New York: Harper and Row, 1974), 139–57.

68. R. Wuthnow, *The Restructuring of American Religion* (Princeton, NJ: Princeton University Press, 1988), 244–67.

69. See R.M. Miller, H.S. Stout, and C.R. Wilson, eds., *Religion and the American Civil War* (Oxford: Oxford University Press, 1998); C.E. O'Leary, *To Die For: The Paradox of American Patriotism* (Princeton, NJ: Princeton University Press, 1999).

70. Pew Forum on Religion & Public Life, *God Bless America: Reflections on Civil Religion After September 11,* February 6, 2002, http://pewforum.org.

71. See M.E. Marty, *Pilgrims in Their Own Land: 500 Years of Religion in America* (New York: Penguin Books, 1984), 274ff.; O'Leary, *To Die For,* 61ff.

72. R. Jewett and J.S. Lawrence, *Captain America and the Crusade against Evil: The Dilemma of Zealous Nationalism* (Grand Rapids, MI: William B. Eerdmans, 2003), 8.

73. D. Butler Bass, *Broken We Kneel: Reflections on Faith and Citizenship* (San Francisco: Jossey-Bass, 2004), 2.

74. Ibid., 9.

75. B. Hankins, "Civil Religion & America's Inclusive Faith," January 18, 2004, http://www.libertymagazine.org.

76. R. Benne, "The American Civil Religion—Destructive, Useless, or Beneficial?" *Journal of Liberal Ethics,* April 2005; for answers to Benne's article, ibid., April and May 2005, http://www.elca.org/jle/articles.

77. M.E. Bailey and K. Lindholm, "Tocqueville and the Rhetoric of Civil Religion in the Presidential Inaugural Addresses," *Christian Scholar's Review* 32, no. 3 (2003): 259–78.

78. G. Monbiot, "Post-9/11 America Is a Religion," July 30, 2003, http://www.alternet.org.

79. Cit. in W. Peterson, "The Case Against Civil Religion," *Eternity,* October 1973, 25.

80. Ibid., 26–27.

81. Ibid., 26.

82. D.B. Kraybill, *Our Star-Spangled Faith* (Scottdale, PA: Herald Press, 1976), 9.

83. Ibid., 20.

84. Ibid., 26.

85. Ibid., 144.

86. Id., "Which God Bless America?" in *Where Was God on Sept. 11? Seeds of Faith and Hope,* eds. D.B. Kraybill and L.G. Peachey (Scottdale, PA: Herald Press, 2002), 159–60.

87. D.E. Nisly, "American Versus Heavenly Citizenship," in *Where Was God on Sept. 11?,* eds. Kraybill and Peachey, 157.

88. R. Detrick, "A Flag in Worship?" in *Where Was God on Sept. 11?,* eds. Kraybill and Peachey, 170.

89. CBS Radio Network, "Flagging Faith," March 21, 2002, http://www.acfnewsource.org/religion/flagging_faith.html.

90. V. Weaver-Zercher, "Why I Don't Fly Old Glory," in *Where Was God on Sept. 11?,* eds. Kraybill and Peachey, 167–68.

91. P. Keim, "My Struggle with the Flag," ibid., 164.

92. D. Domke, *God Willing? Political Fundamentalism in the White House, the "War on Terror," and the Echoing Press* (London: Pluto Press, 2004).

93. J. Wallis, "Dangerous Religion," *Sojourners Magazine,* September–October 2003, 20–26.

94. O. Noti, "Bushs Gott ist ein Götze," in *Sonntagsblick,* March 24, 2003.

95. S. Fath, *Dieu bénisse l'Amérique: La religion de la Maison-Blanche* (Paris: Seuil, 2004), 249.

Chapter 9

1. C.M. Cannon, "Bush and God," *National Journal,* January 3, 2004, 18.

2. "President's Use of Evangelical Christian Language Is Dangerous, Decisive and 'Cripples' Democracy," February 11, 2003, http://www.interfaithalliance.org/News.cfm?ID=4666&c=7.

3. R. Benedetto, "Bush's Approval Rating Drops to Lowest Since 9/11," *USA Today,* September 12, 2003.

4. R. Bernstein, "Foreign Views of U.S. Darken after Sept. 11," *New York Times,* September 11, 2003.

5. "Two Years On," *Economist,* September 13, 2003.

6. The Pew Research Center for the People and the Press, *Anti-Americanism: Causes and Characteristics—Recent Commentary by Andrew Kohut,* December 10, 2003, http://pewforum.org.

7. See Pew Forum on Religion & Public Life, *God and Foreign Policy: The Religions Divide between the U.S. and Europe,* July 10, 2003, http://pewforum.org; E. Gentile, "Collisione transatlantica," *Il Sole-24 Ore,* October 24, 2004; C. Power, "The New Crusade," *Newsweek,* November 8, 2004; P. Ford, "What Place for God in Europe?" *The Christian Science Monitor,* February 22, 2005; Id., "In a Secular Ocean, Waves of Spirituality," ibid., February 23, 2005; Pew Forum on Religion & Public Life, *Secular Europe and Religious America: Implications for Transatlantic Relations,* April 21, 2005, http://pewforum.org.

8. Pew Forum on Religion & Public Life, *God and Foreign Policy.*

9. P. Schneider, "Separated by Civilization: Trans-Atlantic Impasse," *International Herald Tribune,* April 7, 2004.

10. Cit. in T.L. Friedman, "An American in Europe," ibid., January 21, 2005.

11. S.P. Huntington, *Who Are We? The Challenges to America's National Identity* (New York: Simon and Schuster, 2004).

12. Ibid., 365.

13. Ibid., 106.

14. T.L. Friedman, "Two Nations under God," *International Herald Tribune,* November 5, 2004.

15. See R. Dworkin, "The Threat to Patriotism," *The New York Review of Books,* February 28, 2002; B. Moyers, "Welcome to Doomsday," ibid., March 24, 2005.

16. H. Bloom, *The American Religion: The Emergence of the Post-Christian Nation* (New York: Simon and Schuster, 1992), 45.

17. Ibid., 270.

18. M. Silk, "Our New Religious Politics," *Religion in the News* 3, 2005.

19. On the distinction between civil religion and political religion, see E. Gentile, *Politics as Religion,* transl. by G. Staunton (Princeton, NJ: Princeton University Press, 2006).

20. Ibid., xiv–xix, 138–142.

21. A. Wolfe, *The Transformation of American Religion: How We Actually live Our Faith* (New York: Free Press, 2003), 245ff.

22. See M.J. Rozell and G. Whitney, eds., *Religion and the Bush Presidency* (New York: Palgrave McMillan, 2007).

23. M. Silk and J.F. Green, "The GOP's Religion Problem," *Religion in the News,* Winter 2007.

24. B.W. Lynn, *Piety and Politics: The Right-Wing Assault on Religious Freedom* (New York: Harmony Books, 2006).

25. M. Goldberg, *Kingdom Coming: The Rise of Christian Nationalism* (New York: W.W. Norton and C., 2006).

26. D. Kuo, *Tempting Faith: An Inside Story of Political Seduction* (New York: W.W. Norton and C., 2006).

27. Pew Forum on Religion & Public Life, *Clinton and Giuliani Seen as Not Highly Religious; Romney's Religion Raises Concerns,* September 6, 2007, http://pewforum.org ; Id., *Personal Faith and Candidate Image in the 2008 Campaign,* January 31, 2008, http://pewforum.org/events/?EventID=165.

28. Pew Forum on Religion & Public Life, *The Religion Factor in the 2008 Election,* December 4, 2007, http://pewforum.org/events/?EventID=163.

29. Cit. in K. Kernike, "The Christian Mandate," *New York Times,* February 17, 2008.

30. Ibid.

31. Adelle M. Banks and Daniel Burke, "Religious Strategy Heading into Super Tuesday," Religion News Service, January 28, 2008, http://pewforum.org.

32. J. Meacham, *American Gospel: God, the Founding Fathers, and the Making of a Nation* (New York: Random House, 2006), 237.

33. G. Scott Smith, *Faith and The Presidency: From George Washington to George W. Bush* (New York: Random House, 2006), 430.

34. Pew Forum on Religion & Public Life, *The U.S. Religious Landscape Survey 2008,* http://pewforum.org.

35. A. Wolfe, "God's Country: The Changing Face of Religion in America," *International Herald Tribune,* March 1–2, 2008.

Bibliography

Ahlstrom, S.E. *A Religious History of the American People.* New Haven-London: Yale University Press, 1972.

Albanese, C.L. *Sons of the Fathers: The Civil Religion of the American Revolution.* Philadelphia: Temple University Press, 1976.

Alley, R.S. *So Help Me God: Religion and the Presidency, Wilson to Nixon.* Richmond, VA: John Knox Press, 1972.

America Rebounds: A National Study of Public Response to the September 11th Terrorist Attacks: Preliminary Findings. Chicago: NORC, University of Chicago, 2001.

Becker, E. *The Denial of Death.* New York: Free Press, 1973.

Beliefnet (ed.). *From the Ashes: A Spiritual Response to the Attack on America.* N.p.: Rodale, 2001.

Bellah, R.N. *Beyond Belief: Essays on Religion in a Post-Traditional World.* New York: Harper and Row, 1970.

Bellah, R.N. *The Broken Covenant: American Civil Religion in Time of Trial.* New York: The Seabury Press, 1975.

Bellah, R.N., P.E. Hammond (eds.). *Varieties of Civil Religion.* New York: Harper and Row, 1980.

Bellah, R.N., R. Madsen, W.M. Sullivan, Ann Swidler, Steven M. Tipton. *Habits of the Hearts.* New York: Harper and Row, 1985.

Bernstein, R. *Out of the Blue: The Story of September 11, 2001 from Jihad to Ground Zero.* New York: Holt, 2002.

Bodnar, J. (ed.). *Bonds of Affection: Americans Define Their Patriotism.* Princeton, NJ: Princeton University Press, 1996.

Body-Gendrot, S. *La société americaine après le 11 septembre.* Paris: Presses de Science Po, 2002.

Boime, A. *The Unveiling of the National Icons: A Plea for Patriotic Iconoclasm in a Nationalist Era.* Cambridge: Cambridge University Press, 1998.

Boyer, P. *When Time Shall Be No More: Prophecy Belief in Modern American Culture.* Cambridge, MA: Harvard University Press, 1992.

Bradbury, M.L., J.B. Gilbert (eds.). *Transforming Faith: The Sacred and the Secular in Modern American History.* New York: Greenwood Press, 1989.

Brill, S. *After: How America Confronted the September 12 Era.* New York: Simon and Schuster, 2003.

Burbach, R., B. Clarke (eds.). *September 11 and the U.S. War.* San Francisco: City Lights Books and Freedom Voices Press, 2002.

Cabanes, B., J.-M. Pitte. *11 septembre: La Grande Guerre des Américains.* Paris: Armand Colin, 2003.

Calhoun, C., P. Price, A. Timmer (eds.). *Understanding September 11.* New York: The New Press, 2002.

Carter, S.L. *The Culture of Disbelief: How American Law and Politics Trivialize Religious Devotion.* New York: Basic Books, 1993.

Cherry, C. (ed.). *God's New Israel: Religious Interpretations of American Destiny.* Chapel Hill, NC: University of North Carolina Press, 1998.

Clarkson, F. *Eternal Hostility: The Struggle Between Theocracy and Democracy.* Monroe, ME: Common Courage Press, 1997.

Delbanco, A. *The Death of Satan: How Americans Have Lost the Sense of Evil.* New York: Farrar, Strauss and Giroux, 1996.

Dionne, E.J. (ed.). *Community Works: The Revival of Civil Society in America.* Washington, DC: Brookings Institution Press, 1998.

Dionne, E.J., Jr., J.J. DiIulio Jr. (eds.). *What's God Got to Do with the American Experiment?* Washington, DC: Brookings Institution Press, 2000.

Dixon, W.W. *Visions of the Apocalypse: Spectacles of Destruction in American Cinema.* London-New York: Wallflower Press, 2003.

Domke, D. *God Willing? Political Fundamentalism in the White House, the "War on Terror," and the Echoing Press.* London-Ann Arbor: Pluto Press, 2004.

Dupuy, J.-P. *Avions-nous oublié le mal? Penser la politique après le 11 septembre.* Paris: Bayard, 2002.

Eck, D.L. *A New Religious America: How a "Christian Country" Has Become the World's Most Religiously Diverse Nation.* San Francisco-New York: Harper, 2001.

Edel, W. *Defenders of the Faith: Religion and Politics from the Pilgrim Fathers to Ronald Reagan.* New York: Barger, 1987.

Eisenach, E.J. *The Next Religious Establishment: National Identity and Political Theology in Post-Protestant America.* Lanham, MD: Rowman and Littlefield, 2000.

Ellis, R.J. *To the Flag: The Unlikely History of the Pledge of Allegiance.* Lawrence, KS: University Press of Kansas, 2005.

Engeman, Y.T.S., M.P. Zuckert (eds.). *Protestantism and the American Founding.* Notre Dame, IN: University of Notre Dame Press, 2004.

Falk, R. *The Great Terror War.* New York-Northampton: Olive Branch Press, 2003.

Farina, J. (ed.). *Beauty from the Ashes: Spiritual Reflections on the Attack on America.* New York: Crossroad, 2001.

Fogel, R.W. *The Fourth Great Awakening and the Future of Egalitarianism.* Chicago: University of Chicago Press, 2000.

Foote, K.E. *Shadowed Ground: America's Landscapes of Violence and Tragedy.* Austin, TX: University of Texas Press, 1997.

Frachon, A., D. Vernet. *L'Amérique messianique: Les guerres des néo-conservateurs.* Paris: Seuil, 2004.

Fraenkel, B. *Les écrits de septembre: New York 2001.* Paris: Textuel, 2002.

Freiling, T.M. (ed.).*George W. Bush On God and Country.* Washington, DC: Allegiance Press, 2004.

Frum, D. *The Right Man: An Inside Account of the Bush White House.* New York: Random House, 2003.

Fuller, R. *Naming the Antichrist: The History of an American Obsession.* New York-Oxford: Oxford University Press, 1995.

Gehrig, G. *American Civil Religion: An Assessment.* Romeoville, IL: Lewis University, 1981.

Gengor, P. *God and Ronald Reagan: A Spiritual Life.* New York: HarperCollins, 2004.

Goldberg, M. *Kingdom Coming: The Rise of Christian Nationalism.* New York: W.W. Norton and C., 2006.

Goldstein, R.J. *Saving "Old Glory": The History of the American Flag Desecration Controversy.* Boulder, CO: WestView Press, 1995.

Graebner, N. (ed.). *Manifest Destiny.* Indianapolis-New York: Bobbs-Merrill, 1968.

Green, J.C., M.J. Rozell, Clyde Wilcox, (eds.). *The Christian Right in American Politics: Marching to the Millennium.* Washington, DC: Georgetown University Press, 2003.

Greenstein, F.I. (ed.). *The George W. Bush Presidency: An Early Assessment.* Baltimore-London: The John Hopkins University Press, 2003.

Guthrie, W.N. *The Religion of Old Glory.* New York: Doran, 1919.

Hart, R.P. *The Political Pulpit.* West Lafayette, IN: Purdue University Press, 1977.

Hase, T. *Zivilreligion: Religionswissenchaftliche Überlegungen zu einem theoretischen Konzept am Beispiel der USA.* Würzburg: Ergon Verlag, 2001.

Hatcheson, R.G., Jr. *God in the White House: How Religion Has Changed the Modern Presidency.* New York: MacMillan, 1988.

Heclo, H., W.M. McClay (eds.). *Religion Returns to the Public Square: Faith and Policy in America.* Washington, DC: Woodrow Wilson Center Press, 2003.

Henderson, C.P.*The Nixon Theology.* New York: Harper and Row, 1972.

Hershberg, E., K.W. Moore (eds.). *Critical Views of September 11: Analysis from Around the World.* New York: The New Press, 2002.

Hertsgaard, M. *The Eagle's Shadow: Why America Fascinates and Infuriates the World.* New York: Farrar, Strauss and Giroux, 2003.

Hoge, J.F., Jr., G. Rose (eds.). *How Did This Happen? Terrorism and the New War.* New York: Public Affairs, 2001.

Hudson, H.S. (ed.). *Nationalism and Religion.* New York: Harper and Row, 1970.

Hunt, J.G. (ed.). *The Inaugural Addresses of the Presidents.* New York: Gramercy Books, 1997.

Hunter, J.D. *Culture Wars: The Struggle to Define America.* New York: Basic Books, 1991.

Huntington, S.P. *Who Are We: The Challenges to America's National Identity.* New York: Simon and Schuster, 2004.

Hutson, J.H. (ed.). *Religion and the New Republic: Faith in the Founding of America.* Lanham: Rowan and Littlefield, 1989.

Jewett, R., J.S. Lawrence. *Captain America and the Crusade against Evil.* Grand Rapids, MI: Eerdmans, 2003.

Kaplan, E. *With God on Their Side: How Christian Fundamentalists Trampled Science, Policy, and Democracy in George W. Bush's White House.* New York-London: The New Press, 2004.

Kengor, P. *God and George W. Bush: A Spiritual Life.* New York: ReganBooks, 2004.

Kessler, R. *A Matter of Character: Inside the White House of George W. Bush.* New York: Sentinel, 2004.

Kirkpatrick, J.J. *The Reagan Phenomenon, and Other Speeches on Foreign Policy.* Washington, DC: American Institute for Public Policy Research, 1983.

Kohut, A., J.C. Green, S. Keeter, R.C. Toth. *The Diminishing Divide: Religion's Changing Role in American Politics.* Washington DC: Brookings Institution Press, 2000.

Kornbluth, J. E., J. Papin (eds.). *Because We Are Americans: What We Discovered on September 11, 2001.* New York: Warner Books, 2001.

Kosmin, B.A., Seymour P. Lachman. *One Nation Under God: Religion in Contemporary America Society.* New York: Crown Publisher, 1993.

Kraus, J., K.J. McMahon, D.M. Rankin (eds.). *Transformed by Crisis: The Presidency of George W. Bush and American Politics.* New York: Palgrave, 2004.

Kraybill, D., L.G. Peachey (eds.). *Where Was God on Sept. 11?* Scottdale, PA: Herald Press, 2002.

Kuo, D. *Tempting Faith: An Inside Story of Political Seduction.* New York: Free Press, 2006.

Langford, J., L.S. Rouner (eds.). *Walking with God in a Fragile World.* Lanham: Rowan and Littlefield, 2003.

Levison, S. *Constitutional Faith.* Princeton, NJ: Princeton University Press, 1988.

Lieberman, J., M. D'Orso. *In Praise of Public Life.* New York: Simon and Schuster, 2000.

Lieven, A. *America Right or Wrong: An Anatomy of American Nationalism.* Oxford: Oxford University Press, 2004.

Lincoln, B. *Holy Terrors: Thinking About Religion after September 11.* Chicago: University of Chicago Press, 2003.

Linder, R.D., R.V. Pierard. *Twilight of the Saints: Biblical Christianity and Civil Religion in America.* Downers Grove, IL: InterVarsity, 1978.

Linenthal, E.T. *Sacred Ground: Americans and Their Battlefields.* Urbana-Chicago: University of Illinois Press, 1991.

Longley, C. *Chosen People: The Big Idea That Shapes England and America.* London: Hodder and Stoughton, 2002.

Lynn, B.W. *Piety & Politics: The Right-Wing Assault on Religious Freedom.* New York: Harmony Books, 2006.

Mansfield, S. *The Faith of George W. Bush.* New York: Jeremy P.Tacher/Penguin, 2003.

Marling, K.A., John Wetenhall. *Iwo Jima: Monuments, Memories, and the American Hero.* Cambridge, MA: Harvard University Press, 1991.

Martin, W. *With God on Our Side: The Rise of the Religious Right in America.* New York: Broadway Books, 1996.

Marvin, C., D.W. Ingle. *Blood Sacrifice and the Nation: Totem Rituals and the American Flag.* Cambridge: Cambridge University Press, 1999.

Mayo, J.M. *War Memorials as Political Landscape: The American Experience and Beyond.* New York-Westport, CT: Praeger, 1988.

McNall, B.E. *The American Idea of Mission: Concepts of National Purpose and Destiny.* New Brunswick, NJ: Rutgers University Press, 1957.

Meacham, J. *American Gospel: God, the Founding Fathers, and the Making of a Nation.* New York: Random House, 2006.

Merk, F. *Manifest Destiny and Mission in American History.* New York: Vintage Books, 1966.

Metcalf, P., R. Huntington. *Celebrations of Death: The Anthropology of Mortuary Ritual.* Cambridge: Cambridge University Press, 1991.

Meyer, J.F. *Myths in Stone: Religious Dimension of Washington DC.* Berkeley: University of California Press, 2001.

Meyerowitz, J. (ed.). *History and September 11th.* Philadelphia: Temple University Press, 2003.

Micklethwait, J., Adrian Wooldridge. *The Right Nation: Conservative Power in America.* New York: The Penguin Press, 2004.

Miller. W.L. *Piety Along the Potomac: Notes on Politics and Morals in the Fifties.* Boston: Houghton Mifflin, 1964.

Molotosky, I. *The Flag, the Poet & the Song: The Story of the Star-Spangled Banner.* New York: Plume, 2001.

Morone, J.A. *Hellfire Nation: The Politics of Sin in American History.* New Haven-London: Yale University Press, 2003.

Myers, D.G. *The American Paradox: Spiritual Hunger in an Age of Plenty.* New Haven-London: Yale University Press, 2000.

Neiman, S. *Evil in Modern Thought: An Alternative History of Philosophy.* Princeton, NJ: Princeton University Press, 2004.

Neuhaus, R.J. (ed.). *Unsecular America.* Grand Rapids, MI: Eerdmans, 1986.

The 9/11 Report: The National Commission on Terrorist Attacks Upon the United States. New York: St. Martin Press, 2004.

Noll, M.A. (ed.). *Religion and American Politics: From the Colonial Period to the 1980s.* New York-Oxford: Oxford University Press, 1990.

Northcott, M. *An Angel Directs the Storm: Apocalyptic Religion & American Empire.* London-New York: I.B. Taurus, 2004.

Novak, M. *Choosing Presidents: Symbols of Political Leadership.* 2d. ed. New Brunswick: Transaction Publishers, 1992.

O'Brien, C.C. *God and Land: Reflections on Religion and Nationalism.* Cambridge, MA-London: Harvard University Press, 1988.

Pielher, G.K. *Remembering War the American Way.* Washington, DC: Smithsonian Books, 1995.

Pierard, R.V., R.D. Linder. *Civil Religion and the Presidency.* Grand Rapids: Zondervan, 1988.

Potorti, D. (ed.). *September 11th Families for a Peaceful Tomorrow: Turning Our Grief into Action for Peace.* New York: RDV Books, 2003.

Putnam, R. *Bowling Alone: The Collapse and Revival of American Community.* New York: Simon and Schuster, 2000.

Pzszczynski,T., S. Solomon, J. Greenberg (eds.). *Terror in America: The Day Our World Changed.* Washington, DC: American Psychological Association, 2003.

Quaife, M.M. *The Flag of the United States* New York: Grosset and Dunlop, 1942.

The Rebirth of America. Philadelphia: The Arthur S. DeMoss Foundation, 1986.

Reichly, A.J. *Faith in Politics.* Washington, DC: Brookings Institution Press, 2002.

Religion, Ideology and Nationalism in Europe and America: Essay Presented in Honor of Yehoshua Arieli. Jerusalem: The Historical Society of Israel and The Zalman Shazar Center for Jewish History, 1986.

Richey, R.E., D.G. Jones (eds.). *American Civil Religion,* New York: Harper and Row, 1974.

Robertson, J.O. *American Myth, American Reality.* New York: Hill and Wang, 1980.

Rouner, L.S. (ed.). *Civil Religion and Political Theology.* Notre Dame, IN: University of Notre Dame 1986.

Rozell, M.J., G. Whitney (eds.). *Religion and the Bush Presidency.* New York: Palgrave/MacMillan, 2007.

Sardar, Z., M.W. Davies *Why Do People Hate America?* New York: Disinformation, 2002.

Schlesinger, A.M., Jr. (ed.). *The Chief Executive: Inaugural Addresses of the Presidents of the United States from George Washington to Lyndon B. Johnson.* New York: Crown Publisher, 1965.

Schlesinger, A.M., Jr. *The Disuniting of America.* Knoxville, TN: Whittle Direct Book, 1991.

Scott, G.S. *Faith & The Presidency: From George Washington to George W. Bush.* New York: Oxford University Press, 2006.

Segers, M.C. (ed.). *Piety, Politics, and Pluralism: Religion, the Courts, and the 2000 Election.* Lanham: Rowan and Littlefield, 2002.

Sherrill, R.A. (ed.) *Religion and the Life of the Nation: American Recoveries.* Urbana-Chicago: University of Illinois Press, 1990.

Silbertein, S. *War of Words: Language, Politics and 9/11.* London-New York: Routledge, 2002.

Simmons, M., F.A. Thomas (eds.). *9.11.01. African American Leaders Respond to an American Tragedy.* Valley Forge, PA: Judson Press, 2001.

Singer, P. *The President of Good & Evil: Taking George W. Bush Seriously.* London: Granta Books, 2004.

Smith, E.A. (ed.). *The Religion of the Republic.* Philadelphia: Fortress Press, 1971.

Smith, T. *America's Mission: The United States and the Worldwide Struggle for Democracy in the Twentieth Century.* Princeton, NJ: Princeton University Press, 1994.

Strout, C. *The New Heavens and New Earth: Political Religion in America.* New York: Harper and Row, 1974.

Talbott, S., N. Chanda (eds.). *The Age of Terror: America and the World After September 11.* New York: Basic Books, 2001.

Tuveson, E.L., *Redeemer Nation. The Ideas of America's Millennial Role,* The University of Chicago Press, Chicago 1968.

Wallis, J. *God's Politics: Why the Right Gets It Wrong and the Left Doesn't Get It.* New York: HarperCollins, 2005.

Warner, W.L. *The Living and the Dead: A Study of the Symbolic Life of Americans.* New Haven: Yale University Press, 1959.

Weinberg, A.K. *Manifest Destiny: A Study of Nationalist Expansionism in American History.* Chicago: Encounter Paperbacks, 1935.

Wills, G. *Lincoln at Gettysburg.* New York: Simon and Schuster, 1992.

Wills, G. *Under God: Religion and American Politics.* New York: Simon and Schuster, 1990.

Wilson, J.F. *Public Religion in American Culture.* Philadelphia: Temple University Press, 1979.

Wilson, J.F. *Religion and the American Nation: Historiography and History.* Athens-London: University of Georgia Press, 2003.

Wojcik, D. *The End of the World as We Know It: Faith, Fatalism, and Apocalypse in America.* New York: New York University Press, 1997.

Wuthnow, R. *The Struggle for America's Soul: Evangelicals, Liberals, and Secularism.* Grand Rapids, MI: Eerdmans, 1989.

Zelinski, W. *Nation Into State: The Shifting Symbolic Foundations of American Nationalism.* Chapel Hill-London: University of North Carolina Press, 1988.

Index

About the Author and Translators

EMILIO GENTILE is a historian of international reputation. He is the author of 20 books, and his major works and articles have been translated into English, French, and Spanish. He is the author of *Politics as Religion, The Sacralization of Politics in Fascist Italy,* and *The Struggle for Modernity: Nationalism, Futurism, and Fascism.* He is Professor of Contemporary History at the University of Rome "La Sapienza" and has been a visiting professor at the University of Wisconsin–Madison. In 2003, he was awarded the prestigious Hans Sigrist Prize by the University of Berne, Switzerland, for his studies on the sacralization of politics.

JENNIFER PUDNEY is a freelance translator based in Rome, Italy; she has taught translation from Italian into English at Rome's Advanced School for Interpreters and Translators for over 20 years. She is the author of *Written English for Advanced Learners* and the editor of *Edgar Allan Poe: Selected Tales,* both intended for use in Italian universities.

SUZANNE D. JAUS is an American teacher and freelance translator living in Rome, Italy. She has more than 20 years' experience teaching English translation at the University of Padua and Rome's Advanced School for Interpreters and Translators. She has translated several books, among which the most recent are *The Frontier of Hope,* by Renata Broggini, and *La Grande Italia: The Myth of the Nation in the Twentieth Century* (with Jennifer Pudney), by Emilio Gentile.